A Call to Fidelity

Moral Traditions Series

A series edited by James F. Keenan, S.J.

Aquinas and Empowerment: Classical Ethics for Ordinary Lives
G. Simon Harak, S.J., Editor

The Banality of Good and Evil: Moral Lessons from the Shoah and Jewish Tradition
David R. Blumenthal

Bridging the Sacred and the Secular: Selected Writings of John Courtney Murray
John Courtney Murray, S.J.
J. Leon Hooper, S.J., Editor

The Catholic Moral Tradition Today: A Synthesis
Charles E. Curran

Catholic Social Teaching, 1891–Present: A Historical, Theological, and Ethical Analysis
Charles E. Curran

The Christian Case for Virtue Ethics
Joseph J. Kotva, Jr.

The Context of Casuistry
James F. Keenan, S.J., and Thomas A. Shannon, Editors

Democracy on Purpose: Justice and the Reality of God
Franklin I. Gamwell

Ethics and Economics of Assisted Reproduction
Maura A. Ryan

The Ethics of Aquinas
Stephen J. Pope, Editor

The Evolution of Altruism and the Ordering of Love
Stephen J. Pope

The Fellowship of Life: Virtue Ethics and Orthodox Christianity
Joseph Woodill

Feminist Ethics and Natural Law: The End of the Anathemas
Cristina L. H. Traina

Jewish and Catholic Bioethics: An Ecumenical Dialogue
Edmund D. Pellegrino and Alan I. Faden, Editors

John Paul II and the Legacy of *Dignitatis Humanae*
Hermínio Rico, S.J.

Love, Human and Divine: The Heart of Christian Ethics
Edward Collins Vacek, S.J.

Medicine and the Ethics of Care
Diana Fritz Cates and Paul Lauritzen, Editors

The Origins of Moral Theology in the United States: Three Different Approaches
Charles E. Curran

Shaping the Moral Life: An Approach to Moral Theology
Klaus Demmer, M.S.C.
Translated by Roberto Dell'Oro
James F. Keenan, S.J., Editor

Who Count as Persons? Human Identity and the Ethics of Killing
John F. Kavanaugh, S.J.

A Call to Fidelity

On the Moral Theology of Charles E. Curran

James J. Walter
Timothy E. O'Connell
Thomas A. Shannon
Editors

Georgetown University Press
Washington, D.C.

Georgetown University Press, Washington, D.C.

Printed in the United States of America

10 9 8 7 6 5 4 3 2 1 2002

This volume is printed on acid-free offset book paper.

Library of Congress Cataloging-in-Publication Data

A call to fidelity : on the moral theology of Charles E. Curran / edited by James J. Walter, Timothy E. O'Connell, Thomas A. Shannon.

p.cm. — (Moral traditions series)

Includes bibliographical references and index.

ISBN 0-87840-379-5 (alk. paper) — ISBN 0-87840-380-9 (pbk. alk. paper)

1. Curran, Charles E.—Contributions in Christian ethics. 2. Christian ethics.
I. Curran, Charles E. II. Walter, James J. III. O'Connell, Timothy E.
IV. Shannon, Thomas A. (Thomas Anthony), 1940– V. Series.

BX4705.C795 C35 2002
241'.042'092—dc21

2002190224

Contents

Foreword

James J. Walter

Why this book? Two important reasons can be offered. First, it seeks to honor and celebrate the contributions that Charles E. Curran has made to the field of Catholic ethics over the past forty years. Of course, to celebrate his contributions is also to celebrate this man, who has not only given diligently to the discipline of moral theology but also has given generously to so many in the field.

Second, this book seeks to assess the developments on specific topics in contemporary moral theology to which Curran has made particular contributions. To that end, well-known and respected scholars in the field were asked to write essays on topics that will continue to challenge the church and society. The essays are arranged under four headings: fundamental ethics, sexual and medical ethics, social and political ethics, and topics related to dialogue with other traditions and approaches to Catholic ethics.

With a few exceptions, each essay is divided into three parts. The first section of each chapter reviews the recent past (forty years or so) and the current state of the question on the topic under discussion. The second part of each chapter develops Curran's contributions to the topic. Sometimes this section takes the form of themes that Curran has developed in his writings or theoretical constructs that he has offered. In addition, this section assesses from the author's and others' standpoints how helpful or successful Curran's contributions have been. This section presents a critical evaluation of Curran's work. Finally, each essay outlines what the author foresees as the future agenda and challenges that confront society and the church as we move more into the third millennium (the next ten to twenty years).

Examples have the power to reveal. Charles Curran is an example of an individual who has consistently dedicated himself to placing the best scholarship in dialogue with other religious traditions, the social and physical sciences, and his own Catholic tradition. Thus, the most appropriate way for the contributors to this volume to celebrate the writings of our author may be to place his work in critical dialogue with contemporary scholarship.

Examples also have the power to educate, etymologically both in the sense of leading one out of taken-for-granted assumptions (*educere*) and in the sense of forming new thought patterns (*educare*). Charles Curran has been an example of steadfast fidelity—a fidelity frequently tested by criticism and suffering—to his calling as a theologian to educate others. As friends and colleagues, we are deeply thankful for the example of his life and his work.

Charles E. Curran: Catholic Theologian, Priest, Prophet

Daniel C. Maguire

To introduce so dear a friend and so esteemed a colleague, I repair for help to five distinguished, tone-setting keynoters. Each of these keynoters touches themes that reflect the life and the theological mission of Charles E. Curran.

My first keynoter is Avery Cardinal Dulles, S.J. In his presidential address to the Catholic Theological Society of America he said that Vatican II "implicitly taught the legitimacy and even the value of dissent." The council, Dulles said, conceded "that the ordinary magisterium of the Roman Pontiff had fallen into error, and had unjustly harmed the careers of loyal and able theologians." He mentioned John Courtney Murray, Teilhard de Chardin, Henri de Lubac, and Yves Congar. He could surely add the name of Charles E. Curran. Dulles says that certain teachings of the hierarchy "seem to evade in a calculated way the findings of modern scholarship. They are drawn up without broad consultation with the theological community. Instead, a few carefully selected theologians are asked to defend a pre-established position. . . ." Dulles aligns himself with theologians who do not limit the term "magisterium" to the hierarchy. He speaks of "two magisteria—that of the pastors and that of the theologians." These two magisteria are "complementary and mutually corrective." The theological magisterium may critique the hierarchical magisterium. Dulles concludes, "We shall insist on the right, where we think it important for the good of the Church, to urge positions at variance with those that are presently official."[1]

Elsewhere—and relevant to our purposes here—Dulles, speaking at the Catholic University of America, wondered whether Thomas Aquinas, "if he were alive today... would be welcome" at the Catholic University of America. Once again, he insists that the "magisterium of the professors" relies "not on formal authority but rather on the force of reasons." He aligns himself with St. Thomas Aquinas's view that "with the growth of the great universities the bishops could no longer exercise direct control over the content of theological teaching." "Their role," Dulles insists, "was primarily pastoral, rather than academic."[2]

My next keynoter is Thomas Aquinas himself, the saintly theologian who exemplified theology done *ex corde ecclesiae*. Thomas drew a sharp and still-useful distinction between the *officium praelationis* of bishops and the *officium magisterii* of theologians.[3] Thomas also distinguished the *magisterium cathedrae pastoralis* of the bishops and the *magisterium cathedrae magistralis* of the theologians.[4] What Aquinas is saying here, as Cardinal Dulles observes, is that the hierarchy does not monopolize the charism of truth and "the theologian is a genuine teacher, not a mouthpiece or apologist for higher officers."[5]

My third keynoter is Joseph Cardinal Ratzinger, who also put in words the truth that Charles Curran has lived: "The Church is not the petrification of what once was, but its living presence in every age. The Church's dimension is therefore the present and the future no less than the past."[6]

My fourth keynoter is Paul Lehmann, then professor of Christian ethics at Union Theological Seminary in New York. Lehmann was invited to give the inaugural address at the dedication of a new church and educational building in Towson, Maryland. The pastor, a former student, introduced Dr. Lehmann with pride. Lehmann mounted the pulpit, looked out into the sea of joyful faces in that beamingly well-lit building, and began with these words: "Do you know what you have built here? A resplendent mausoleum. It stands incandescent in the glow of its own irrelevance as the dynamics of the time rush to pass it by." After the pastor was revived, Dr. Lehmann went on to argue that it need not be so if the church could read the signs of the times and respond with courage.

My final keynoter is professor Terence McCaughey, a theologian at Trinity College, Dublin. The See of Dublin was newly vacant and a group of Catholic professors were gathered in a pub near the college, expressing their hopes that a progressive and powerful leader would fill the archiepiscopal chair. McCaughey was the lone Protestant in the group. When he heard their aspirations, he replied with a twinkle: "I hope you get a terrible bishop here who provides no leadership at all. Then, maybe, at last, you Catholics will respond to your baptismal promises to grow into a mature adulthood in the very image of God." The point was taken but no offense was felt in a pub atmosphere that was flowing with sanctifying grace.

AN UNLIKELY REVOLUTIONARY

Charles Curran was born in March 1934. He was ordained a priest in the Catholic diocese of Rochester, New York. Throughout his career, he has taught moral theology at St. Bernard's College in Rochester (1961–65), the Catholic University of America (1965–89), Cornell University (1987–88), the University of Southern California (1988–90), and Auburn University (1990–91). Since 1991 he has been Elizabeth Scurlock University Professor of Human Values at Southern Methodist University in Dallas. He has been a prolific scholar; the impressive list of his scholarly publications appears in the back of this volume.

Charles Curran did not set out to be a theologian, much less a revolutionary one. His goal was to be a priest. He was an obedient, rule-abiding seminarian. When he was ordered to do graduate studies with a professorship as its goal, that same obedience kicked in with gusto. Sent back to Rome for a doctorate, he proceeded to earn two—one from the Gregorian University and one from the Alfonsiana, where he met his mentor, Bernard Häring. When he was assigned to teach moral theology at St. Bernard's Seminary in Rochester, he obeyed a norm that few followed: For the first three weeks he lectured only in Latin. No student suffering through that would ever have guessed they were listening to a theologian who would turn the ecclesiastical world on end. (Using the good ears that are the mark of any effective theologian, he heeded the pleas of his students and changed to English.)

As a student of theology, Curran was docile. His only serious disagreements with the preconciliar theology he was learning were on the issues of religious freedom and the necessity of baptism for the salvation of infants. His dissertations at the two universities contained no hint of rebellion. Bernard Häring was a major influence on the Curran we now know. Like Curran, Häring was a priest with heartfelt pastoral concerns. Häring was biblically grounded and opposed to the separation of spiritual theology from moral theology, and open to the thinking of philosophers like Max Scheler. Curran identified with all of this, and it animated his theological career. In Curran's words, "What appealed so profoundly to me was the wholeness of Häring's approach which was mirrored in his own life and personality."[7] Curran's students could say the same.

In a sense, Curran as theologian did better than Häring in joining solid, cutting-edge scholarship with pastoral concern for a holistic and livable moral theology. Häring's later work became more homiletic and less rigorous—a point conceded by Curran. Curran's work did no such thing. The pastoral concerns were always present, but the rigor has perdured.

Curran listened to more than his students. In parish work he was educated by the *sensus fidelium* (a source of truth in Catholic faith) and saw that uninformed theories were imposing on good people yokes that were not sweet and unnecessary burdens that were not light. He had gotten top grades defending those theories in examinations in Rome. His postdoctoral education was now honing his critical skills. Experience is the plasma of theory, and Curran's theology was refreshed by this experiential infusion. He realized early on that the two key issues for the reform of Catholic moral theology (*theologia semper reformanda:* theology is always in need of reform) were natural law and hierarchical authority. Narrow, physicalist notions of natural law were a straightjacket that crushed a legitimate pluralism on specific moral issues, and hierarchical control of theology is a perennial challenge in Catholic theology.

Soon Curran's growing critical sense showed in his teaching and writing, and it was noticed. Harassment began. Officials of the diocese of Rochester began to caution him about his teaching, and in 1965 he was removed from the faculty at St. Bernard's Seminary. He moved to the Catholic University of America. Church officials who thought that the loss of the seminary post would bend Curran failed to realize that they were dealing with prophetic steel.

With the relentless honesty that marks his life and work, Curran continued to live out his calling. On April 17, 1967, the axe fell. He was called to the rector's office. There the rector, Bishop McDonald, flanked by all the executive officers of the university, announced that the board of trustees (including twenty cardinals, archbishops, and bishops) had voted not to renew Curran's contract. Curran subsequently learned that the Apostolic Delegate, Archbishop Vagnozzi, participated in this action because, in Curran's words, "Rome wanted to make an example out of a liberal American priest, and I was chosen."

I was in Curran's room when his Rochester bishop, Fulton Sheen, called and I heard Curran say to him that he would be content working in a parish. The priesthood was his first and enduring love. Prophecy trumps priesthood, however, when the ecclesiological stakes are as high as they were in this case. The silencing of theologians was well under way in the backlash to Vatican II, and resistance was a duty. The university community rallied behind Curran. First the theology department voted unanimously that "we cannot and will not function unless and until Fr. Curran is reinstated. We invite our colleagues in other schools of the university to join with us in our protest." They did—and for the first time since the Middle Ages a faculty voted to close the entire university and go on strike. The board of trustees buckled, and Curran was reinstated and promoted with tenure.

It was a *kairos* moment, but sadly such moments are rare. Curran predicted in 1975 that if the Vatican tried again to remove him he would get no such support. When the Vatican successfully did so ten years later, there was no effectual response from the university or the theological community at large even though at the time Curran held a tenured full professorship. No other Catholic university opened its doors to this distinguished scholar—past president of the Catholic Theological Society of America, the Society of Christian Ethics, and the American Theological Society and winner of the prestigious John Courtney Murray award for theological excellence. None of his honorary doctorates are from Catholic universities. Something of the loneliness of the prophet was put upon those gentle shoulders: "Because I felt thy hand upon me, I have sat alone" (Jer. 15:17). "For twenty-three years . . . I have been . . . taking pains to speak to you, but you have not listened" (Jer. 25:3).

The Vatican cannot really be blamed for this eerie shunning. Its action made no theological sense, yet it has been accepted as a defining intervention. In a letter dated July 25, 1986, Cardinal Ratzinger told Curran, "you will no longer be considered suitable nor eligible to exercise the function of a Professor of Catholic Theology." In a previous letter, Ratzinger said that Curran's views "violate the conditions necessary for a professor to be called a Catholic theologian." This language indicates the misuse of a juridical paradigm in defining scholarly credentials. In statecraft, this juridicism would make sense; in defining credentials it amounts to a crude nominalism. If a state were to decommission an ambassador, the decommissioned officer could no longer be considered or "called" an ambassador of that state. Curran *is* a Catholic theologian, however. He is not an Islamic theologian or an expert on Tibetan Buddhism. He has all "the conditions necessary for a professor to be called a Catholic theologian." When he speaks and writes, he speaks as what he is. *Operatio sequitur esse.*

The disedifying message from the Catholic academe is that oppression in timid times is metastatic.[8] That Curran holds the distinguished Elizabeth Scurlock Chair of Human Values at Southern Methodist University is a tribute to that university and a message about Catholic academe. One may hope that this volume and other Curran volumes published by Georgetown University Press are a vernal harbinger of a better season.

Curran returned to his work at Catholic University after the 1967 strike. One year later came the encyclical *Humanae vitae,* condemning all forms of artificial birth control. It was reported that the encyclical would appear on Monday morning, July 29, 1968. Curran and several American Catholic theologians predicted that the pope would have to respect mainstream Catholic theological opinion and allow for some openness on the question. We were wrong. Curran, undaunted by the agonies of the preceding year, led the reaction. After a group of ten theologians carefully studied every word of the encyclical, they drafted a letter on Curran's shaky little typewriter that gently but firmly dissented from the papal absolutism. The letter eventually was signed by more than 600 theologians. It was promulgated widely in the national and international press. With admirable restraint (not emulated by others in the Vatican), Pope Paul VI commented that he saw that his encyclical had engendered "a lively debate."

With this letter, Curran's fate was sealed. The Vatican inquisition, acting without the open and due process procedures that are regarded as essential to all civilized contemporary systems of law, moved toward Curran's expulsion. Joseph Cardinal Ratzinger, in a letter to Curran on September 17, 1985, stated that the results of the inquiry on Curran had been presented to "the Sovereign Pontiff in an audience granted to the undersigned Cardinal Prefect on June 28, 1985, and were confirmed by him." Cardinal Ratzinger and the pope objected to Curran's positions on contraception, sterilization, abortion, mercy death, masturbation, premarital sexual ethics, homosexuality, and divorce. (With the exception of mercy death, all of the issues were in the realm of what I have called pelvic orthodoxy, which in the past century has unduly distracted the Vatican from the moral challenges of biblical religion.) Curran was ordered to "retract" his views on all of these complex issues within "two months."

In previous correspondence and meetings with Vatican officials, Curran had labored to explain his views on these matters. His views are not in any sense radical and indeed are shared by the mainstream of *auctores probati* (tested authors) in the Catholic and broader Christian and ecumenical communities. Here we see that the Curran drama is not the story of a single man. The underlying story is retrenchment by the Vatican from the doctrinal advances of the Second Vatican Council. The Decree on Ecumenism in that council recognized that on certain dogmatic questions agreement among Christians was not imminent. On the level of moral debates, however, dialogue could and should commence. "The ecumenical dialogue could start with discussions concerning the application of the gospel to moral questions."[9] This perspective cohered with the Council's acknowledgment that Protestant bodies are truly "ecclesial," animated by the same Spirit, displaying signs of even heroic holiness, and skilled in their knowledge of the scriptures. Respect for the views of such Christians is the obvious conclusion—and, as the Council said, *especially in moral matters*. There is broad and deep agreement among Christian scholars regarding the legitimacy of pluralism on all of the issues on which Curran was condemned.[10] Thus, the critique of Curran also was a critique of the doctrinal progress made in the Second Vatican Council and a step back in ecumenism. That is why the Curran saga is ecclesiological in its dimensions and not merely personal.

WHY CURRAN?

When the Vatican decided to stifle the reformation of moral theology that began before Vatican II, it chose as its principal target Charles E. Curran. This choice was not made by chance. Curran is a thoroughly Roman Catholic theologian. One of his prophetic traits is a dynamic traditionalism. The prophets of Israel derived much of their power from their sense of history. They reminded people of the exciting revolution that brought Israel into being. They sought reform from within the Israelitic story, putting these words into the mouth of God: "I remember the unfailing devotion of your youth, the love of your bridal days, when you followed me in the wilderness, through a land unsown" (Jer. 2:2).

Charles Curran shows that the word *Catholic* can be a growing moral and spiritual experience, not a crust sloughed off by the rush of time. There is great strength in the Catholic ethical tradition, and Curran, two doctorates deep in it, has never forgotten or stopped loving those formative strengths. He was a perfect target because he is so Catholic. He recalls for Catholics the achievements of the past, the bridal days of Catholic thought. By a kind of homeopathy he seeks cures from within the tradition itself, and this approach stings those who resist such reform because it proves that the tradition embodies change and calls for humility.

With his passion for the Catholic story, Curran has developed into the premiere historian of Catholic ethical theory.[11] Perhaps better than any contemporary moral theologian, he knows what the tradition contains to remedy its ills. This knowledge should make him beloved of all who love the Church because he shows that the struggling company of believers has the resurrection power to recover repeatedly from the incessant deaths caused by sin and weakness.

Catholic social theory did blaze a trail "in the wilderness, through a land unsown" in its social justice theory. Protestant theologian Emil Brunner acknowledged this conclusion when he wrote in 1945 that "while the Catholic Church, drawing on centuries of tradition, possesses an impressive systematic theory of justice, Protestant Christianity has had none for some three hundred years past."[12] Curran draws on that history in his social ethics and in his critique of procedures within the church. His recognition of the role in ethics of empirical situational analysis is as Catholic as Thomas Aquinas. "Human actions are right or wrong according to their circumstances," wrote Thomas.[13] Curran's respect for the Catholic ethical principle *ubi dubium ibi libertas* (where there is doubt there is freedom) is in line with the "moral systems" (Probabilism, Equiprobabilism) championed by the Dominicans, Jesuits, and Redemptorists.

In Curran's own words: "I am a committed Christian believer belonging to the Roman Catholic Church."[14] "I am deeply committed to the Church on a very profound level."[15] "My own theological ethics stands firmly within the tradition of Roman Catholic theology."[16] The horizon of Curran's theology "is formed by the fivefold Christian mysteries of creation, sin, incarnation, redemption, and resurrection destiny." He continues: "Any approach to Christian ethics which forgets one of these elements or overemphasizes one element is in my judgment inadequate."[17]

If so faithful a Catholic demonstrates the reformability of moral theology and the legitimacy of ethical pluralism within Catholic moral theology, he is more of a threat to the fear-filled immobilists than anyone who is identifiable as a renegade or an outrider. Curran was a natural target for the Vatican and simultaneously—in a sad irony—one of the best witnesses to the vitality of distinctively Catholic thought. As the church grew and management clung to what Cardinal Dulles called "pre-established positions," many Catholics left the church to grow elsewhere, grateful for the riches they got there and healing from the bruises they sustained. That may be the truest choice for many. Many others, like Curran, stay and function like healthy blood in a diseased organism, paying in the process a great price.

SEQUELS AND CHALLENGES

Moral theologians who are worthy of the name raise more questions than they answer. They turn soil where others must plant, or they busy themselves with one furrow and leave others unplowed. This book celebrates one of the great moralists of our time. Charles Curran's life demands encores from his audiences. Curran himself points to two areas in the Catholic tradition where more—much more—remains to be done: Catholic social theory has lain too fallow and has not been effectively directed toward changing the economic and cultural structures of our society, and Catholic theology is still hobbled by its failure to clarify the distinct roles of hierarchy and scholarship.

As Emil Brunner observed, Catholic social justice theory—drawn from Hebraic, Greek, and Roman antiquity and developed in the writings of Thomas Aquinas, the modern popes, liberation and modern feminist theology, and Latin and United States bishops' writings on the economy—is a treasury. It is loaded with subversive bite, but it has been doing too little biting. When Jimmy Carter was running for the presidency, he called Charles Curran to get advice on what was important to Catholics. Was he calling about American racism, the overwhelming of political power by corporate power (of the 100 largest economies in the world, 50 are corporations), the destruction of the environment, the 40 million people who die every year from poverty-related causes (the equivalent of 300 jumbo jet crashes every day, with half the passengers being children), or about the sexist poisoning of our political and economic structures?[18] No. He was calling about abortion—the only issue he regarded as "a Catholic issue." Carter was not insulting Catholics. He was simply reading them and judging where they were morally serious—and recall that he is a shrewd enough observer to move from a peanut farm to the White House. As Curran says, Catholic social teaching often does not appear "at the level of the pulpit and in the daily lives" of Catholics.[19] The aforementioned issues are screamingly relevant to Catholic social teaching, but they have not become "Catholic issues."

Look Around

The first rule of ethics is *circumspice:* Look around. As Hitler built the Third Reich and planned the holocaust, many theologians—not all—were doing abstruse work on the subsistent relations within the Trinity; they were not *looking around.* Looking around today, we see a new holocaust threatening all of the foundational elements of life on earth: water, topsoil, and air. If current trends continue, we will not. We are well on our way to killing this generous host of an earth. Not surprisingly, in solidarity with the decedent earth, people are dying too. In poverty the rule seems to be "women and children first." Four million babies die yearly from diarrhea in what is euphemistically called the "developing world." Dr.

Noeleen Heyzer of the United Nations says, "Poverty has a female face." Women constitute 70 percent of the world's 1.3 billion absolute poor; they own less than 1 percent of the world's property but contribute two-thirds of the world's working hours.[20] Microbes and viruses that found a life for themselves in the forests have accepted deforesting humans as their new hosts. As Joel Cohen says, "The wild beasts of this century and the next are microbial, not carnivorous."[21] More than thirty new diseases have been identified since 1973, many of them relating to our gluttonous and ecologically dangerous lifestyles.[22]

Overconsumption by the elite is the prime demon. A finite earth cannot hold infinite numbers. Thomas Aquinas saw and wrote that the number of children should not exceed the resources of the community. He even added that this standard should be assured by law as needed. Thomas said that if the generation of children were to exceed what we call today the "carrying capacity" of the territory, civil chaos would result.[23] His insight was that the same fertility that is the greatest blessing also can be a curse. As Gennifer Mitchell says:

> Over the next 25 years, some 3 billion people—a number equal to the entire world population in 1960—will enter their reproductive years, but only about 1.8 billion will leave that phase of life. Assuming that the couples in this reproductive bulge begin to have children at a fairly early ages, which is the global norm, the global population would still expand by 1.7 billion, even if all of those couples had only two children—the long-term replacement rate.[24]

Most of that increase will occur in the overstressed poor world. That is a painful problem.[25]

The elitist illusion is that we can make nations—or parts of them—into gated communities, veiling from our eyes the decay and the huddled and hungry masses, but we can't. Poisons are as globalized as capital. They come to us in the strawberries and the rain. Professor David Orr gives us some of the scary data: Male sperm counts worldwide have fallen by 50 percent since 1938. Human breast milk often contains more toxins than are permissible in milk sold by dairies, signaling that some toxins have to be permitted by the dairies in our dirty world. At death some human bodies contain enough toxins and heavy metals to be classified as hazardous waste.[26] Jeremiah warned us that it is hard to escape the effects of moral malignancy: "Do you think that you can be exempt? No, you cannot be exempt" (Jer. 25:5, 29).

Catholic social theory must address all of this with passion, or it is a magnificent irrelevancy.

Regnum, Sacerdotium et Studium

Religions always teeter on the edge of magic, and they slip over that edge with unfortunate frequency. Christians have struggled with magic on the issue of how we come to know the truth; at times they have done so with heroic success. The early church was confident that the truth could be known because the Spirit of Truth was breathing through the ecclesial community. Even into the early Middle Ages, the terms "inspiration" and even "revelation" were used rather promiscuously to describe the utterances of Fathers, councils, and outstanding churchmen. The Spirit was perceived as "instructing," "dictating," and "preaching" through the councils. Even disciplinary decrees were credited directly to the Holy Spirit.

This unnuanced confidence in the active illuminating presence of God took a new form in the heavily juridical ecclesiology that grew out of the eleventh- and twelfth-century reforms. After studying the period closely, Yves Congar finds in this period "the transition from an appreciation of the ever-active presence of God to that of juridical powers put at the free disposal of, and perhaps even handed over as its property to, 'the Church,' i.e., the hierarchy."[27] Gradually the lubricious term "assistance" replaced "inspiration" and "revelation" to explain the teaching power of the hierarchy. The term has never been developed or blessed by critical theology. Suarez even opined that it was "equivalent to revelation."[28] The First Vatican Council added its weight to this confusion when it defined the possibility of making infallible statements through the medium of fallible language. The preparatory committee, the Deputation of the Faith, raised the question of whether the pope had to use ordinary means to reach his infallible conclusions. The answer was that the efficacious nature of "assistance" is such that even a negligent pope would be impeded from making a pronouncement that would be wrong or destructive. "The protection of Christ and the divine assistance promised to the successors of Peter is such an efficacious cause that the judgment of the supreme pontiff, if it were in error and destructive of the church, would be impeded."[29] Pope Paul VI capped this sad theology by saying that the hierarchical magisterium could teach "without the aid of theology" because it "represents Jesus Christ the teacher and is his quasi-instrument."[30] Pope John Paul II's *Veritatis splendor* is in the grips of the same undeveloped "assistance" theology.[31]

TENTATIO DEI

This assistance theology, which is liable to charges of magic (achieving effects without appropriate causation), can be corrected, following Curran's example, by the Catholic tradition itself. Catholic moral theology has condemned the rash expectation of divine assistance when one has not used the ordinary means to the desired end. This expectation, in effect, challenges God to supply for your negligence. Jesuit theologians Noldin and Schmitt give the clear example of the priest who relies on God's assistance rather than preparing his sermon; they call this behavior a mortal sin of presumption.[32] Henry Davis, S.J., says such tempting of God is a "sin against faith and religion."[33] To expect bishops or popes who are not professional theologians to stand in judgment on theologians—while the bishops rely not on study or expertise but on the assistance of God—tempts God and violates a healthy Catholic understanding of responsible conduct. This radical flaw emerges most recently in the *Ex corde ecclesiae* decree that would put theologians' thinking under the control of bishops, based on this "assistance" that the bishops avowedly have and the theologians do not.

A major struggle of Charles Curran's life will end in failure if today's Catholic theologians do not return to the glorious achievement of Catholic Christianity at the time of the first universities. In *Censure and Heresy at the University of Paris: 1200–1400,* J. M. Thijssen writes, "When around 1200 the University of Paris gradually emerged, its appearance marked the birth of the *studium* as a new social order alongside *regnum* and *sacerdotium,* the powers of kingship and priesthood."[34] The title *doctor* "which in the early church, designated the bishops . . . was now reserved for theologians."[35] As a result of this successful distinction between what Aquinas called the *"officium praelationis"* and the *"officium magisterii,"* "academic heresies and errors were demonstrated in a process of rational discourse, by cognitive criteria that were provided by experts."[36] The fallibility of bishops in doctrine was known to the heroes of this moment. The condemnation of Aquinas by Bishop Stephen Tempier in 1277 had to be recanted by Bishop Stephen of Bourret in 1325. On the basis of that episode, Godfrey of Fontaines said that a theologian should not comply with a teaching of a bishop if he saw it as untrue. If he was certain of its untruth, the theologian should speak out publicly even if people are shocked by his disobedience.[37]

Like all breakthroughs, this advance was not perfect or full-blown. Ideals always have a rough birthing. The ideal of freedom in early America would take many amendments and struggles to bring it to term—and it is not yet fully born. Academic freedom in the modern sense flowered in nineteenth-century Germany, not in thirteenth-century Paris or Bologna. Yet the seeds were sown back there. Pioneers such as William of Ockham saw that only truth has authority, and doctrinal authority has to be based on cognitive criteria, not on institutional power.[38]

Many people wonder today whether the term "Catholic university" is a contradiction in terms. Such doubts thrive because of the timidity and infidelity of contemporary Catholic theologians who have not been worthy of their thirteenth- and fourteenth-century predecessors. The struggle of those prophets was not just for the freedom of theologians. At that time freedom for theology meant freedom for the whole academe, so these trailblazers fought for the freedoms relished in every modern university today. Theirs was a budding belief, Cardinal Newman thought, that the true university is a place where many minds compete freely together. A Catholic university, true to its own history, should be the freest place on earth. It is sin and scandal when this is not so. I have visited the University of Bologna, which was among the first of the European universities. It has preserved some of the original columns. I wanted to hug them or kneel before them because I was standing in a precious and holy place where the bush of learning was epochally set ablaze.

Charles Curran stands in the line of those great battlers for the freedom and the integrity of the human search for truth. He is an amalgam of courage, intelligence, and balance the likes of which only rarely treads this earth. We are forever and happily in his debt.

NOTES

1. Avery Dulles, S.J., "Presidential Address: The Theologian and The Magisterium," *Proceedings of the Catholic Theological Society of America* 31 (1976): 235–46. Eight years before Dulles' presidential address I argued for the distinction between the hierarchical magisterium and the theological magisterium and spoke of the two magisteria as "mutually corrective" in "Moral Absolutes and the Magisterium," in *Absolutes in Moral Theology,* ed. Charles E. Curran (Washington, D.C.: Corpus Instrumentorum, 1968), 57–107. The term "official teaching" is theologically defective. The question is not what teaching is official in the sense of what is taught by officials but what teaching is true.
2. Avery Dulles, S.J., "The Revolutionary Spirit of Thomas Aquinas," *Origins* 4 (February 13, 1975): 543.
3. Thomas Aquinas, *In 4 Sent.,* D. 19, q. 2, qua. 2, ad 4.

4. *Quodlibet* 3, q. 4, art. 1. *Contra impugnantes Dei cultum et religionem,* chap. 2.
5. Dulles, "Presidential Address," 243.
6. Joseph Ratzinger, "The Dignity of the Human Person," in *Documents of Vatican II,* vol. 5, ed. Herbert Vorgrimler (New York: Herder and Herder, 1969), 116.
7. Charles E. Curran, *Ongoing Revisions: Studies in Moral Theology* (Notre Dame, Ind.: Fides, 1975), 265.
8. Visibly missing in the reaction to *Ex corde ecclesiae* is the New Testament virtue of *parresia* (παρρησια). See Acts 4:13. This theological virtue rises *"ex magna animi constantia firmaque veritatis persuasione."* One who has this virtue *"non veretur aliquid aut dicere aut clare dicere."* Francis Zorell, S.J., *Lexicon Graecum Novi Testamenti* (Paris: Lethielleux, 1931), 1012.
9. "Decree on Ecumenism," in *Documents of Vatican II,* Walter M. Abbott, S.J., General Editor (Herder and Herder: New York, 1966), vol. 23, 365. See also vol. 3, 345–46.
10. There is also broad and deep agreement on these issues among the world's non-Christian religions. See Daniel C. Maguire, *Sacred Choices: The Right to Contraception and Abortion in Ten World Religions* (Minneapolis: Fortress Press, 2001). Of these religions the Second Vatican Council, in the "Decree on the Missionary Activity of the Church," said, "truth and grace are to be found among the nations, as a sort of secret presence of God." Walter M. Abbott, *Documents of Vatican II,* vol. 9, 595–96.
11. See, for example, his *Moral Theology at the End of the Century: The Pere Marquette Lecture in Theology, 1999* (Milwaukee, Wisc.: Marquette University Press, 1999).
12. Emil Brunner, *Justice and the Social Order* (London: Lutterworth, 1945), 7.
13. Thomas Aquinas, *Summa Theologiae,* I II q. 18, a. 3. Throughout this *Quaestio* 18, Thomas makes the point that morality must be judged *"secundum diversa,"* according to diverse circumstances. Some circumstances "enter into the principal condition of the object in such wise that they determine the moral species" (a. 10). The rational mean of the virtues, the fulcrum for the balanced understanding of a virtue, is "according to the diverse circumstances" (I II q. 64, a. 1, ad 2).
14. Curran, *Ongoing Revisions,* 291–92.
15. Ibid., 293.
16. Ibid., 283.
17. Ibid., 287.
18. For a study that is the empirical verification of the doctrine of original sin, see Clive Ponting, *A Green History of the World: The Environment and the Collapse of Great Civilizations* (New York: Penguin Books, 1991).

19. Curran, *Ongoing Revisions*, 290–91.

20. Noeleen Heyzer, *The Balancing Act: Population, Development, and Women in an Era of Globalization* (Chicago and New Delhi: John D. and Catherine T. MacArthur Foundation, 1996), 16–17.

21. Joel E. Cohen, "Population Growth and the Earth's Human Carrying Capacity," *Science* 269 (July 21, 1996): 34.

22. See Anne E. Platt, *Infecting Ourselves: How Environmental and Social Disruption Trigger Disease* (Washington, D.C.: Worldwatch Paper, 1996), 6.

23. Thomas Aquinas, *Omnia Opera: Sententia Libri Politicorum* (Rome: Ad Sanctae Sabinae, 1971), Book II, chap. 15; also, chaps 6, 13, 17. On the thorny problem of governmental regulation of fertility, see Daniel C. Maguire and Larry L. Rasmussen, *Ethics for a Small Planet: New Horizons on Population, Consumption, and Ecology* (Albany: State University of New York Press, 1998), 10–18, for my comments on "China and the Draconian Critical Mass."

24. Gennifer D. Mitchell, "Before the Next Doubling," *Worldwatch* 11 (January/February 1998): 23.

25. John Bongaarts of the Population Council, letter in *New York Times*, November 9, 1997.

26. See David W. Orr, *Ecological Literacy: Education and the Transition to a Postmodern World* (Albany: State University of New York, 1992), 3–5, and *Earth In Mind: On Education, Environment and the Human Prospect* (Washington, D.C.: Island Press, 1994), 1–3.

27. Yves Congar, *Tradition et les Traditions* (Paris: Librairie Artheme Fayard, 1960), 164. Congar notes that this switch is undermined by a chastening look at history. He cites "*. . . le problème de certaines contradictions ou divergences entre un énoncé et un autre: comment était-ce possible, si tous venaient du méme Saint-Esprit?*" (". . . the problem of contradictions and divergences between one pronouncement and another: How was this possible if all these pronouncements came from the same Holy Spirit?"), 165

28. "*. . . aequivalet revelationi vel consummat illam, ut ita dicam*" (". . . is equivalent to revelation or completes it, so to speak"). Suarez, *De Fide*, disp. III, sect. 2, n. 11 (*Opera*, ed. Vives, vol. 12), 100.

29. *Sacrorum Concilorum Nova et Amplissima Collectio*, ed. Giovanni Domenico Mansi, Jean Baptiste Martin, and Louis Petit (Paris: H. Welter, 1927), 52, 1214.

30. *Acta Apostolicae Sedis* 58 (1966): 892–96.

31. This same mischievous "assistance theology" is employed by Bishop John M. D'Arcy in his "*Ex Corde Ecclesiae:* From the Heart of the Church," in *Today's Catholic* (September 5, 1999): 12–17, to defend the mysterious power of single local bishops to evaluate the theology of professors from dozens of different

areas of expertise in deciding their worthiness of a "mandate." This astonishing feat is to be achieved "by the help of the Holy Spirit." The "ultimate criterion of truth"—"the standard"—is the hierarchical magisterium.

32. H. Noldin and A. Schmitt, *Summa Theologiae Moralis: De Praeceptis Dei et Ecclesiae* (New York: Pustet, 1941) sect. 173, p. 168.

33. Henry Davis, S.J., *Moral and Pastoral Theology,* vol. 2 (London and New York: Sheed & Ward, 1949), 84.

34. J. M. H. Thijssen, *Censure and Heresy at the University of Paris: 1200–1400* (Philadelphia: University of Pennsylvania Press, 1998), 94.

35. Ibid., 112.

36. Ibid., 115.

37. Godfrey of Fontaines, *Quodlibet VII* 404–5. Quoted in Thijssen, *Censure and Heresy at the University of Paris,* 92.

38. See Thijssen's conclusions, *Censure and Heresy at the University of Paris,* 112.

PART I

Fundamental Moral Theology

CHAPTER 1

The Moral Person: Moral Anthropology and the Virtues

Timothy E. O'Connell

Through the centuries, moral theology has concerned itself with two areas of inquiry. On one hand, it reflected on the nature of moral acts and the objective quality of particular acts as right or wrong. On the other hand, it sought to identify the qualities and characteristics of the right-living moral person. In other words, moral theology dealt both with actions and with agents, with objectivity and subjectivity. The topic of this chapter is the second of these concerns: the moral person.

In the Middle Ages, discussion of the human person as moral agent exhibited considerable sophistication. The twin foundations of human authenticity—knowledge and freedom—were explored in detail, and obstacles to full human flourishing, gathered under the rubric of "impediments," were detailed with insight. All in all, that tradition provided an admirably nuanced picture of the human person.

Recent scholarly exploration has identified several inadequacies with this traditional understanding and has sought to respond to these lacunae with additions to and modifications of the tradition. This chapter first outlines two series of developments that have enriched and modified the traditional understanding of the moral person. Second, it points out the substantial contribution to the process made by Charles E. Curran. Third, it specifies several issues that remain current and provide an agenda that is likely to occupy moral theology in coming years.

RECENT DEVELOPMENTS

Although the Catholic moral tradition of the past several centuries did seek to understand and describe the moral person, that attempt was hobbled by its choice of starting point. The person was understood fundamentally as an agent, as a doer of deeds.[1] As a result, personal identity, for all practical purposes, was equated with personal action. The central qualities of the human were equated with the central requirements for reasonable action: knowledge and freedom.[2]

This perspective resonated with (as it was actually prompted by) medieval philosophical anthropology. As these philosophical perspectives evolved, however, this standpoint became less satisfying. Rene Descartes' seventeenth-century "turn to the interior," followed by the Enlightenment's emphasis on human rights and individual dignity, encouraged a view of the person as transcending action, even as it supports action. The Catholic Church's resistance to secular developments in the intertwined sectors of philosophy and politics meant, however, that these new perspectives were not quickly incorporated into theological discussions. It remained for twentieth-century theology to undertake this development. Two different initiatives deserve special mention.

Fundamental Option

One initiative involved an intensified focus on the human person as such, utilizing the categories of continental transcendental philosophy. A major figure in this process was Karl Rahner, who proposed a distinction of "levels" within the human person: transcendental and categorical. Similarly, Rahner argued for a "person as subject" that is within and beneath "person as agent." Then, in the course of hundreds of essays, he wove these perspectives into the whole range of theological concerns: creation, sin, grace, redemption, and the rest.[3]

With particular attention to moral decision making, Rahner suggested the existence of a "fundamental stance" that is both shaped by individual action and undergirds that action as being the person's self-definition.[4] On the presumption that this fundamental stance is not given with the existence of the person but rather is an achievement, Rahner posited the existence of a "fundamental option"—a transcendental inner act whereby, in the midst of making fully engaged particular "categorical" actions, a person may embrace a self-definition and assume a radical moral identity.

This Rahnerian anthropology was integrated even more fully into the discussions of Catholic moral theology by Josef Fuchs, who presented and developed these ideas in his textbook of fundamental moral theology and in a large number of essays;[5] by Bernard Häring;[6] and by a growing circle of Catholic theologians.[7]

The potential of this approach for distortion has been noted by some commentators, including the Roman Catholic magisterium.[8] Popular discussions of fundamental option, at least, have the tendency to imagine it as separated from the person's categorical acts, as if a person could freely and intentionally choose to act abusively and destructively toward his or her neighbor and nonetheless maintain "in the heart" a rightly ordered, genuinely loving fundamental stance. Careful review of presentations by the aforementioned scholars makes clear, however, that this distortion is nowhere embraced and consistently rejected.[9] Properly understood, there is an integrity (a wholeness) between the transcendental and categorical levels of the self. The integrity is not complete because the presence of original sin means that there can be a lack of categorical freedom—an undue influence of addictions, weaknesses, and misunderstandings, and the like. In the absence of major mental illness, however, this integrity is not altogether absent, either. For that reason, this overall initiative, whereby focus on the person as agent is complemented by focus on the abiding and underlying nature of the person as subject, has become widely appreciated and utilized.

Virtue

The second initiative likewise shifted the focus from moral agency to the abiding reality of the moral person. In that regard, it also responded to the "shift to the interior" of modern philosophy and contemporary culture. Ironically, however, this initiative did so by returning to an overlooked theme of ancient and medieval thought: the centrality of virtue.

As is well known, Thomas Aquinas organized his discussion of specific moral questions by gathering them under the various moral virtues. Moreover, Aquinas' choice was not arbitrary. It expressed a conviction of his theological anthropology that people act in accord with their nature—both their intrinsic nature and their nature as cultivated and developed through life. Thus, for Aquinas the development of virtues was a central project of the moral life.

In this approach, Aquinas was quite different from later manualists, who often used the Ten Commandments, rather than the virtues, as the organizing principle for their discussions of specific moral concerns. Again, this election was not arbitrary; it reflected a dominating concern for concrete moral behavior, with the rightness and wrongness of specific actions, along with a relative disinterest in deeper anthropological and theological issues. Thus, whatever its initial motivation, the move from virtues to commandments presumed and encouraged the shift from moral person to moral agency as the pivotal theme of fundamental moral theology.

In recent decades, this second development in theological reflection on the moral person has involved retrieval of an appreciation for the virtues and the anthropological emphasis on abiding personhood that it implies. Many authors contributed to this development. The initial impetus seems to have come from James Gustafson. In *Christ and the Moral Life* Gustafson calls for a focus on the underlying attitudes and dispositions that distinguish Christian ethics from the wholesome attitudes and actions of others.[10] Stanley Hauerwas often is credited with moving the issue to center stage for Christian ethicists. Preferring the term "character" for the way it emphasizes central personal moral identity, Hauerwas nevertheless mined the insights and approaches of Aquinas for their relevance to the moral project.[11] Other authors, including Romanus Cessario[12] and Jean Porter,[13] contributed to this development by providing rich historical studies of Aquinas's writings. Philosopher Alasdair MacIntyre deepened and popularized the development with his landmark *After Virtue*.[14]

The central insight of this development (as with the notion of fundamental option) is that there is a dialectical relationship between personhood and action, such that each influences and modifies the other. Following Aquinas, "virtue" can be understood as a moral habit, and "habit" can be described as an inclination toward and facility for actions of a particular kind. "Natural athletes," for example, have an ingrained facility for engaging in sport. This facility makes playing the game enjoyable and thus prompts an inclination to do so. This inclination, in turn, leads to concrete and repeated actions. That is, for such athletes their ingrained facility generates an inclination for action that leads in turn to action itself. Thus, the habit leads organically to action.

At the same time, the inclination to play a sport, for whatever reason (to impress one's friends, for example)—and even if one is not particularly skillful—if acted upon, generally improves one's facility. That is, one gets better at the game. Action nurtures the habit, helping facility and, therefore, inclination to grow. Thus, habit and action have a dialectical relationship in which each cultivates the other.

If habits are an inclination toward and facility for various kinds of action, virtues are habits whose object is a particular sort of action—namely, action as finally right or wrong. Virtues are "moral habits," an inclination toward and facility for acting uprightly. If this is true, however—if virtues are a particular case of habits—then in this ethical sphere the dialectical relationship can be expected to recur. On one hand, one's virtues (and vices) influence one's behavior. If one has a "native" facility for honest communication, and thus an inclination toward truthfulness, one is more likely to act truthfully, even at high personal cost. At the same time, the act of telling the truth, repeatedly and in varied circumstances, increases one's facility for such communication and thus one's inclination to behave in such a manner. Ultimately, the virtue may grow.

Spokespersons for this focus on the virtues argue that a moral vision that looks solely at action divorces action from the person who initiates it and, more important, misconstrues the way in which actions occur. This approach misses the fact that actions occur not only as responses to behavioral alternatives but also as expressions of personal identity. Instead, these authors call for attention to the person who exists within action, who initiates action, and who is shaped by action. They call for attention to the cultivation of the virtues—indeed, of Christian character.[15]

CONTRIBUTION OF CHARLES E. CURRAN

> The Catholic manuals of moral theology paid comparatively little attention to the moral person because they were primarily concerned with sinful acts. However, the Catholic theological tradition in general recognizes the significance of the person and also the different aspects within the person.[16]
>
> In keeping with the Catholic teaching on grace and the virtues, one distinguishes between the basic orientation of the total person and the virtues that modify and dispose the person with regard to her multiple relationships.[17]

These statements of Curran's make clear that he is well aware of the issue that opened this chapter's discussion: the tendency in much of the Catholic tradition to ignore the dynamics of the human person in favor of a one-sided focus on human action. Moreover, he regards the two initiatives discussed above as part of the solution: a focus on fundamental orientation and a return to the theology of the virtues. A review of Curran's published scholarship reveals a detailed series of contributions through which he has participated in this renewal.

Fundamental Option

Curran's engagement of the notion of the fundamental option is particularly interesting. He clearly was aware of the European developments that brought this idea to the fore. As long ago as 1968, Curran used the idea as a way to make sense of the fact that the Catholic tradition has long held that masturbation is an objectively serious misuse of human sexuality even though statistical evidence suggests that the overwhelming majority of human persons—including many whose behavior otherwise suggests a generous and loving approach to life—engage in this behavior. What shall we make of this paradox?

Curran suggests that for various reasons the assertion that masturbation involves "objectively grave matter" is not convincing. In this regard, his argument is about the objective character of the action and not the nature of the moral person. Yet as one element of his argument he also utilizes the notion of the fundamental option:

> Does the act of masturbation so involve the core of the person that man generally makes a fundamental option with regard to it? The empirical evidence . . . indicates that masturbation, especially among adolescents, does not involve a fundamental option. Since masturbatory activity is symptomatic, it can have many different meanings. The ambiguous nature of masturbation argues against the theory that masturbation always involves grave matter.[18]

Thus, Curran is aware of the notion of fundamental option and is willing to make use of it. Nonetheless, what is really intriguing is his mixed feeling about this concept.

Over the years, Curran has made relatively little use of the idea of fundamental option in his writings. This may be partly because his interests often have focused elsewhere. One wonders, however, if something more is at stake. That suspicion is confirmed in his recent book, *The Catholic Moral Tradition Today,* in which he provides an overview of all the major themes of fundamental moral theology.

> Contemporary moral theology has also recognized that the basic orientation and fundamental commitment of the Christian person motivates and influences who the person is as subject and what the person does as agent.
>
> One popular school of contemporary moral theology has developed this basic orientation and fundamental commitment in terms of the fundamental option based on a Rahnerian approach.[19]

Expanding on this opening comment, Curran proceeds to summarize this idea with clarity and conciseness. He then offers some evaluative comments:

> Rahner's transcendental anthropology has been criticized by Johann Baptist Metz for its failure to include the social and political dimensions of human existence. There is merit in this criticism. I also think the fundamental option downplays the historical, social, cultural, and political dimensions of our lives. I want to insist on the person as subject and agent in the multiplicity of our relationships. . . . Proponents of the fundamental option theory claim to recognize to some degree these multiple relationships. . . . However, the person as subject remains too "transcendental" in this interpretation and becomes separated from concrete social and historical reality.[20]

Thus, Curran finds the anthropological schema underlying fundamental option, inherited from transcendental philosophy, too ahistorical and unenculturated for his taste. He fears that it distances the two levels of the person in a way that contradicts the powerful experience of human wholeness—of the ways in which concrete circumstances affect the very identity of the person. As much as spokespersons for fundamental option may struggle to maintain the interactions of the levels of the person that they envision, the pivotal distinction between "transcendental" and "categorical" ultimately may make that impossible.

Curran's concern is the disconnection of transcendental from categorical, of fundamental option from the specificity of individual moral choices. Is this not the very objection lodged against the theory by some magisterial statements? Curran is quick to say that it is not. In showing why it is not, he offers a helpful and concise summary of his position.

> Although I have some hesitations about the theory of fundamental option, I do not share John Paul II's criticism of it in the encyclical *Veritatis splendor.* The pope accuses proponents of the fundamental option of separating that option from concrete behavioral acts. Such a charge distorts what its proponents are really saying. The theory distinguishes the transcendental and categorical aspects, but it does not separate them. But it does, I repeat, downplay the relational and historical aspects of salvation and of the human subject.[21]

Virtue

> That virtue has played an important role in Catholic moral theology is exemplified in the work of Thomas Aquinas. Here virtue is understood as a good habit or stable disposition inclining the person toward the good. The manuals of moral theology, however, with their narrow focus paid basically no attention to virtue.[22]

Curran begins another chapter of his book—the chapter that follows his discussion of fundamental option—with the foregoing words. Again, we are made aware that he is cognizant of this initiative in Christian anthropology. Again, we discover that he is familiar with those who have made particular contributions to this initiative, as he discusses the work of Hauerwas, Porter, Cessario, and others.

We also discover a certain demurral in Curran's exploration of this theme. It is true that a careful reading of his text fails to find any specific objections to the assertions of those who have sought to bring character and virtue to the fore in their understanding of the moral person. Nonetheless, there is a sense that these insights are marginal to the vision that Curran himself espouses.

> The realities of historical consciousness, social location, diversity, pluralism, and individual vocations must also influence our interpretation of the virtues. Is it possible to propose that the virtues can still characterize Christian life in the midst of such diversity and pluralism?. . . One can spell out the virtues of the Christian life common to all Christians but only in the sense of a loosely arranged minimum common to all.[23]

Curran then proceeds to present a sort of meditation on some of the qualities that could or should characterize the Christian in our time. Although there is much to admire in the meditation, it does not represent any kind of exhaustive treatment of virtues as aspects of mature Christian personhood. Even less does it offer an anthropology of Christian character as the source of and product of ongoing moral behavior.

What is the reason for the apparent disconnect between Curran's theological anthropology and these contemporary discussions of character and virtue? The answer may be discerned in a comment he makes as he introduces his meditation on the various virtues.

> The relationality-responsibility model influences how one understands the virtues—both the general virtues that affect our basic orientation and all our relationships and the particular virtues that modify our particular relationships with God, neighbor, world, or self.[24]

The answer is the "relationality-responsibility model."

Relationality-Responsibility Model

Curran has been exploring and utilizing the notions of relationality and responsibility as central, defining themes in moral theology for more than thirty years. The earliest reference seems to be in 1968, when a chapter titled "Christian Responsibility" concludes that "a moral methodology must be developed which sees the morality of actions not merely in terms of the nature and purposes of individual faculties or substances but rather in relation to other beings as persons."[25] The earliest conjoining of the two terms seems to have occurred in 1972, when he declared that "in contemporary Catholic moral theology the responsibility and relationality motif has emerged as most fundamental."[26] Additional discussions occur in 1977, 1979, 1982, and 1988.[27] In Curran's latest consideration of themes from fundamental moral theology, *The Catholic Moral Tradition Today,* he again outlines in considerable detail his thoughts on this topic. I base my summary of the theme on this most recent presentation.

The quotation from Curran that served as the transition to this section of our study stands within his chapter on "Person"; it explains his attitude on the theme of virtue by appealing to the "relationality-responsibility model." For that very reason, it is noteworthy that his substantive presentation of this theme does *not* occur in the chapter discussing "Person." Instead it is found in an earlier chapter titled "Model," wherein he presents his understanding of morality as a whole. That is, for Curran the conjoined ideas of relationality and responsibility are, in the first instance, a lens through which we can understand morality as an overall project. Nevertheless, his presentations make clear that he has adopted this model of morality because he believes it most adequately reflects his understanding of the human person. Hence, his thoughts on this topic fit well in the agenda with which we are concerned here.

> Historically, and especially in the area of philosophical ethics, two models [of the moral life] have been prominent—the deontological and the teleological. The deontological sees the moral life primarily in terms of duty, law, or obligation. The teleological model understands the moral life as seeking ends or goals. A third and newer model was developed by H. Richard Niebuhr, who spoke of it as the responsibility model. I will develop this third model as a relationality-responsibility model.[28]

Here Curran introduces his approach, situates it within the classic discussions of morality, and gives primary credit to Niebuhr. I do not rehearse the classic distinctions, to which Curran devotes more than ten pages, nor do I enter into Niebuhr's thought. Some additional details about Curran's synthesis are important, however.

From the start Curran shows how his model of morality is rooted in his vision of the person.

> The relationality-responsibility approach is my name for a third model which, in my judgment, is the most adequate model for Christian ethics. In general this approach sees the human person in multiple relationships with God, neighbor, world, and self. These multiple relationships impinge on the moral reality of the person.[29]

Curran then declares that "scriptural, theological, and philosophical arguments can be made to show the centrality of a relationality-responsibility model,"[30] and the remainder of his presentation does precisely that. He explores biblical themes including creation and sin, arguing that they imply both the centrality of relationship (the human connection with all that is) and the challenge of responsibility (response-ability—interactive engagement with a dynamic environment). He enters the theological realm, reflecting on the doctrine of the Trinity and the theology of grace, and he turns to philosophy, presenting a pivotal assertion:

> Contemporary philosophical approaches support the relationality-responsibility model. Consider the great diversity and particularity existing in our world. In the midst of such diversity the deontological and teleological models do not seem adequate. There appears to be no detailed law that all people should follow. There seem to be no built-in ends or goals that all should seek. However, in this situation, the danger arises that everyone does one's own thing. Some type of relationality-responsibility approach seems to be the best way to avoid tribalism and chaos in the midst of the particularity and diversity of our global existence today.[31]

Finally, Curran adds a comment that telegraphs again his discomfort with the idea of fundamental option:

> Karl Rahner and Bernard Lonergan, two of the most influential Catholic theologians in the second half of the twentieth century, stressed the role of the subject in their philosophy and theology. This emphasis on the subject naturally brings the concept of responsibility to the fore. However, we are very aware today that the person is not a self-creator but a person with limited creativity and initiative in the context of multiple relationships. Persons are not totally determined by these relationships, but their freedom and creativity are limited by these realities. Such an anthropology constitutes one more reason for adopting a relationality-responsibility model.[32]

Moving on from this overview of theological sources, Curran attempts to show the emergence of this model in contemporary church life.

Although he freely acknowledges that ecclesial practice is inconsistent, he nonetheless finds evidence of the model in Catholic social teaching and in the evolving practice of the Sacrament of Penance. Building on his earlier writings in which he had highlighted the fundamentally different way in which the Church engages social ethics, on one hand, and sexual ethics, on the other, he concludes the chapter by suggesting how the use of the relationality-responsibility model might help address the latter topic.

Summary

In sum, then, Curran's contribution to the initiatives of others in enriching the view of the human person is twofold. First, Curran has helped to communicate these other initiatives by faithfully reporting them and by engaging in dialogue with them. Throughout the years and in virtually all of his writings, he has taken pains to present the newest thoughts on particular questions, offering bibliographic information and intellectual exploration. Second, he has contributed by critiquing those initiatives and offering adjustments and alternatives. Utilizing American sources more than did the presenters of fundamental option, and contemporary historical and cultural perspectives more than did the retrievers of virtue ethics, Curran has consistently urged his relationality-responsibility vision of the person.

At the same time, Curran's various presentations of this vision have been measured in pages, not books. When he embraces the notion of the person as responsible, he roots himself in Niebuhr and accepts this alternative image. As it comes from Niebuhr, however, the idea is more seminal than fully formed.[33] Moreover, Curran does not expand on Niebuhr so much as he adopts the notion. For example, he does not explore at length the signs of responsibility or the dynamics by which it is developed in the person.

Similarly, when Curran emphasizes the relational character of the person, he is utilizing an insight that is widely appreciated in Anglo-American philosophy.[34] Again, however, he does not delve into the ramifications of this question, such as how the person is constituted by relations and what are the qualities of dialectical relationship between an individual and those to whom he or she is related.

Many unanswered questions remain. These questions provide issues regarding the theology of person that will occupy scholars in the coming years.

FUTURE ISSUES

In presenting the anthropological alternative known as "the relationality-responsibility model," Charles Curran has put his finger on the lens that will focus a wide range of issues for the future. Curran is not alone in using the language of responsibility and relationality, of course. By adopting it consistently and remaining faithful to it through the years, however, he has helped to keep it front and center as a way of engaging anew the perennial questions of human personhood.

For the future, three issues seem to demand further attention. First, with regard to the notion of responsibility, there is the question of how human persons develop, change, and grow. The insight that the human world lives within time and must be viewed with historical consciousness is hardly new.[35] For all that, however, much work remains to be done in identifying just how this development takes place. What this means is that the insights of the social scientists—especially developmental psychologists—will need to be incorporated into the study. Interestingly, most of the classic sources on this idea are philosophers and theologians. The scholars whose direct object of attention is the shaping of responsibility, on the other hand, are social scientists—and they have much to contribute.

To give a simple example, traditional Catholic theology of conscience started from the idea of synderesis, the fundamental sense of right and wrong, and asserted that this sense is integral to the human person from the beginning.[36] Observers of contemporary culture wonder if this is true, however; certainly there seems to be ample evidence of a lack of a sense of responsibility. Perhaps we should speak of a human "capacity for responsibility" that can be cultivated, rather than an ingrained sense that is present from the beginning. Or perhaps we should conclude that the original "light of conscience" can be easily extinguished by negative life experiences. One thing is clear: Dialogue between theologians and social scientists would shed much light on this question. Thus, the notion of "responsibility" cannot be taken as a fully formed perspective. Instead, it remains an invitation to serious scholarly exploration.

Second, there is the question of "relationality." Again, much more work needs to be done on understanding exactly how relationships contribute to and influence personal moral posture. Again, the efforts of social scientists will be very beneficial, though in this case it appears that social psychologists and sociologists will be particularly helpful. For example, the philosophical assertions of people such as Macmurray that persons are constituted by their relationships are powerfully confirmed by the empirical studies of scholars such as Albert Bandura and George Herbert Mead.[37] Authors of this sort present compelling evidence that personal moral priorities, even one's abiding moral character, are expressive not simply of the values of the person but also of the commitments of the groups with which the person identifies. Indeed, on the basis of their research one can assert that values are not, in the first instance, the possession of individuals; they are the possessions of groups. People live up to or down to the groups with whom they identify.[38] The studies of scholars from these fields, then, can provide clarity and impact to assertions of "relationality" such as Curran's, helping us discover precisely what significance they have in particular circumstances.

Third, in reference to both responsibility and relationality, much more work needs to be done on the role played by imagination and by those tools of imagination, narrative, and gesture. The fact that narrative, in particular, is important was trumpeted by Stanley Hauerwas as part of his emphasis on character ethics as long ago as 1981.[39] The theme has been developed extensively by scholars in other theological disciplines.[40] Again, however, the precise dynamics by which narratives influence and support the development of individual virtues, moral character, and, at the most substantive level, the identity of the moral person have not been identified.

With regard to the impact of nonverbal communications, even less has been done. An initial exploration has been attempted by Thomas Driver,[41] but more is needed. The overall significance of body language and gesture, as communicative and formative of personal values, needs to be explored, and the potency of rituals to carry the value priorities of communities needs to be examined. At this point one can say only that their import for the shaping of moral persons is significant. With regard to how that import is actualized, however, relatively little is known.

CONCLUSION

Who is the moral person? The question would seem to be a paragon of simplicity because in answering it we ultimately are simply describing ourselves. Yet it is a question that seems never to be finally solved. Perhaps, indeed, it is by nature a perennial question that must be answered anew by each generation—not because earlier answers are false but simply because they are interim.

If that is true, Christian ethics has participated richly in the reexamination of the question in our time. And Charles Curran has contributed thoughtfully and substantively to the exploration. New, more appropriate answers have emerged. Although they do not contradict the answers of the past, they do translate and enrich those answers with insights prompted by the cultural experience of our time.

These answers are no less final than their predecessors, however. As a consequence, in coming years contributors to Christian ethics will be invited to renew the conversation, to retrieve the wisdom of the past, and to refract fresh experiences and fresh insights into new wisdom. So it goes on, in the endless effort to understand ourselves in wisdom and in faith.

NOTES

1. For example, Henry Davis, *Moral and Pastoral Theology,* vol. 1 (New York: Sheed & Ward, 1958), 11; Hieronymous Noldin, *Summa Theologiae Moralis,* vol. 1 (Innsbruck, Austria: Rauch, 1957–60), 15–100.
2. See Timothy E. O'Connell, *Principles for a Catholic Morality,* 2d ed. (San Francisco: Harper and Row, 1990), 51–102. The ideas described here are developed at length in O'Connell's book, which also provides an extensive bibliography on the topic.
3. For example, Karl Rahner, "The Theological Concept of Concupiscentia," in *Theological Investigations I* (Baltimore: Helicon, 1961), 347–82; "The Dignity and Freedom of Man," in *Theological Investigations II* (Baltimore: Helicon, 1963), 235–63; "Guilt and its Remission: The Borderland between Theology and Psychotherapy," in *Theological Investigations II* (Baltimore: Helicon, 1963), 265–81; "Some Thoughts on a Good Intention," in *Theological Investigations III* (New York: Seabury, 1974), 105–28; and "Justified and Sinner at the Same Time," in *Theological Investigations VI* (Baltimore: Helicon, 1969), 218–30. See also Timothy E. O'Connell, "The Question of *Grundentscheidung,*" *Philosophy and Theology* 10 (1996): 143–68.
4. To the best of my knowledge, this precise term does not exist in Rahner's corpus. He speaks of *Grundfreiheit* (basic freedom), which grounds and actualizes *Grundentscheidung* (basic choice). French translations of his works rendered the latter German term as *option fondamentale,* which led to the common English terminology. Similarly, it seems appropriate to term the abiding actuation of basic freedom as "fundamental stance."
5. Josef Fuchs, *Theologia Moralis Generalis,* vol. 2 (Rome: Gregorian University, 1963 and 1967), 4. See also "Basic Freedom and Morality," *Human Values and Christian Morality* (Dublin: Gill and Macmillan, 1970), 92–111; "Sin and Conversion," *Theology Digest* 14 (1966): 292–301. See also Timothy E. O'Connell, *Changing Roman Catholic Moral Theology: A Study in Josef Fuchs* (Ann Arbor, Mich.: University Microfilms, 1974), 231–312.

6. Bernard Häring, *Free and Faithful in Christ,* vol. 1 (New York: Seabury, 1978), 162–222.

7. For example, John Glaser, "Transition Between Grace and Sin: Fresh Perspectives," *Theological Studies* 29 (1968): 260–74; Richard McCormick, "The Moral Theology of Vatican II," in *The Future of Ethics and Moral Theology,* ed. Don Brezine and James V. McGlynn (Chicago: Argus, 1968), 7–18; Norbert Rigali, "The Moral Act," *Horizons* 10 (1983): 252–66; Ronald Modras, "Implications of Rahner's Anthropology for Fundamental Theology," *Horizons* 12 (1985): 70–90.

8. See "Declaration on Certain Questions Concerning Sexual Ethics," Sacred Congregation for the Doctrine of the Faith (December 29, 1975), sect. 10, and *Veritatis splendor,* encyclical letter of John Paul II (August 6, 1993), sect. 63–70.

9. A point acknowledged by the magisterium. The "Declaration" says so clearly, and *Veritatis splendor* by its description of a distorted view that no one holds implies as much.

10. James Gustafson, *Christ and the Moral Life* (Notre Dame, Ind.: University of Notre Dame Press, 1968).

11. Stanley Hauerwas, *Vision and Virtue* (Notre Dame, Ind.: Fides, 1974); *Character and the Christian Life* (San Antonio, Tex.: Trinity University Press, 1975); and *A Community of Character* (Notre Dame, Ind.: University of Notre Dame Press, 1981).

12. Romanus Cessario, *The Moral Virtues and Theological Ethics* (Notre Dame, Ind.: University of Notre Dame Press, 1991).

13. Jean Porter, *Recovery of Virtue: The Relevance of Aquinas for Christian Ethics* (Louisville, Ky.: Westminster/John Knox, 1990), and "The Unity of the Virtues and the Ambiguity of Goodness: A Reappraisal of Aquinas' Theory of the Virtues," *Journal of Religious Ethics* 21 (1993): 137–64. An excellent, concise presentation of Aquinas's understanding of virtues appears in Jean Porter, *Moral Action and Christian Ethics* (Cambridge: Cambridge University Press, 1995), 138–43.

14. Alasdair MacIntyre, *After Virtue* (Notre Dame, Ind.: University of Notre Dame Press, 1981).

15. See also James Keenan, "Virtue Ethics: Setting the Agenda," *Thought* 67 (June 1992): 115–125; "Proposing Cardinal Virtues," *Theological Studies* 56 (1995): 709–29; *Virtues for Ordinary Christians* (Kansas City, Mo.: Sheed & Ward, 1996); "How Catholic are the Virtues?" *America* (June 7, 1997): 16–22.

16. Charles E. Curran, *The Catholic Moral Tradition Today* (Washington, D.C.: Georgetown University Press, 1999), 87.

17. Ibid., 89.

18. Charles E. Curran, "Masturbation and Objectively Grave Matter," in *A New Look at Christian Morality* (Notre Dame, Ind.: Fides, 1968), 207.
19. Curran, *The Catholic Moral Tradition, 95ff.*
20. Ibid., 97.
21. Ibid., 98.
22. Ibid., 110
23. Ibid., 112.
24. Ibid., 113.
25. Curran, *A New Look at Christian Morality,* 244.
26. Charles E. Curran, *Catholic Moral Theology in Dialogue* (Notre Dame, Ind.: Fides, 1972), 32. This statement comes at the end of an extended discussion of the idea (pp. 28–32). In these pages Curran cites three sources for this idea: Jonsen, Häring, and especially Niebuhr—sources he cites repeatedly in subsequent years. See Albert R. Jonsen, *Responsibility in Modern Religious Ethics* (Washington/Cleveland: Corpus Books, 1968); Bernard Häring, *The Law of Christ,* 3 vols. (Westminster, Md.: Newman, 1961, 1963, 1965); H. Richard Niebuhr, *The Responsible Self* (New York: Harper and Row, 1963).
27. Charles E. Curran, *Themes in Fundamental Moral Theology* (Notre Dame, Ind.: University of Notre Dame Press, 1977), 136–39; *Transition and Tradition in Moral Theology* (Notre Dame, Ind.: University of Notre Dame Press, 1979), *4ff; Moral Theology: A Continuing Journey* (Notre Dame, Ind.: University of Notre Dame Press, 1982), 44–47; *Tensions in Moral Theology* (Notre Dame, Ind.: University of Notre Dame Press, 1988), 96–100.
28. Curran, *The Catholic Moral Tradition Today,* 60.
29. Ibid., 73.
30. Ibid.
31. Ibid., 76.
32. Ibid., 77.
33. *The Responsible Self,* for example, was developed from lectures Niebuhr delivered in 1960 and was published posthumously in 1963. It carries the telling subtitle, "An Essay in Christian Moral Philosophy."
34. Perhaps most notably by John Macmurray, *The Self as Agent* (London: Faber and Faber, 1957), and *Persons in Relation* (London: Faber and Faber, 1961), which represent the Gifford Lectures of 1953–54.
35. For example, see Bernard Lonergan, "The Transition from a Classicist World-View to Historical-Mindedness," in *Law for Liberty,* ed. J. E. Biechler (Baltimore: Helicon, 1967), 126–33; Bernard Häring, "Dynamism and Continuity in a Personalistic Approach to Natural Law," in *Norm and Context in Christian Ethics,* ed. G. H. Outka and P. Ramsey (New York: Scribner, 1968), 199–218.

Curran himself has highlighted this fact. See, for example, "Natural Law and Contemporary Moral Theology," in *Contemporary Problems in Moral Theology* (Notre Dame, Ind.: Fides, 1970), 97–158, especially 116–36.

36. For example, Timothy E. O'Connell, *Principles for a Catholic Morality,* 2d ed. (San Francisco: HarperCollins, 1990), 110, where synderesis is termed "conscience/1."

37. Albert Bandura, *Social Foundations of Thought and Action: A Social Cognitive Theory* (Englewood Cliffs, N.J.: Prentice Hall, 1986). Mead's thought is presented in Ruth A. Wallace and Alison Wolf, *Contemporary Sociological Theory,* 3d ed. (Englewood Cliffs, N.J.: Prentice Hall, 1991).

38. These ideas are developed at length in Timothy E. O'Connell, *Making Disciples: A Handbook of Christian Moral Formation* (New York: Crossroad, 1998), 75–101.

39. Stanley Hauerwas, *A Community of Character* (Notre Dame, Ind.: University of Notre Dame Press, 1981), especially 9–35 and 129–52. See also Stanley Hauerwas and L. Gregory Jones, *Why Narrative* (Grand Rapids, Mich.: Eerdmans, 1989).

40. John Dominic Crossan, *The Dark Interval Towards a Theology of Story* (Niles, Ill.: Argus Communications, 1975); John Shea, *Stories of God* (Chicago: Thomas More Association, 1978); William Bausch, *Storytelling: Imagination and Faith* (Mystic, Conn.: Twenty Third, 1984); Terrence Tilley, *Story Theology* (Collegeville, Minn.: Liturgical, 1985).

41. Thomas Driver, *The Magic of Ritual* (New York: HarperSanFrancisco, 1991).

CHAPTER 2

The Moral Agent: Actions and Normative Decision Making

James F. Keenan, S.J.

MORAL THEOLOGY SINCE VATICAN II

Before Vatican II, moral theologians began to innovate moral theology to become much more attuned both to Jesus' call to discipleship and the contemporary world. Dom Odon Lottin studied the historical development of scholastic thought from the eleventh through fourteenth centuries (particularly on moral psychology and epistemology);[1] with that appreciation of history, he offered a fundamental moral theology that specifically took account of the developmental nature of personal moral growth.[2] Fritz Tillmann left biblical studies for moral theology to write about the call to discipleship and the threefold love of God, neighbor, and self.[3] Gerard Gilleman did a dissertation on charity as the foundation of the moral life to reintegrate the ascetical life with the moral life, with the former serving as the animating force for the latter.[4] Theodor Steinbüchel integrated graced human freedom and the call to decision making into key elements for realizing the call to pursue moral truth.[5] These scholars renovated the foundations of moral theology by reintegrating moral theology with the other fields of theology: biblical, dogmatic, historical, and ascetical theology.

On these foundations, Bernard Häring established a major synthesis of the notion of moral truth as an ontological reality, maintaining, like those before him, that moral truth is to be realized from the depths of persons.[6] His position emerged from an appreciation of his predecessors and from his own wartime experiences that convinced him that in crises, people reason from the depths of their personal commitments. He found moral truth not primarily in what persons say but in how they live.[7]

These early innovators were not particularly known for their writings on moral reasoning, however. This was partly a consequence of the fact that unlike the contemporary manualists who located moral truth in prescribed propositions, these theologians recognized moral truth in the person. Because they were so interested in the person and became, in turn, defenders of conscience, they were reluctant to conclude debates—unlike their manualist counterparts John Ford and Gerald Kelly, who seemed eager to resolve all sorts of problems. The latters' deductive, principle-based, manualist casuistry allowed them to devise solutions for a host of topics dealing with death and dying, military activities, marital relations, and reproductive issues.[8]

Deferring to the personal conscience of the Christian disciple, moral theologians developed a method for what a conscientious decision would look like. One of the most interesting expressions of such a decision appeared in the majority report of the papal commission on birth control. This report recognized that moral truth regarding birth control can be articulated most appropriately by married persons who in conscience need to determine whether and when the serious issue of birth control ought to be a means toward realizing themselves as responsible parents. In presenting the report, Josef Fuchs explained that the locus for finding moral truth had shifted from manualists' propositions to personal reality: "Many confuse objective morality with the prescriptions of the Church. We have to realize that reality is what is. And we grow to understand it with our reason, aided by law. We have to educate people to assume responsibility and not just to follow the law."[9]

Whereas those manualist moral theologians from the 1930s to the 1960s were known for the very foundations of the paradigm they proposed, in many ways those from the 1960s through the 1970s were known predominantly for repudiating the existing manualist paradigm. This dismantling of the manualist logic occurred in several ways.

First, responding to Vatican II's call to renovate moral theology *(Optatam Totius 16)*, the innovators perceived in the wake of *Humanae vitae* that the notion of moral absolutes in general and intrinsic evil in particular had to be critiqued and rejected, rather than assumed. Of the many critiques of absolutes, three are particularly noteworthy because of their distinctive strategies. The first was Charles Curran's edited collection, *Absolutes in Moral Theology?* The second was embodied in individual articles penned by various major scholars. For instance, Josef Fuchs argued that no specific moral judgment could be rendered by the simple direct application of an a priori, universal principle; the morally objective judgment was achieved by adequately understanding and responding to the multiple demands emergent in any particular situation.[10] The third was John Dedek's historical study of the development of the concept of intrinsic evil. Dedek found that the concept of intrinsic evil originated with none other than Thomas Aquinas's greatest historical detractor, Durandus of St. Pourçain, O.P.[11]

With the claims of intrinsic evil somewhat undermined, Peter Knauer introduced an argument for a form of moral reasoning. By invoking the principle of double effect and removing the force of the first condition—that is, that the morally right action could not be an intrinsic evil—Knauer argued that the principle collapses into its fourth condition: proportionate reason.[12] Bruno Schüller disputed Knauer's claims,[13] and Schüller's student, Lucius Ugorji, provided a rigorous study of the use of the principle in manualist thought.[14] The instinct to develop a method of moral reasoning by eliminating the force of intrinsic evil remained intact, however, and Louis Janssens offered a way of reasoning morally that aimed to reduce the amount of ontic evil in the world.[15] Janssens provided an incipient method of moral reasoning that, he argued, was compatible with an ontological notion of moral truth that Janssens called personalism. In response to these Europeans, moral theologians in the United States began to develop a form of this method of moral reasoning, calling it proportionalism.[16] Richard McCormick became its most thoughtful and loquacious proponent.[17]

Proportionalism was a temporary attempt to develop a system of moral reasoning; it had strong manualist instincts because it was essentially manualist logic *sans* intrinsic evil. It preserved the proper mediating function of rules in Christian ethics,[18] engaged circumstances, and weighed premoral values. As such, it focused on actions that could be permitted and values to be protected, but it never engaged directly any of the incipient virtue theory that was emerging at this time. Furthermore, although proportionalists engaged the notion of "doing evil to achieve good," for the most part they reflected on cases that followed the constraining manualist agenda of avoiding evil rather than the more embracing pursuit of the good.

Two other concepts that belonged to manualist moral reasoning also were subject to considerable scrutiny: the claim of consistency as a relevant truth standard and the putative difference between indirect and direct action. Like *Humanae vitae,* the classicist paradigm depended on consistency: If a truth claim was universally true, it was true geographically and historically. Through historical studies of usury and contraception, John Noonan demonstrated, as Lottin did before him, that moral propositional utterances are subject in their formulation to the historical contexts out of which they were originally formulated and in which they are later applied.[19] Noonan's work served as an impetus to investigate other problematic claims of consistency. Giovanni Cappelli illustrated the inconsistency of church teachings on masturbation through the first millennium; in fact, he argued that, contrary to manualists' claims, church concern about masturbation often was relatively insignificant.[20] More recently, Mark Jordan examined seven medieval texts on homosexuality and concluded that far from being consistent, the tradition's teaching was completely incoherent.[21] Bernard Hoose highlighted how conservative claims to continuous church teaching on matters of life and death, sexuality, and even crime and punishment in fact were neither accurate nor really traditional.[22] Behind these works were claims not simply of inconsistency, contradiction, and even incoherence but also that continuity with the tradition was not itself a guarantor of the truth of any teaching.

Regarding the difference between direct and indirect, Curran in the United States and Bruno Schüller in Germany argued powerfully against the normative claims of the difference.[23] As we shall see later, this critique, along with the previous one, freed moral theologians to rethink the foundations of moral reasoning. Interestingly, they both criticized their colleague Richard McCormick, who of the three was the proportionalist. This critique indicated again how proportionalism's logic was closely related to manualist thought, despite objections otherwise.[24]

While many moralists critiqued the manualists' claims, others took the long view and presented historical investigations. Four lines of investigation are particularly noteworthy.

First, Louis Vereecke provided many moral theologians with the foundations for reflecting on the history of morals.[25] In particular, he helped moral theologians see that prior to the manualist period (which so often regarded the conscience as perplexed, scrupulous, doubtful, or erroneous), moral theologians were worried about protecting the responsible freedom of the conscience. At the same time, Eric D'Arcy[26] and Philippe Delhaye[27] offered their investigations with a particular appreciation for St. Paul's validation of the conscience as not only judge but also moral legislator.

This positive, forward-looking view of conscience subsequently was developed in several important ways. John Glaser helpfully distinguished the conscience from the superego and thereby liberated the conscience from the darker interpretations it often had.[28] Sydney Callahan provided an inclusive, holistic view of the conscience and its capabilities for development.[29] Paul Valadier offered a significant historical apology for the conscience as not a threat to but a constitutive component for the development of our living tradition.[30] Anne Patrick brought a liberating feminist perspective to conscience and provided narratives of "truth-tellers" who serve as worthy models for the moral life.[31] Finally, Linda Hogan provided a robust, unapologetic defense of the primacy of the conscience within the Catholic tradition.[32]

Second, John Mahoney offered a study of the making of moral theology and emphasized the tradition's obsession with sin that, Mahoney claimed, ironically was poorly developed. While suggesting the need for more theological reflection on sin, he advanced an argument for a moral theology that was better integrated with spirituality. Here he saw that the former's traditional fixation on avoiding evil ought to be wedded with the latter's interest in the pursuit of the good. An integrated spiritual and moral theology would recapitulate the first principle of the natural law: to do good and avoid evil. Furthermore, Mahoney argued that moral reasoning should be more fully animated by the Spirit and that the notion of "discernment" ought to be more fully incorporated into moral reasoning.[33]

Just as theologians were trying to reconsider methods of moral reasoning, so were philosophers. Stuart Hampshire raised questions about reasoning and objectivity and discussed the particular perspective of the moral agent as different from the moral observer, arguing that the agent had privileged information about the influence that an action could have on the agent's own self.[34] Similarly, Stephen Toulmin studied the structure of an agent's moral reasoning, analyzing the deepest epistemological motivations in an agent.[35] Both were effectively engaging the personalism of moral reasoning as relevant for the attainment of right moral judgment.

These efforts led philosophers to look to history—and here we find the third major contribution, in which Toulmin worked with Albert Jonsen to present an historical study and philosophical defense of high casuistry (1560–1660).[36] This method of moral reasoning was based on the analogical method of comparing new cases with paradigm cases; the latter served as truth standards, much as principles later did in manualist thought. This inductive reasoning was highly context dependent (contrary to the authors' own claims)[37] and extraordinarily sensitive to circumstances. Principles and rules served as moral guides much as maxims do today. The integrity of casuistry, however, depended on the cogency of its argument from which one could derive "internal certitude" and on the authority and credibility of the argument's own author from which one derived "external certitude."

Finally, Jean Porter demonstrated that from the twelfth century, the scholastics' idea of natural law was embedded in the world of theology.[38] In particular, the schoolmen routinely turned to revelation to justify their appeals to natural law and to derive some of the moral content of natural law. This more inclusive and somewhat eclectic way of advancing moral argument validated in many ways the attempts to bridge moral reasoning with the Gospels and with spirituality, but it also suggested that natural law had other potential bedfellows. Pamela Hall demonstrated the mutual affinity between narrative ethics and natural law.[39] Similarly, Lisa Sowle Cahill developed a cogent demonstration of what natural law would look like from a feminist perspective,[40] and Cristina Traina advanced that case in her new work.[41]

Before closing this section, I must nod toward virtue ethics—specifically to another important contribution by Jean Porter in recovering Thomas Aquinas's account of the virtues.[42] This work helped us see the relevance of character development in the determination of right action. Virtue ethics still needs to demonstrate its concrete expressions of moral reasoning, however. The only significant attempt in this direction was Daniel Mark Nelson's work on prudence, which claimed that prudence effectively articulates the norms of natural law.[43] Nelson's claim still needs to be historically and philosophically substantiated, however.

CHARLES CURRAN'S CONTRIBUTIONS

In a manner of summing up the foregoing, Charles Curran writes, "Moral theology can no longer consider the action apart from the person who places the action."[44] Similarly, we cannot consider theologians' writings apart from themselves or their actions. In this section, I consider Curran—the person and his writings. I begin by recognizing that Curran's attempts to protect his teaching position at the Catholic University of America are specific expressions of his commitment to and defense of the very method of decision making outlined above: If the morally right judgment is determined by adequately discerning and responding to the many claims of a specific situation, we must have the intellectual and academic freedom to entertain those claims.[45]

Moreover, if moral theologians do not defend that freedom, they also fail at their primary task:

> Moral theologians must become more aware of their proper function. In the past we moralists spent most of our time interpreting the documents of the magisterium for the Christian people. Today the Vatican Council and theologians are beginning to recognize the importance of the experience of Christian people. Theologians must also interpret the experience of Christian people for the magisterium.[46]

Curran's defense of academic freedom is a defense of the moral theologians' duties to reason rightly and to reflect on the experience of others.

Another way of expressing these concerns is by talking about the defense of the conscience. In 1965, Curran provided a good description of its dreadful state in the Roman Catholic tradition:

> The defects of the manualistic treatises on conscience are great. Briefly, legalism, extrinsicism, impersonalism, and an ethic of obligation characterize such considerations of conscience. Positive law and objective considerations are greatly exaggerated. Conscience becomes negative, oppressive, and sin-orientated. The dire consequences are not restricted merely to the intellectual and theoretical plane. History and empirical studies show that the linking of introspection with a legalistic approach to morality provides fertile ground for the formation of the scrupulous conscience. Unfortunately, in everyday Catholic life, the average Catholic equates Christian morality with Mass on Sunday, no meat on Friday, and the need to obey what the Church teaches about sex.[47]

Curran's first interests were to take our understanding of conscience out of the manualists' negative, essentialist nature. Conscience hinges instead on a personal self-understanding as fundamentally relational, for "conscience must act in accord with the nature and person of man."[48]

Curran brought this notion of relational self-understanding to the conscience by developing it in light of Häring's own work. Curran proposed two specific characteristics of the conscience:

> A communitarian conscience recognizes man's relationship with his fellow men in the kingdom of God. A communitarian conscience avoids excessive individualism and the opposite extreme of mass hypnosis. A creative conscience, attuned to the Spirit, throws off the shackles of stultifying legalism.[49]

For Curran, the person's conscience stands in relation not only to self and neighbor, but also to God. Again, that relationship can only be understood as personal. "The basis of Christian morality, however, is not man's relation to an abstract principle, but to a person, *the* person, God."[50] Curran then places this multi-relational self-understanding of the conscience, creatively attuned to the Spirit, within the context of the Church. He does that in his new synthesis,[51] but he has almost always held that: "Salvation comes to man in community, as a member of the Church, the new Israel."[52]

Curran incorporated this relational self-understanding into a relational-responsibility model of moral reasoning.[53] In one of the many ways in which he illustrated how this model expressed its reasoning, Curran asked: "Should sexual morality be grounded solely in the nature and finality of the sexual faculty itself?" He answered:

> The sexual faculty should never be absolutized and seen only in itself, but in relationship to the person and the person's relationship to others. Thus, in the matter of artificial contraception for spouses, the good of the person or the good of the marriage relationship justifies interfering with the faculty or its act.[54]

In this simple explanation we see what differentiates Curran from proportionalism. As noted above, proportionalism was a revision of manualism; Curran described it as somewhere "between the two extremes of total consequentialism and the physicalism of the Catholic tradition."[55] Yet although he defended proportionalism against critics who seemed not to understand it,[56] and although he held "a chastened Aristotelian-Thomistic approach" that promoted basic human goods such as life, justice, and perhaps solidarity,[57] he supported these goods precisely because they express relational responsibilities. For this reason, he often has showed throughout his theology a special predilection for justice.[58]

Curran criticized proportionalism and all of teleology, just as he criticized deontology.[59] He advocated—as the sexual faculty case demonstrates—an understanding of the ways we are related to one another and the responsibilities that arise from these relations. Thus, whereas Bruno Schüller and Richard McCormick routinely divided ethics into teleology and deontology, Curran recognized a third area: responsibility. I have always understood and preferred another threefold division: an act-oriented ethics (here manualists and proportionalists are included because both express goods attached to particular ways of acting as their primary concern), a duty or a responsibility ethics (here are Kantians and American responsibility ethicists who define moral logic in terms of particular social duties or responsibilities), and finally virtue ethics (embodied by those who define their moral logic primarily in terms of specific character traits to be pursued). Either triad is helpful to a point because Curran has warned us against neat, all-inclusive approaches.[60] Indeed, virtue ethicists have incorporated social ways of being related into their ethics,[61] just as Curran recently has inserted the virtues into his relational-responsibility model.[62]

Curran's insistence on relational responsibility distinguishes him not only from the manualists, as well as the proportionalists and virtue ethicists, but also from European innovators who insisted on an autonomous conscience. He criticized these thinkers: "Conscience and human freedom are not completely autonomous. In practice man rejects the complete autonomy of conscience. In the eyes of the world, Adolf Eichmann and the Nazis were guilty of crimes against humanity despite the plea of a clear conscience."[63] Eventually Curran's European colleagues reformed their own position to argue that the autonomous conscience had to belong to a person who was constitutively relational.[64]

Essential for Curran's relational responsibility is dialogue. This dialogue is based on a historicist assumption that to discover the truth, we must continue to learn.[65] As a theologian, Curran consistently has committed himself to this need for dialogue. For instance, he has encouraged dialogue with Protestants in general[66] and Paul Ramsey specifically.[67] In the multivolume *Readings in Moral Theology,* Curran has fashioned a dialogue of sorts by bringing into conversation a variety of contributors on numerous topics. Likewise, when many theologians who were more closely connected to the Vatican were interested in ending the dialogue surrounding contraception and moral absolutes, Curran responded by inviting into discussion theologians and ethicists to converse on these issues. These dialogues created far more of an impact on renewal than any singular contribution.[68]

Dialogue requires the willingness to learn:

> Dialogue is not monologue. Dialogue presupposes that Catholics can learn from all these others. The call for dialogue presupposes the historical and pilgrim nature of the Church that does not possess all the answers but is open to the search for truth. The need for ongoing dialogue and ongoing search for truth contrast sharply with the classicist view of reality and truth.[69]

Curran has lamented the magisterium's inability to let go of the classicist, manualist method and enter into dialogue: "Unfortunately, all the changes in man's understanding of himself and his world have had little or no effect as yet on moral theology."[70]

Dialogue can lead to critique, and Curran is especially critical of attempts to respond to contemporary issues that use manualist insights or implicitly accommodate those insights by employing pastoral solutions. He criticized McCormick for believing that the distinction between direct and indirect had normative significance. In that same volume, Curran similarly critiqued Paul Ramsey.[71] Curran has argued against those who assume the distinction as a casuistic device without exploring the question of its normativity. For instance, although the manualists offered an indirect abortion to resolve the case of an ectopic pregnancy, they were not able to offer a right resolution for any other life-threatening pregnancy, simply because manualist logic had deigned that there could be no direct taking of fetal life. Yet what is the difference between a direct and indirect abortion other than the difference that manualists constructed?

Curran also applied his critique of the direct and indirect distinction to the purported difference between commission and omission, specifically in the matter of the care of people who are dying.[72] Curran also criticized those who employed pastoral solutions without examining whether the manualist or magisterial claims were legitimate. For instance, commenting on Josef Fuchs—who asked whether there is "grave subjective guilt" in the act of masturbation—Curran wrote:

> The "objectively grave-subjectively not culpable" approach offers a good pastoral solution for the priest or confessor. However, theologians must ask the further question: Does the confessional experience of a frequent lack of subjective guilt indicate that the matter itself might not be objectively grave?[73]

Likewise, he criticized those who appropriated these pastoral solutions to the question of contraception:

> Such pastoral solutions might help solve the perplexed conscience of the individual person, but they do nothing to alleviate, and in fact ultimately perpetuate, the social problems connected with overpopulation in many parts of the globe. For the sake of truth and the best interests of the Church and all mankind, I have concluded that it is necessary to take the more radical solution which maintains that the papal teaching on this point is in error.[74]

His argument against assuming these manualist devices or pastoral solutions without addressing underlying claims was most clearly expressed in his position on sterilization:

> My disagreement with the accepted teaching goes to the most basic and fundamental level—the stewardship which man has over his sexuality and generative functions. Those who disagree primarily by questioning the concept of direct and indirect or the principle of totality without going to the ultimate level do not, in my judgment, adequately come to grips with the question of sterilization.[75]

Each of these positions is an instantiation of Curran's firm commitment to a realistic relational-responsibility ethics: He refuses to appropriate the manualist method or its distinctions or accompanying complex pastoral solutions because inevitably they do not adequately engage the reality of an agent's objective relational responsibility.

This realism has led Curran to several other considerations; I mention only two. First, he has rigorously critiqued a naive physicalist interpretation of natural law.[76] Although he has validated natural law,[77] he has insisted that the reality of the natural law is fundamentally relational.[78] This view of a natural law that is based on the human person as relational, Curran argues, is gathering more and more support from Catholic and Protestant ethicists.[79]

To understand what natural law requires, Curran adds, we need an inductive method of moral reasoning that is open to change and development, dependent on empirical data, and looking for resolution in moral, as opposed to absolute, certitude.[80] This type of moral reasoning is considerably like high casuistry. In fact, Curran has acknowledged a certain symmetry between his thought and this form of casuistry.[81] His attraction to casuistry is related not simply to its evident congruence with his thought but also to the fact that in reality human beings "are more likely to choose a more experiential and less discursive approach to decision making."[82]

Realism also has led Curran to consider compromise. Here he reflects on humanity with its limitations and sin, awaiting the full realization of the kingdom. In that context, he acknowledges that our judgments must be prudential: They cannot exceed what we cannot realize in the here and now. Whereas I have never fully understood what he means by sin in this context (between someone compromising in sin or someone compromising because of the effects of humanity's sinful condition, I take the latter—as I think he does), his realistic compromise affords us an important insight into the very nature of the virtue of prudence.[83]

FUTURE CHALLENGES

> Openness to the Spirit is completely incompatible with irresponsibility and a selfish seeking of the easiest way out of a given situation. Contemporary theology needs to develop the treatise on the rules for the discretion of the Spirit. The discernment of the Spirit is a most important factor in the moral life of the contemporary Christian.[84]

When we turn to the Spirit, we get a glimpse of the future challenges that await us in light of the legacy of the innovators in general and Curran in particular. Edward Vacek[85] and William Spohn[86]—writing on the foundations of Christian ethics being rooted in the love of God and Christian spirituality, respectively—remind us of what Gilleman, Häring, Mahoney, Curran, and others have claimed: that in the Spirit we find the possibility of a more integrated, positive, and relational moral theology.

For all the integration and foundation that we have developed, however, we need now to offer to the people of God an integrated moral theology that is ordinary, accessible, readable, and pertinent. We need to make more of our writing practical. We need to apply these insights to relevant but familiar and not fantastic cases to illustrate exactly what an inductive, analogically based method of moral reasoning looks like.[87] In fact, Curran himself—who recently has acknowledged the value of casuistry—could demonstrate for us what that casuistry would look like in a relational-responsibility model.

Similarly, virtue ethicists and other innovators who write about relational anthropologies as the foundation for Christian ethics need to demonstrate how character informs the process of moral reasoning—and they need to do this for their own colleagues as well as for a broader readership. Could they not also turn to casuistry?

We live now in a church that has never had a better-educated membership, yet the moral theology that most Catholics know, unfortunately, is still the manualist method as conveyed by the magisterium. We moral theologians need to be led by the Spirit into the ordinary lives of church members. If Charles Curran is right that our task is to interpret their experiences, we should, in turn, be able to engage them more frequently than we presently do.

NOTES

1. Odon Lottin, *Psychologie et morale aux XII et XIII siècles* (Louvain, Belgium: Abbaye du Mont César, 1942–1957).

2. Odon Lottin, *Morale fondamentale* (Tournai, Belgium: Declée & Cie, 1954); Mary Jo Iozzio, *Self-Determination and the Moral Act: A Study of the Contributions of Odon Lottin, O.S.B.* (Leuven, Belgium: Peeters, 1995).
3. Fritz Tillmann, *Die katholische Sittenlehre: die Idee der Nachfolge Christi* (Düsseldorf, Germany: L. Schwann, 1934); *Handbuch der katholischen Sittenlehre* (Dusseldorf, Germany: L. Schwann, 1934–1938); *The Master Calls: A Handbook of Christian Living* (Baltimore: Helicon, 1960).
4. Gerard Gilleman, *Le primat de la charité en théologie morale: essai méthodologique* (Louvain, Belgium: E. Nauwelaerts, 1952); *The Primacy of Charity* (Westminster, Md.: Newman, 1959).
5. Theodor Steinbüchel, *Existenzialismus und christliches Ethos* (Heidelberg, Germany: F. H. Kerle, 1948); *Religion und Moral* (Frankfurt am Main, Germany: Knecht, 1950).
6. Bernard Häring, *Das Gesetz Christi: Moraltheologie, dargestellt fur Priester und Laien* (Freiburg, Germany: E. Wesel, 1958); *The Law of Christ* (Westminster, Md.: Newman, 1961).
7. Bernard Häring, *Embattled Witness: Memories of a Time of War* (New York: Seabury, 1976).
8. John Ford and Gerald Kelly, *Contemporary Moral Theology* (Westminster, Md.: Newman, 1964).
9. Robert Kaiser, *The Politics of Sex and Religion* (Kansas City, Mo.: Leaven, 1985), 154; the papal commission report is in the appendix of Kaiser's book.
10. Josef Fuchs, "The Absoluteness of Behavioral Moral Norms," in *Personal Responsibility and Christian Morality* (Washington, D.C.: Georgetown University Press, 1983), 115–42.
11. John Dedek, "Intrinsically Evil Acts: The Emergence of a Doctrine," *Recherches de theologie ancienne et medievale* 50 (1983): 191–226; "Intrinsically Evil Acts: An Historical Study of the Mind of St. Thomas," *Thomist* 43 (1979): 385–413; "Moral Absolutes in the Predecessors of St. Thomas," *Theological Studies* 38 (1977): 654–80.
12. Peter Knauer, "The Hermeneutic Function of the Principle of Double-Effect," in *Readings in Moral Theology, No. 1,* ed. Richard McCormick and Charles Curran (New York: Paulist Press, 1979), 1–39.
13. Bruno Schüller, "The Double Effect in Catholic Thought: A Reevaluation," in *Doing Evil to Achieve Good,* ed. Richard McCormick and Paul Ramsey (Chicago: Loyola University Press, 1978), 165–91.
14. Lucius Ugorji, *The Principle of Double Effect* (Frankfurt am Main, Germany: Peter Lang, 1985).
15. Louis Janssens, "Personalist Morals," *Louvain Studies* (1970–71): 5–16; "Ontic Evil and Moral Evil," *Louvain Studies* 4 (1972–73): 115–56; "Norms and

Priorities in a Love Ethics," *Louvain Studies* 6 (1976–77): 207–38; "Ontic Good and Evil: Premoral Values and Disvalues," *Louvain Studies* 12 (1987): 62–82.

16. Bernard Hoose, *Proportionalism: The American Debate and its European Roots* (Washington D.C.: Georgetown University Press, 1987).
17. Richard McCormick, *Notes in Moral Theology 1965–1980* (Washington, D.C.: University Press of America, 1981); *Notes in Moral Theology 1981–84* (Washington, D.C.: University Press of America, 1985). See James J. Walter, "The Foundation and Formulation of Norms," in *Moral Theology: Challenges for the Future,* ed. Charles Curran (New York: Paulist Press, 1990), 125–54.
18. See Curran on mediation in Catholic thinking: *The Catholic Moral Tradition Today: A Synthesis* (Washington, D.C.: Georgetown University Press, 1999), 10–14 (hereafter *Synthesis*).
19. John Noonan, *Contraception: A History of Its Treatment by the Catholic Theologians and Canonists* (Cambridge, Mass.: Harvard University Press, 1965); *The Scholastic Analysis of Usury* (Cambridge, Mass.: Harvard University Press, 1957).
20. Giovanni Cappelli, *Autoerotismo: un problema nei primi secoli cristiani?* (Bologna, Italy: Edizioni Dehoniane, 1986).
21. Mark Jordan, *The Invention of Sodomy in Christian Theology* (Chicago: University of Chicago Press, 1997).
22. Bernard Hoose, *Received Wisdom: Reviewing the Role of Tradition in Christian Ethics* (London: Geoffrey Chapman, 1994).
23. Charles Curran, *Ongoing Revision: Studies in Moral Theology* (Notre Dame, Ind.: Fides, 1975), 205–7; Bruno Schüller, "Direct Killing/Indirect Killing," *Readings in Moral Theology, No. 1,* 138–57.
24. John Connery, "Catholic Ethics: Has the Norm for Rule-Making Changed?" *Theological Studies* 42 (1981): 232–50; John Connery, "The Teleology of Proportionate Reason," *Theological Studies* 44 (1983): 489–96.
25. Louis Vereecke, *De Guillaume D'Ockham à Saint Alphonse de Liguori* (Rome: Collegium S. Alfonsi de Urbe, 1986)
26. Eric D'Arcy, *Conscience and its Right to Freedom* (London: Sheed & Ward, 1961).
27. Philippe Delhaye, *The Christian Conscience* (New York: Desclée, 1968).
28. John Glaser, "Conscience and Superego," *Theological Studies* 32 (1971): 30–47.
29. Sydney Callahan, *In Good Conscience: Reason and Emotion in Moral Decision Making* (San Francisco: HarperSanFrancisco, 1991).
30. Paul Valadier, *Eloge de la conscience* (Paris: Seuil, 1994).
31. Anne Patrick, *Liberating Conscience* (New York: Continuum, 1996).

32. Linda Hogan, *Confronting the Truth: Conscience in the Catholic Tradition* (New York: Paulist Press, 2001).
33. John Mahoney, *The Making of Moral Theology* (New York: Oxford University Press, 1987); *Seeking the Spirit* (London: Sheed & Ward, 1981). See Norbert Rigali, "The Unity of the Moral Order," *Chicago Studies* 8 (1969): 125–43; "Christian Ethics and Perfection," *Chicago Studies* 14 (1975): 227–40; "The Future of Christian Morality," *Chicago Studies* 20 (1981): 281–89. See also Richard Gula, *The Good Life* (New York: Paulist Press, 1999).
34. Stuart Hampshire, *Thought and Action* (Notre Dame, Ind.: University of Notre Dame Press, 1983).
35. Stephen Toulmin, *The Place of Reason in Ethics* (Chicago: University of Chicago Press, 1986).
36. Albert R. Jonsen and Stephen Toulmin, *The Abuse of Casuistry: A History of Moral Reasoning* (Berkeley: University of California Press, 1988).
37. *The Context of Casuistry*, ed. James Keenan and Thomas A. Shannon (Washington, D.C.: Georgetown University Press, 1995); *Conscience and Casuistry in Early Modern Europe*, ed. Edmund Leites (New York: Cambridge University Press, 1988); Richard Miller, *Casuistry and Modern Ethics* (Chicago: University of Chicago Press, 1996).
38. Jean Porter, *Natural and Divine Law: Reclaiming the Tradition for Christian Ethics* (Grand Rapids, Mich.: Eerdmans, 1999).
39. Pamela Hall, *Narrative and the Natural Law: An Interpretation of Thomistic Ethics* (Notre Dame, Ind.: University of Notre Dame Press, 1994).
40. Lisa Sowle Cahill, *Between the Sexes* (Philadelphia: Fortress, 1985); *Sex, Gender, and Christian Ethics* (New York: Cambridge University Press, 1996).
41. Cristina Traina, *Feminist Ethics and Natural Law* (Washington, D.C.: Georgetown University Press,1999).
42. Jean Porter, *The Recovery of Virtue* (Louisville, Ky.: Westminster/John Knox, 1990).
43. Daniel Mark Nelson, *The Priority of Prudence* (University Park: Pennsylvania State University Press, 1991).
44. Charles Curran, *A New Look at Christian Morality* (Notre Dame, Ind.: Fides, 1968), 200–216, at 203.
45. Charles Curran, *Faithful Dissent* (Kansas City, Mo.: Sheed & Ward, 1986).
46. Curran, *A New Look*, 215. Similarly, Josef Fuchs writes, moral theologians "know that they are under obligation to the People of God." *Christian Ethics in a Secular Arena* (Washington, D.C.: Georgetown University Press, 1984), 138.
47. Charles Curran, *Christian Morality Today* (Notre Dame, Ind.: Fides, 1966), 16.
48. Ibid., 18.
49. Ibid., 21.

50. Ibid., 18.
51. Curran, *Synthesis,* 1–29.
52. Curran, *A New Look,* 145–57, at 151.
53. Charles Curran, *Moral Theology: A Continuing Journey* (Notre Dame, Ind.: University of Notre Dame Press, 1982), 35–60; *Tensions in Moral Theology* (Notre Dame, Ind.: University of Notre Dame Press, 1988), 87–109; *History and Contemporary Issues* (New York: Continuum, 1996), 246–50; *Synthesis,* 60–86.
54. Curran, *Synthesis,* 82.
55. Ibid., 157.
56. Ibid., 155–60.
57. Ibid., 161–62.
58. See, for instance, Charles Curran, *Contemporary Problems in Moral Theology* (Notre Dame, Ind.: Fides, 1970), 145.
59. Curran, *Moral Theology: A Continuing Journey,* 35–60; *Synthesis,* 60–73.
60. Charles Curran, *Ongoing Revisions: Studies in Moral Theology* (Notre Dame, Ind.: Fides, 1975), 190.
61. James Keenan, "Proposing Cardinal Virtues," *Theological Studies* 56, no. 4 (1995): 709–29.
62. Curran, *Synthesis,* 110–36.
63. Curran, *Christian Morality Today,* 18.
64. James Keenan and Thomas Kopfensteiner, "Moral Theology out of Western Europe," *Theological Studies* 59 (1998): 107–35.
65. Similarly, we need constant conversion: "Conversion is not just a once for all time action, but rather a continual conversion is the law of life for the Christian." Curran, *A New Look,* 149.
66. Charles Curran, *New Perspectives in Moral Theology* (Notre Dame, Ind.: University of Notre Dame Press, 1976), 5–37.
67. Curran, *Ongoing Revisions,* 229–59.
68. *Absolutes in Moral Theology?* ed. Charles Curran (Washington, D.C.: Pilgrim, 1968); *Contraception: Authority and Dissent,* ed. Charles Curran (New York: Herder and Herder, 1969).
69. Charles Curran, "Absolute Norms and Medical Ethics," in *Absolutes in Moral Theology?* 108–53, at 131.
70. Ibid., 1–18, at 10.
71. Curran, *Ongoing Revision,* 258–59. See Peter Black and James Keenan, "The Evolving Self-understanding of the Moral Theologian: 1900–2000," *Studia Moralia* 39 (2001): 291–327.

72. Curran, *Ongoing Revisions,* 208, note 66. He refers the reader to his *Politics, Medicine and Christian Ethics: A Dialogue with Paul Ramsey* (Philadelphia: Fortress Press, 1973) 152–63.

73. Curran, *A New Look,* 200–216, at 203.

74. Curran, "Introduction," in *Contraception: Authority and Dissent,* 12–14, at 14.

75. Curran, *New Perspectives,* 194–211, at 203. For a similar rigorous, thoroughgoing critique, see Kevin Kelly, *New Directions in Sexual Morality* (London: Geoffrey Chapman, 1998).

76. Curran, *A New Look,* 75–84; *Directions in Fundamental Moral Theology* (Notre Dame, Ind.: University of Notre Dame Press, 1985), 257–78; *Contemporary Problems,* 104–16; Ongoing Revisions, 229–59, 245–59; *Synthesis,* 152–55.

77. "A morality based on the reality of man and his history in the world definitely is a valid source of ethical knowledge." Curran, "Absolute Norms and Medical Ethics," 108–53, at 150.

78. "The contemporary view sees reality more in terms of relations than of substance and nature." Curran, *Contemporary Problems,* 133.

79. Curran, "Absolute Norms and Medical Ethics," 108–53, at 150–53.

80. Curran, *Contemporary Problems,* 124–31.

81. Curran, *Synthesis,* 164–65.

82. Ibid., 164.

83. Curran, *Ongoing Revisions,* 187–89; *Contemporary Problems,* 97–102; *Moral Theology: A Continuing Journey,* 53.

84. Curran, *Directions in Fundamental Moral Theology,* 212.

85. Edward Vacek, *Love, Human and Divine: The Heart of Christian Ethics* (Washington, D.C.: Georgetown University Press, 1995).

86. William Spohn, *Go and Do Likewise* (New York: Continuum, 1999).

87. In addition to works by Richard Gula and Kevin Kelly, see Margaret Farley, *Personal Commitments* (San Francisco: Harper, 1986); Patrick T. McCormick and Russell B. Connors, *Character Choices and Community* (New York: Paulist Press, 1999); Timothy O'Connell, *Good People, Tough Choices: Making the Right Decisions Every Day* (Allen, Tex.: Thomas More, 1999).

CHAPTER 3

Ethics, Ecclesiology, and the Grace of Self-Doubt

Margaret A. Farley

What is the influence of ecclesiology on ethics, or ethics on ecclesiology? The tempting answer to both of these questions, framed almost anywhere we want to look in the long history of the Roman Catholic Church, is simple: There is no influence, one way or the other. Theological construals of what the church is or should be have little to do with the content of moral theology, and moral theology (or ethics)[1] is seldom brought to bear on our understandings of the church. If we limit the questions to the recent history of Catholic theology (say, from the middle of the twentieth century to the beginning of the twenty-first) the answer seems even clearer. Ecclesiology and ethics share a common context—the church—but they seldom if ever interact.

However tempting such a response may be, the historical and contemporary situations are much more complex. In the past or the present, if theologies of church as such do not shape moral theology and vice versa, the actual mode of life in the church does influence its moral discernment and teaching, and—at least to some extent—our understandings of church have influence on its life. We can say more than this, however. In an important sense the twentieth century was the century for ecclesiology, and the last third of the century frequently has been described as the "age of ethics." Therefore it was inevitable that theological paths would cross—that ethical assessments would be made of the church itself, as well as of theologies of church, and that interpretations of the nature and function of the church would play a role in ethical debates.

It is instructive to trace twentieth-century interactions between ecclesiologists and church leaders and between church leaders and moral theologians. The most dramatic interactions are adversarial, and the debates turn less often on issues of morality than on issues of church authority. Though some of the participants play more than one role, the adversaries frequently are church leaders and moral theologians, with ecclesiology providing the main lines of the no-longer-surprising plot. A more sobering interpretation of the drama, however, recognizes this as only a subplot. The major story is about what happens to the vast numbers of faithful members of the Catholic Church—largely observers of the subplot, though relentlessly drawn into it, with their lives at stake. A key question raised by this story is: Why is the church's teaching on many ethical issues so divisive or so ineffective? Or, to narrow the question more fairly: Why does the official teaching of the church on certain ethical issues appear to be unconvincing to so many of its members?

The answer to this question may be embedded in the story itself, or it may be obscured by the more visible onstage actions that are part of the subplot. This essay explores the lines of the subplot, in search of an understanding of the main one. It begins with the work of Charles E. Curran—the moral theologian whose life and writings, more than any of his peers, are at the center of the subplot and whose own work suggests interpretations of the story as a whole. The essay then moves to the broader stage of developments in the Roman Catholic tradition since Vatican II—developments in ecclesiology, moral theology, the writings and actions of church leaders, and the general life of the church. The final section of the essay addresses directly the question of "reception" on the part of the faithful—the internalization, or not, of official church teachings. Here I examine the concept of "self-doubt" on the part of everyone involved in relation to the experience of moral obligation—a set of considerations whose relevance will, I hope, become clearer as we proceed. These are all large tasks, so I make no pretense in this essay of pursuing them further than to suggest possible renderings of the story and interpretations of its meaning.

CHARLES E. CURRAN: THE MEETING OF ECCLESIOLOGY AND ETHICS

Of the almost three dozen books authored by Charles Curran as well as the dozen and a half edited or co-edited by him, by my count only four do not address some aspect of the relationship between ecclesiology and ethics. Throughout most of his more than thirty-five years of thinking about this relationship, Curran provides brief, sometimes repeated, considerations that nonetheless add up to a whole that he himself has not yet drawn together completely.[2] These considerations cover methodological issues in moral theology, a basic theology of the teaching function and office of the church, the relation between theologians and the hierarchical magisterium, justification of dissent from noninfallible but official church teachings, and general considerations of power in the church (including considerations of church/state relations). Curran provides historical overviews of these issues, critical analyses, and constructive recommendations for the ways in which church leaders and theologians should relate. Overall, it seems fair to say that for Curran the ultimate issue in all of this is moral discernment in the church—the capacitation of the church as a moral community that lives in the world.

Curran's path to this central issue is direct but not simple. At the very beginning of his academic career, he wrote doctoral dissertations on the limits of moral knowledge available through natural law[3] and on the medical treatment of women after rape.[4] His attention is later drawn to the troubling questions of the relation between ecclesiology and ethics and between church leaders and ethicists because of the difficulties encountered by theologians and others regarding the teaching of the church on artificial contraception. His own experience of struggle with church authorities over this and other normative ethical questions stands as a kind of defining moment for the post–Vatican II church—and surely for Curran's own professional life. The documentation of this shared struggle is itself a significant contribution to any efforts to address these troubling issues.[5]

Limitations on the roles of church leaders and moral theologians are at the heart of Curran's theological perspective on the teaching function of the church. Although he has never hesitated to affirm the need for some kind of hierarchical structure in the church, Curran has long been opposed to "hierarchology"—the theological commitment to a "pyramid" structure of the church whereby absolute authority exists at the top. Consistent with and part and parcel of this rejection of total hierarchy, Curran again and again reiterates a view of the teaching function of the church as broader than the church's teaching office.[6] Function and office are not to be conflated; they are not identical. Rather, the teaching function includes all of the church's members in a way that is analogous to the priesthood of all believers. Just as there are "different kinds of sharing in the priesthood of Jesus," so "all share in some way in the teaching function of Jesus."[7] Correlatively, all are learners, one from the other. "There can be no absolute division between the hierarchy as the teaching church and the rest of the faithful as the learning church."[8] If there is some role for everyone in the teaching function of the church, then all roles have their limits; all are part of a whole.

The task of theologians is carried out within the whole of the teaching and learning church. It is a limited task—limited by its very nature (as a discipline of learning), by the diverse ministries of theology and church leadership, and by its dependence on and service of the faithful. Theologians must look to the sources of insight into Christian faith—scripture, tradition, reason, and experience (not just their own experience but the experience of others in the church).[9] They also must listen to and respect the judgments articulated by hierarchical church authorities as they, too, interpret scripture and tradition and relate to the whole church.

Similarly, the task and authority of those who hold teaching offices in the church are limited—by the same sources to which theologians must turn, by the need to listen and learn from all members of the church, and by important dependence on the work of theologians in the past and in the present. The limited nature of the church's teaching office correlates with Curran's general understanding of the nature of the church. His is a post–Vatican II ecclesiology that emphasizes the sacramental and communal aspects of the church and seeks to move from a juridical model to a model imaged as the People of God.[10] It remains important for the Roman Catholic tradition to affirm the visible nature of the church, and hence the significance of structure. Yet this is a pilgrim church, "between the times" and in continual need of reform, including a reform of its institutional structure. In the aftermath of Vatican II, Curran was arguing for the decentralization of power in the church, fuller participation by all members, and collegiality with coresponsibility—within the hierarchy and between the hierarchy and theologians.[11]

The issue of dissent, including public dissent on the part of theologians, was the issue that sharpened Curran's articulation of the limits of the teaching office of the church. He interpreted his own positions regarding artificial contraception, divorce and remarriage, homosexuality, and related issues (particularly in sexual ethics) as faithful, justifiable dissent from official church teachings of the time. Vatican authorities judged that his dissent was not legitimate, and their discipline was to deny him his faculty position as a Catholic theologian at the Catholic University of America. Curran's defense of his and others' dissent was not an appeal to freedom of conscience but to a theology of the church's teaching function and office.[12] He and other theologians, canonists, and church historians argued that there is a long and honorable tradition of Roman Catholic theology and practice that allows and can even welcome dissent that is both respectful of the hierarchical teaching office and offers carefully reasoned alternative positions.[13]

What lies behind a theological justification of dissent, as well as behind the limitations of the teaching office, ultimately is the nature of moral knowledge. Curran notes repeatedly throughout his writings the many ways in which knowledge of specific moral norms is contingent, limited, subject to error, not conducive to certitude. In a tradition that generally has eschewed voluntaristic divine or ecclesiastical command theories, there is a long-standing and deep conviction that moral obligation depends on moral insight.[14] That is, the sheer will of a lawgiver is not a sufficient ground for moral obligation. Even God's commands—from God's wisdom as well as God's will—have a content whose meaning ordinarily and at least to some degree is accessible to those who receive them. Creation is revelatory of moral claims; scripture and tradition provide lenses for interpreting God's will; grace heals, in part, the injuries to mind and heart that are the result of sin; graced human reason, therefore, is capable of moral discernment. Yet moral discernment is difficult, imperfect, likely to be diverse, and never completed. Except for extremely important general moral convictions, the church and each person in it must continue the process of discerning and deliberating about what we should do and how we should live together.

Like Thomas Aquinas, Curran believes that moral knowledge is more subject to contingencies the closer it gets to particulars. Hence, whatever infallible powers the teaching church may have, they do not reach to the problems of particular ethical norms. Processes of discernment and deliberation inevitably include disagreement, mistakes, reversals, new insights, and conversions of both heart and mind.[15] Moral certainty, therefore, comes in degrees, and dissent against noninfallible official church teachings can be not only justifiable but beneficial for the process as a whole. This does not mean that moral insight is finally unattainable or that the church must be timid in articulating basic moral obligations and aspirations. It means that "the church can and does speak with a greater degree of certitude on the level of more general values, goals, attitudes, dispositions and norms" than when it speaks on specific issues; for the latter, it "must realize that its statements cannot claim to have absolute certitude."[16]

If the teaching and learning functions of the whole church are to serve effectively the church's mission to the world, it will not be because human limitations in moral knowing are completely transcended. The assistance of the Holy Spirit is real, but it does not work by magically overwhelming human capacities. The truth that the church as a community holds and shares with generations of believers is not the totality of all truth; it is not a truth that is once and for all fully possessed.[17] The moral insight that believers achieve is always partial, always the object of further search in ever-new human situations. There is a legitimate presumption in favor of the church's official teachings, but it is not sufficient to begin and end with this presumption. For if this teaching is about particular moral norms, then it is noninfallible teaching—which is to say that it may be wrong. Moreover, the presumption will be weakened if those in a teaching office do not properly carry out their role in relation to the roles of others in the church.[18]

Given these understandings of the church, its participative teaching function, and the nature of moral knowledge, Curran recommends requisite strategies for communal moral discernment. First is epistemic humility. The church—in particular, its leaders—must remove the "albatross of certitude" that prevents it from relating the gospel message more effectively to the modern (and postmodern) world.[19] Accepting the limits of moral insight, the church can more graciously acknowledge the legitimacy of disagreement and dissent. It can live as a community of moral conviction (regarding basic moral obligations such as love of enemies, compassion for the poor, prohibitions against genocide, and so forth); this church also can risk recognizing itself, however, as a "community of moral doubt," in need of the insights of others on troubling particular moral issues.[20] In accordance with this perspective, the church can shape and use its structures in ways that best serve the requirements of learning as well as teaching—activating all levels of its life, local and universal, and enabling the voices of its members. Its laws can be assessed and valued insofar as they genuinely build the life of the community and bear witness to its faith and its love.[21]

Not surprisingly, Curran's more specific recommendations address the all-too-frequent tensions between hierarchical authorities and Catholic theologians. He wrote in 1982 that the primary responsibility for checking errors in theology rests with the theological community, whose obligation as a community of scholars is to assess rigorously the work of its members. The hierarchical teaching office does have a "judicial function" in relation to the work of theologians, but judicial interventions should be reserved to a category of "last resort," made only after consultation with theologians of more than one school of theology; begin at the local level, so that diversity in cultural experience and praxis can be taken into account; and follow due process in every case.[22]

Curran insisted, then, that theologians must be self-critical and open to dialogue with all other theologians in the church. In 1992, however, he followed Richard McCormick in identifying corrective attitudes and actions also required of the hierarchy.[23] Holders of the hierarchical teaching office must acknowledge different levels of church teaching, admit past mistakes, refuse to collapse the teaching role of bishops into the teaching role of the papacy, consult widely on moral matters, recognize that discernment is a process, revise procedures for overseeing theological work, and overall introduce a more communal form of discernment in the church.[24]

I suggested earlier that Curran's ultimate concern in all of his considerations of the relationship between ecclesiology and ethics has been capacitation of the church as a moral community with internal responsibilities and a mission in and to the world. We may now be at a point at which the force of that judgment becomes clear. Church structures serve a "discerning church"[25] when they facilitate effective and creative moral discourse and when they nurture the moral lives of individuals and the church as a whole. Because of the limited nature of moral knowledge as well as the intrinsic significance of communal participation, teaching and learning thrive when church leaders, theologians, and all of the faithful collaborate in the discernment and fulfillment of moral obligations. No longer theorized as a "perfect society" sufficient unto itself with an unchanging and absolute hierarchical order, the church is nonetheless a "unique community,"[26] one in which moral deliberation and action can be nurtured. Inerrancy in moral matters is guaranteed not by the grace of office but by a decentralized church in which inclusive "catholicity," functioning through different levels of authority and diverse ministries, offers an "antidote" to many of the risks of error that beset even graced humanity.

For these reasons, Curran laments the inattention given to the moral formation of the church community, or even to theological reflection on the "ecclesial context" of the moral life of believers.[27] He insists on the utter importance of the role of the faithful in discernment and action[28] and provides brief analyses of relevant aspects of moral experience, decision making, judgment, and the formation of conscience in the context of the church.[29] I return to these concerns in the final section of this chapter. For now, however, it is useful to turn to the broader stage on which ecclesiology and moral theology have been developing since Vatican II. This discussion will help place Curran's work in theological and ecclesial context, but it also will provide a fuller background for pursuing questions of the requirements for moral discourse in a discerning church.

ECCLESIOLOGY AND ETHICS: THE POST–VATICAN II STRUGGLE

The twentieth century marks an extraordinary move by ecclesiology to the center of the theological stage. Surveys of the important writings abound, some focusing on the relationship of ecclesiology to ethics.[30] There is no need to repeat these surveys here, but it is important not to underestimate the ecclesiological sea changes that have taken place and the intensity of the theological conflicts that surged before and in the aftermath of Vatican II. This council produced two constitutions that focused entirely on the church—one dogmatic *(Lumen gentium)* and the other pastoral *(Gaudium et spes);* most of its other documents address ecclesiological issues as well. The council did not happen in a vacuum, nor did the sea changes it brought about begin or end with the council itself. One need only think of names such as Emile Mersch, Henri de Lubac, Yves Congar, and Karl Rahner—and later Hans Küng, Edward Schillebeeckx, Avery Dulles, Rosemary Radford Ruether, Leonardo Boff, Hans Urs von Balthasar, and many others—to remember the kind of theological work, precisely in ecclesiology, that preceded and followed the council. Though the fortunes of theologies of the mystical body, historical studies of church reform, and critiques of church structures have risen and fallen more than once, this work informed the council and became part of the debates in its wake.

The council said very little explicitly about ethics, but what it said about the church—its life and its practices—had great influence on developments in the method and substance of ethical thought. Issues such as the meaning of church as the People of God, the role of the laity in the church, the church as a world church, religious liberty, the function of the local church in relation to the church universal, openness of the church to the world, ecumenism, development of doctrine, and the church as pilgrim church each yielded new questions about a theology of communion, cultural diversity, freedom of conscience, the core and peripheral status of truths, the "sense of the faithful" as source and confirmation of church teaching, the church's mission, corporate responsibility, and on and on. All of these questions are questions not only for ecclesiology but for ethics. They have been extended with an urgency pressed in political theologies, liberation theologies, and the many forms of feminist theology, where the line between systematic and moral theology has been usefully blurred for some time.

In pursuit of the overall questions of this essay, I focus on only two of the major ecclesiological issues that have preoccupied the church and its theologians since Vatican II and today are fraught with difficulties and conflicts. These issues are of clear importance for moral theology, and they have implications for nearly every other issue, large or small, that I have identified above. The first has to do with ecclesiological concepts of "communion." The second is embedded in the many debates about teaching authority in the church. These two issues are not unrelated because church structures and functions are inseparable from whatever it means for the Roman Catholic Church to be a community.

Communion and Its Discontents

By far the dominant paradigm for the church coming out of Vatican II was that of the People of God.[31] Countering the narrowly institutional representations of the church that held sway through most of the second millenium, this image represented new understandings of the church's relation to God and, even more important, the possibility of newly structured relationships among its members. It was not in opposition to an earlier twentieth-century Mystical Body of Christ theology, though it added historicity, visibility, and mission to what might otherwise be too mystical, organic, and spiritual a view of the church. Moreover, although the Body of Christ and People of God images could both accommodate democratic tendencies, organic metaphors (frequently part of the meaning of "Body of Christ") generally proved less conducive than covenantal ones (frequently intrinsic to understandings of "People of God") in this regard.

In some ways the concept of "communion" has worked well with the People of God paradigm. It provided "interiority" comparable to the Body of Christ metaphor, it could combine respect for the dignity of the individual with a concern for the common good, and it incorporated notions of diversity in community. Significant contributions to a theology of communion (or *koinonia,* community) were made by Catholic theologians such as Charles Journet, Henri de Lubac, Yves Congar,[32] and later Heribert Mühlen[33] and J. M. R. Tillard.[34] For all of these thinkers, an ecclesiology of communion included a vertical meaning (the church and its members in communion with God) and a horizontal meaning (the members called to communion with another in the church). It therefore was lodged in and incorporated doctrines of the Trinity and Incarnation on one hand and the Risen Christ and Eucharist on the other.[35]

The richness of the concept of *communio* has had wide appeal, but its very breadth and depth can mask serious differences in theological perspectives. When it has focused on "community," for example, it has served a new theological communitarianism, particularly in ecumenical circles. It also has shown the limits of too narrow an appeal to communitarianism.

Since 1992 the World Council of Churches (WCC) has attempted to address the divide between its projects on Faith and Order and on Life and Work. Concern to achieve a unified voice on issues of peace and justice prompted a study of the relationship between ecclesiology and ethics.[36] Strongly influenced by ethicists such as Stanley Hauerwas, John Howard Yoder, and John Milbank, this work focused on the question of the formation of community *(koinonia)*. The insights from this study have been valuable for Protestants, Orthodox Christians, and Roman Catholics alike.[37] Yet the tendency of the study to cede discussion of church-dividing ethical issues to discussion of the church itself *as* a social ethic did not fulfill the hopes of all WCC participants. For many Roman Catholic readers of the study, moreover, the integration of mission in the world, solidarity with the poor, and universal concerns for justice are not yet adequate. Missing too are many of the creative insights of feminist scholars, Catholic and Protestant, on the nature of the church community and its tasks in relation to the world.[38]

Theologies of *communio* have had other important implications for ecumenism—some of them equally relevant to ethics, and equally controversial. For example, there is the question of the relationship of all Christian churches to one another. Congar argued that a view of the church that gives priority to communion can accommodate unity and diversity among the Christian traditions.[39] From an eschatological point of view, there are degrees of unity. Yet there is already present among Christians a unity sufficient to be called "communion" and, as I have maintained elsewhere, sufficient to allow Christians to welcome one another to their Table.[40] This view, of course, is disputed and is not represented in current official church teachings. It remains a troubling issue for communion ecclesiology and for ethics.

Finally, a theology of communion has exacerbated some already disputed questions about relationships intrinsic to the Roman Catholic Church. These issues range from the relationships of local churches with one another and with the papacy to relationships between the hierarchy and Catholic theologians. They are simultaneously issues of structural viability, diversity, and doctrinal development in a church that is deeply, if mysteriously, communal. They take us to the second major issue for ecclesiology and ethics.

Authority and Its Afflictions

Ironies abound in the history of the Roman Catholic Church, but the ironies of the post–Vatican II era surely are among the greatest. Two theologies of church battled with each other prior to the council. One appeared generally more persuasive in the council; to some extent, these same two theologies continue to battle after the council. "Descending" ecclesiology affirms the centralization of authority and power in the church, favors expanding the reach of claims of infallibility, regards some church structures as absolutely unchangeable, is wary of pluralism, and continues to consider the church a bulwark against the dangers of much of contemporary society. "Ascending" ecclesiology (the approach generally taken in Vatican II) presses for decentralization, resists what it calls "creeping infallibility," regards structure in the church as a modifiable instrument, considers pluralism inevitable in a "world church," and wants openness to the world in its radical need and in some of its achievements. Such descriptions are overly simple, no doubt, and no theologian would feel comfortable being placed completely in one school or the other. Yet at least the issues of development of doctrine, reform of the papacy, the authority of *Humanae vitae* and *Evangelium vitae,* historical aspects of church structure, uniformity and diversity, the hierarchy of truths, and so on, are often debated precisely along these lines.[41] Current struggles over the implementation of John Paul II's 1990 *Ex corde ecclesiae* exhibit the divide as clearly as anything else—a divide in which, on one hand, *communio* is interpreted in interior spiritual terms amenable to decentralization of authority in the church, and, on the other, communion theology is aligned with juridical structures and a centralized, hierarchical view of the teaching function of the church.[42]

Although sharp debates engage theologians on both sides of these issues, attention has been focused in recent years on what I describe as a subplot in the story of the relationship between ecclesiology and ethics—that is, the theological and political struggle between many church leaders and many moral theologians. The ecclesiological spotlight here is on authority, both teaching and governing. As the action unfolds, we see a mounting effort on the part of church leaders to maintain one official voice on controversial moral (and other theological) issues. Document after document has attempted to settle once and for all the moral questions that continue to divide the teaching office of the church from the work of many theologians.[43] Along with multiple investigations of individual theologians, there have been still more documents aimed precisely at tightening the reins on theologians in the exercise of their craft.[44]

However one interprets or evaluates these documents, they relegate to the shadows the deeper questions that press the church—its leaders and its theologians—regarding moral discernment and teaching. For example, should moral disputes, questions of moral truth, be settled by the command of those currently holding hierarchical power, or does this kind of ecclesiastical discipline contradict the very nature of moral discernment and moral insight? Is the ultimate authority of the church located in a central *sedes* that extends with absolute power to all corners of the church and to each individual's conscience? Or is the church first a community and second a structured community whose roles and offices derive their authority only as they serve the community well? Is the Catholic Church built on a tradition wherein moral insight must be informed, critiqued, nurtured, chastened, but finally freed for communal and individual moral action? Moreover, can moral questions have different answers in diverse cultures (all part of a world church) without yielding a full-scale moral relativism? Can disagreements be accommodated, sometimes within the same (even dominant) culture of the church without a loss of unity so serious that the church's prophetic witness is compromised?

As we have seen, much of the hard work on such questions has been done by systematic theologians and church historians such as Tillard, Congar, Rahner, and Dulles.[45] These questions, however, are of utmost importance for moral theologians who—along with colleagues in other theological disciplines—continue the work of Häring, Curran, McCormick, and many others. A small essay such as this is no place to adjudicate large questions, but I turn now to an issue that is relevant to all of them: reception of moral teachings by the faithful members of the church. My interest, however, is not finally in reception as such but in what it provides as a vantage point for an ecclesiology of a morally discerning and acting church.

THE GRACE OF SELF-DOUBT

Although "reception" as a theological concept has various historical and contemporary connotations,[46] I assume it to mean acceptance and internalization of church teachings by faithful members of the church. In this sense, it is essentially connected with an active notion of the *sensus fidelium*—that is, the whole church searching for and sharing insights into what it believes and how it should act on what it believes. My concern is reception of the moral teachings of the church and participation of the faithful in the discernment and deliberation that lead to these teachings. The first step in my brief analysis is to consider once again the nature of moral knowledge.

We have already noted in relation to Charles Curran's work the generally accepted Catholic conviction that human reason is capable of some genuine moral insight, especially when it is graced by the power of the Holy Spirit. We also have noted that moral insight, rather than blind surrender to command, is at the heart of Catholic traditional understandings of moral obligation. It is important to say more than this, however—for example, that a descriptive analysis of the experience of moral obligation reveals the following elements: an experience of a *claim* that is addressed to one's *freedom,* experienced as *unconditional,* perceived to be *justifiable,* and experienced as both a *liberating appeal and an obligating demand.*[47] Insofar as moral obligation emerges in this kind of experience, moral obligations "make sense" to those who have these experiences; in other words, they are in some way and to some degree intelligible. For those who stand in the Catholic tradition, this "making sense" has almost everything to do with interpreting concrete reality in light of reason and revelation.[48]

Because there is something that must be understood or recognized (something intelligible) at the heart of the experience of moral obligation, it is not possible to separate the question of moral "authority" from the question of moral "truth" (or "content" or "meaning").[49] Unless an individual recognizes the moral claim as genuine (based in the concrete realities that are confronted), there will be no experience of obligation; if there is one, it will be the pragmatic (not moral) obligation to avoid punishment or to reap a reward, depending on one's response to what is perceived as a (nonmoral) claim. Similarly, it is not possible for persons to experience moral obligation in response to the teaching or command of another unless they recognize the "truth" in what is being communicated—unless it makes some "sense." This does not mean that we need to discern for and by ourselves the answer to every moral question before we can recognize it when it comes from another, or that we cannot learn from others—those we recognize as "authorities" because we have learned to trust their wisdom, their experience, or even their designation as authorities within our communities. Ultimately we learn from others because they help make transparent the truth for which we seek.

If moral insight comes in a recognition of some moral truth, it is not possible for persons (especially persons in a tradition that affirms this approach to moral matters) to experience moral obligation simply because they are told that they ought to.[50] They may do something only because they have been commanded to do so, but their response is a moral response only if they recognize a moral claim. The truth or genuineness of a moral claim—no matter how difficult its content—makes a nonviolent appeal to the human subject.[51] As such, it does not coerce the human person but obligates her; in this process, it also frees her to do what is most true to herself.[52]

If we add to this interpretation of moral obligation an acknowledgment of the limitations in all moral insight (Curran's position, but also affirmed by most, perhaps all, contemporary Catholic moral theologians), we come close to explaining the pluralism among Catholics regarding particular moral questions. With some key issues such as artificial contraception, same-sex relationships, and second marriage after divorce, the diversity among Roman Catholics is not merely a matter of differing intellectual opinions but of profoundly divergent experiences of moral obligation. How, then, shall a discerning church accommodate such differences? Shall it tolerate them, engage them in an ongoing process of moral discernment, or repudiate those that differ from the present teachings of central church leaders? Theological and moral pluralism on such matters seems inevitable, even though consensus is a worthy goal for the church to pursue. Insofar as unanimity is desirable, however, how may it be sought in ways that respect the nature of moral knowledge and capacitate a faith community for moral discernment?

Participants in the Catholic tradition believe that they are assisted by the Holy Spirit in their efforts to discern actions that are faithful to God's plan for creation. One of the least recognized gifts of the Spirit, however, may be what I will call the "grace of self-doubt." If all co-believers are to participate in moral discernment in the church, and if the limited contribution of each requires the participation of the others, then all—laity, clergy, theologians, church leaders—have need of the grace of self-doubt. There are obvious objections to be made to such an assertion: Self-doubt is hardly grace-ful; it is a debility that can distract us, undermine our capacity for discernment, and cut the nerve of our action. Those with real power never yield to self-doubt, and those who do yield are doomed to ineffectiveness and despair. How, then, can the church raise a unified prophetic voice if it is infected with self-doubt?

These objections may be accurate. There are different forms of self-doubt, however. There is the kind that must be overcome and the kind that must be achieved with grace. Often they are correlated with positions of powerlessness and power. It is not a grace for anyone to doubt fundamentally his or her own self-worth, or the value of her experience and the possibility of his insight. There are forms of insecurity that require transformation into strength. There also is a graced self-doubt, however, necessary perhaps especially for those who are in positions of power. If the greatest temptation of religious persons is self-righteousness, the second greatest is the grasping for certitude—fighting self-doubt in ways that shut the mind and sometimes close the heart. The grace of self-doubt is what allows for epistemic humility, the basic condition for communal as well as individual moral discernment (affirmed not only by Curran but by all who have understood the lessons of our age and the limits of moral epistemology). It is a grace that is accessible to those who struggle for understanding, those who have come to see things differently from what was once seen, those who have experienced the complexity of translating convictions into action.

This is not a grace for calling into question every fundamental conviction we have achieved. It will not foster doubt, for example, about the dignity of human persons or the trustworthiness of God's promises. It is a grace for recognizing the contingencies of moral knowledge when we stretch toward the particular and the concrete. It allows us to listen to the experience of others, take seriously reasons that are alternative to our own, rethink our own last word. It assumes a shared search for moral insight, and it promotes (though it does not guarantee) a shared conviction in the end. Absent such grace, it is not surprising that a church's teaching will remain divisive and ineffective, unconvincing to many within the church and without. Perhaps, then, we have come to a clue for interpreting the main plot of the story of ethics and ecclesiology in the twenty-first century of the Catholic Church.

It is unlikely that official moral teachings can be received and affirmed by members of the church whose experiences of moral obligation are dismissed or denied. Theologians oppose one another and/or church leaders, reaching impasse after impasse, slowing the process of genuine discernment. Church leaders judge those who disagree with them as "dissenters," legitimate or not, rather than as necessary participants in the search for moral truth. Ironically, the voice of the church is thereby muted because it does not represent the wisdom of a genuinely discerning church. Is this last claim really so? No amount of the grace of self-doubt will solve all of the problems of moral disagreement, so is it not better to raise a voice that is unified, even if it can be so only by silencing opposition?

The response to this objection can only be that one voice cannot in fact speak for a divided church. The responsibility of church leaders is to hear all voices, mediate them, and finally speak with humility, even—on some questions—provisionally if necessary. This can constitute in itself an important witness in a church and a world that know all too well how complex are the specific moral issues to be faced. Such an approach need not compromise a prophetic response to massive problems of war, racism, dying refugees, a threatened environment. It need not soften the Catholic tradition's commitments to respect human life, promote human well-being, and honor the sacred in all created realities. It can forge cross-cultural discourse and sustain a mission of justice in the world. The unanimity that emerges from diversity is powerful and will not be broken by the best of all efforts at moral discernment.

The church needs the structural flexibility to serve such an aim and such a process. Curran and major ecclesiologists have pointed in the right direction. The central and minor plots of the large drama of ecclesiology and ethics need not be either institutionally or personally tragic. Infused with the grace of self-doubt as well as the courage of conviction, this ought to be a story of faithful discernment, corporate responsibility, and persuasive guidance for a future whose moral questions can only be more and more demanding.

NOTES

1. Unless otherwise indicated, I use the terms "ethics" and "moral theology" interchangeably. Without burdening the text with descriptives, both refer to the theological discipline of reflecting on questions of morality within the Roman Catholic tradition. This is a kind of shorthand, of course, and when necessary I augment it with clarifying distinctions or designations.
2. I say this despite the more lengthy treatment Curran gives to these matters in at least three of his later works: *The Living Tradition of Catholic Moral Theology* (Notre Dame, Ind.: University of Notre Dame Press, 1992), chaps. 5–6; *Church and Morality* (Minneapolis: Fortress, 1993); and *The Catholic Moral Tradition Today: A Synthesis* (Washington, D.C.: Georgetown University Press, 1999), chapters 1, 2, and 8.
3. Charles E. Curran, *Invincible Ignorance of the Natural Law According to St. Alphonsus* (Rome: Academia Alfonsiana, 1961).
4. Charles E. Curran, *The Prevention of Conception after Rape: An Historical Theological Study* (Rome: Pontificia Universitas Gregoriana, 1961).
5. Charles E. Curran, Robert E. Hunt, and the subject professors, with John F. Hunt and Terrence R. Connolly, *Dissent In and For the Church: Theologians and* Humanae Vitae (New York: Sheed & Ward, 1969); Charles E. Curran, *Faithful Dissent* (Kansas City, Mo.: Sheed & Ward, 1986).
6. See for example, Charles E. Curran, *Themes in Fundamental Moral Theology* (Notre Dame, Ind.: University of Notre Dame Press, 1977), 114; *Moral Theology: A Continuing Journey* (Notre Dame, Ind.: University of Notre Dame Press, 1982), 4; *Catholic Moral Tradition Today*, 197–98.
7. Curran, *Moral Theology: A Continuing Journey*, 4.

8. Ibid.

9. Curran, *Catholic Moral Tradition Today,* 47–55.

10. Curran et al., *Dissent In and For the Church,* 96–97; Charles E. Curran, *Critical Concerns in Moral Theology* (Notre Dame, Ind.: University of Notre Dame Press, 1984), chap. 1; *Toward an American Catholic Moral Theology* (Notre Dame, Ind.: University of Notre Dame Press, 1987), 150–57; *Living Tradition of Catholic Moral Theology; Catholic Moral Tradition Today,* chap. 1.

11. Curran et al., *Dissent In and For the Church,* 96–97; Curran, *Catholic Moral Theology in Dialogue* (Notre Dame, Ind.: Fides, 1972; reprinted by University of Notre Dame, 1976), chap. 5.

12. Charles E. Curran, ed., *Contraception: Authority and Dissent* (New York: Herder & Herder, 1969), 11.

13. Ibid., 9–15; Curran et al., *Dissent In and For the Church,* 133*ff.;* Curran, *Themes in Fundamental Moral Theology,* 111.

14. Curran frequently notes two strands in the Catholic tradition—strands identified with Aquinas on one hand and Scotus and Suarez on the other. The former strand regards law primarily as an ordinance of reason, and the latter considers it primarily in terms of the will of the legislator. The former has prevailed in the Catholic tradition overall, certainly in the contemporary period. See, e.g., Charles E. Curran, *A New Look at Christian Morality* (Notre Dame, Ind.: Fides, 1968), 128–30; *Contemporary Problems in Moral Theology* (Notre Dame, Ind.: Fides, 1970), 138–42; *Directions in Fundamental Moral Theology* (Notre Dame, Ind.: University of Notre Dame Press, 1985), 200–202; *Toward an American Catholic Moral Theology,* 157–58; *Catholic Moral Tradition Today,* 1.

15. Charles E. Curran, *Directions in Catholic Social Ethics* (Notre Dame, Ind.: University of Notre Dame Press, 1985), 119–23; *Living Tradition of Catholic Moral Theology,* 114–20.

16. Charles E. Curran, *New Perspectives in Moral Theology* (Notre Dame, Ind.: Fides, 1974), 154–55.

17. Curran, *Living Tradition of Catholic Moral Theology,* 112.

18. Ibid., 120.

19. Curran, *New Perspectives in Moral Theology,* 155.

20. Curran, *Church and Morality,* 10–11.

21. Curran, *Directions in Fundamental Moral Theology,* 199.

22. Curran, *Moral Theology: A Continuing Journey,* 9–10.

23. Richard A. McCormick, *The Critical Calling: Reflections on Moral Dilemmas since Vatican II* (Washington, D.C.: Georgetown University Press, 1989), 142–45.

24. Curran, *Living Tradition of Catholic Moral Theology,* 126–29.

25. Curran, *Church and Morality,* 46.

26. Curran, *Directions in Fundamental Moral Theology,* 199; *Toward an American Catholic Moral Theology,* 167. For the rejection of "perfect society" notions of the church, see Curran, *New Perspectives in Moral Theology,* 146; *Critical Concerns in Moral Theology* (Notre Dame, Ind.: University of Notre Dame Press, 1984), 26.

27. Curran, *Catholic Moral Tradition Today,* 2–3.

28. Curran, *Living Tradition of Catholic Moral Theology,* 120–22.

29. Curran, *Catholic Moral Theology in Dialogue,* 174; *Living Tradition of Catholic Moral Theology,* 120–22; *Catholic Moral Tradition Today,* chap. 7.

30. I am particularly dependent on essays by Avery Dulles, "A Half Century of Ecclesiology," *Theological Studies* 50 (September 1989): 419–42; Mary E. Hines, "Community for Liberation," in *Freeing Theology: The Essentials of Theology in Feminist Perspective,* ed. Catherine Mowry LaCugna (New York: HarperCollins, 1993), 161–84; and Richard A. McCormick, "Moral Theology 1940–1989: An Overview," *Theological Studies* 50 (March 1989): 3–24. Curran also provides many useful historical overviews throughout his writings, e.g., *Transition and Tradition in Moral Theology* (Notre Dame, Ind.: University of Notre Dame Press, 1979), 3–28; *Toward an American Catholic Moral Theology,* 157–61; *The Origins of Moral Theology in the United States: Three Different Approaches* (Washington, D.C.: Georgetown University Press, 1992); *Living Tradition of Catholic Moral Theology,* 103–25; *Moral Theology at the End of the Century* (Milwaukee, Wisc.: Marquette University, 1999); *Catholic Moral Tradition Today,* chaps. 1 and 8. An excellent overall resource is Charles E. Curran and Richard A. McCormick, eds., *Readings in Moral Theology No. 3: The Magisterium and Morality* (New York: Paulist Press, 1982).

31. Others have noted this, but the landmark work of Avery Dulles helped to situate this in the context of the council as well as in a broader historical and theological context. See Avery Dulles, *Models of the Church* (New York: Doubleday, 1974), especially chaps. 1 and 3.

32. For succinct but thoughtful overviews of the relevant works of Journet, de Lubac, and Congar, see Dennis M. Doyle, "Journet, Congar, and the Roots of Communion Ecclesiology," *Theological Studies* 58 (September 1997): 461–79, and "Henri de Lubac and the Roots of Communion Ecclesiology," *Theological Studies* 60 (June 1999): 209–27.

33. Heribert Mühlen, *Une Persona mystica,* 3d ed. (Paderborn, Germany: Schöningh, 1968).

34. J. M. R. Tillard, *Church of Churches: An Ecclesiology of Communion,* trans. R. C. Peaux (Collegeville, Minn.: Liturgical Press, 1992); see also Tillard's "The Church of God is a Communion: The Ecclesiological Perspective of Vatican II," *One In Christ* 17 (1981): 117–31.

35. See, e.g., Tillard, "The Church of God is a Communion," 118–25.

36. For useful insights into the WCC process, see Lewis S. Mudge, "Ecclesiology and Ethics in Current Ecumenical Debate," *Ecumenical Review* 48 (January 1996): 11–27; Lewis S. Mudge, "Towards a Hermeneutic of the Household: 'Ecclesiology and Ethics' after Harare," *Ecumenical Review* 51 (July 1999): 243–55; Werner Schwartz, "Church and Ethical Orientation: Moral Formation in the People of God," *Ecumenical Review* 51 (July 1999): 256–65; Arne Rasmusson, "Ecclesiology and Ethics: The Difficulties of Ecclesial Moral Reflection," *Ecumenical Review* 52 (April 2000): 180–94.

37. Reports of the consultations of the study are available in Thomas F. Best and Martin Robra, eds., *Ecclesiology and Ethics: Ethical Engagement, Moral Formation, and the Nature of the Church* (Geneva, Switzerland: WCC Publications, 1997).

38. See, for example, Rosemary Radford Ruether, *Women-Church: Theology and Practice of Feminist Liturgical Communities* (New York: Harper & Row, 1985), esp. chap. 5; Letty M. Russell, *Church in the Round: Feminist Interpretation of the Church* (Louisville, Ky.: Westminster/John Knox, 1993); Serene Jones, *Feminist Theory and Christian Theology: Cartographies of Grace* (Minneapolis: Fortress, 2000), chaps. 6–7.

39. Yves Congar, *Diversity and Communion* (Mystic, Conn.: Twenty-Third, 1982).

40. Margaret A. Farley, "No One Goes Away Hungry from the Table of the Lord: Eucharistic Sharing in Ecumenical Contexts," in *Practice What You Preach,* ed. James Keenan and Joseph Kotva (Kansas City, Mo.: Sheed & Ward, 1999), 186–201.

41. See, e.g., Avery Dulles, "Catholic Doctrine: Between Revelation and Theology," *Catholic Theological Society of America Proceedings* 54 (1999): 83–91; Richard A. McCormick, "Moral Doctrine: Stability and Development," *Catholic Theological Society of America Proceedings* 54 (1999): 92–100; John R. Quinn, *The Reform of the Papacy: The Costly Call to Christian Unity* (New York: Crossroad, 1999); Francis A. Sullivan, "The Doctrinal Weight of *Evangelium Vitae,*" *Theological Studies* 56 (September 1995): 560–65; Congar, *Diversity and Communion,* parts I and III; Tillard, "The Church of God is a Communion," 124–25; Hines, "Community for Liberation," 164–67; Germain Grisez and Francis A. Sullivan, "Quaestio Disputata: The Ordinary Magisterium's Infallibility," *Theological Studies* 55 (December 1994): 720–38. The 1985 Synod of Bishops attempted to accommodate various ecclesiologies, though it did not by any means resolve the major divide. See Synod of Bishops, "The Final Report," *Origins* 15 (December 19, 1985): 444–50.

42. The first view is anticipated in the 1990 *Report of the Catholic Theological Society of America on the Profession of Faith and the Oath of Fidelity.* The second is articulated in J. Augustine Di Noia, "Ecclesiology of Communion and Catholic Higher Education," *Origins 29* (October 7, 1999): 268–72.

43. Consider, for example, not only *Humanae vitae* but the 1992 *Catechism of the Catholic Church, Ordinatio sacerdotalis* (1994), *Evangelium vitae* (1995), and countless papal letters and documents from the Congregation for the Doctrine of the Faith regarding issues in sexual ethics.

44. Dramatic examples include the revised "Profession of Faith and Oath of Fidelity" mandated by the Congregation for the Doctrine of the Faith in 1989; *Veritatis splendor* in 1993, which identified not only nonnegotiable moral teachings but attacked whole schools of thought that were judged to foster departures from official teachings; *Ad tuendam fidem* in 1998, which established new canonical categories to restrict dissent; and the Vatican insistence on specific ordinances for the implementation of *Ex corde ecclesiae,* approved by the American bishops in 2001. An exception to this list of examples is the set of guidelines worked out between U.S. bishops and theologians, "Doctrinal Responsibilities: Approaches to Promoting Cooperation and Resolving Misunderstandings Between Bishops and Theologians," *Origins* 19 (June 29, 1989): 97–110.

45. Space limitations alone prevent me from incorporating the monumental work of persons such as Francis A. Sullivan in *Magisterium: Teaching Authority in the Catholic Church* (New York: Paulist Press, 1983), and *Creative Fidelity: Weighing and Interpreting Documents of the Magisterium* (New York: Paulist Press, 1996), as well as John W. O'Malley, *Tradition and Transition: Historical Perspectives on Vatican II* (Wilmington, Del.: Michael Glazier, 1989), and Ladislas M. Örsy, *The Church: Learning and Teaching* (Wilmington, Del.: Michael Glazier, 1987). It also is difficult to overestimate the contribution of biblical scholars such as Elisabeth Schüssler Fiorenza, *Discipleship of Equals: A Critical Feminist Ekklesia-logy of Liberation* (New York: Crossroad, 1993).

46. For a succinct discussion of its meanings, see Lucien Richard, "Reflections on Dissent and Reception," in *The Church in the Nineties: Its Legacy, Its Future,* ed. Pierre M. Hegy (Collegeville, Minn.: Liturgical Press, 1993), 6–14. We need here, of course, a full-scale discussion of Canon 750, which on some readings gives very little importance to "reception" but on others points to the essential role of "Christ's faithful" in the very possibility of an ordinary universal magisterium.

47. Of course, this means that any particular experience of moral obligation could be a mistake. That is, the claim might be misinterpreted; one might not be actually free to respond to the claim; it might not be unconditional; and it might prove to be unjustified. I am not trying to describe the grounds for unconditionality, freedom, or justifiability, only to describe what does occur in our experience. A full description of this experience must wait for my forthcoming work on the experience of free choice. The elements I note here should not be surprising, however, in that they intend to integrate what many others have partially identified.

48. I am not unique in taking this position. It is what can be generally understood as one form of a Catholic natural law approach.

49. I put "truth" within quotation marks to indicate its generally contested meaning and possibility. The questions surrounding this term are beyond the scope of this essay, but I do not think they vitiate the use I make of it here. I have treated this issue at somewhat greater length regarding the use of scripture as a source for theology and ethics. See Margaret A. Farley, "Feminist Consciousness and the Interpretation of Scripture," in *Feminist Interpretation of the Bible,* ed. Letty M. Russell and Shannon Clarkson (Philadelphia: Westminster, 1985), 41–51.

50. I do not dispute the fact that those who believe that the root of moral obligation is solely or primarily in the authority of the commander will not necessarily need the command to make sense. This is certainly true of those whose religious and moral framework is based on a full-blown divine command theory. In this case, however, the basis of a moral command "making sense" is precisely that it comes from a recognized legitimate commander. This is not what characterizes much of the Roman Catholic tradition of moral theology. Hence, it is even notable that traditional Catholic interpretations of the Abraham and Isaac story tend to differ from traditional Protestant ones.

51. I draw here on a characterization of "truth" provided by Paul Ricoeur, *Essays on Biblical Interpretation,* ed. Lewis S. Mudge (Philadelphia: Fortress, 1980), 95.

52. I realize that I prescind here from many urgent philosophical questions about the nature of the human subject and the very possibility of becoming a self. In this brief essay, I can do no other.

CHAPTER 4

Moral Theology and Academic Freedom: The New Context

James A. Coriden

When Charles Curran was very young he went off to school, and he has yet to return. Curran has spent his entire adult life studying, and helping others to study, Roman Catholic moral theology in institutions of higher learning. In those many years, while Curran has engaged nearly every issue within the wide scope of moral theology, he also has shared fully in the life and issues of the academic communities in which he learned and taught.

This essay briefly explores three issues related to the academic setting of moral theology: the changed academic scene within which Catholic moralists now function, the new dynamics within that arena, and the separation of moral theology from canon law; academic freedom within Catholic colleges and universities, its rationale, and the canonical requirement of a *mandatum* for teachers of theological disciplines; and institutional autonomy and Catholic identity in higher education—the urgency of the question, a theological framework and practical actions to address it, and its implications for moral theology. I identify the significant contributions of Charles Curran as I engage each topic.[1] I raise these topics in a preliminary way that invites further exploration.

A RADICALLY ALTERED SCENE

David Tracy identified three "publics," or reference groups, for theological discourse: the wider society, the academy, and the church. Tracy insists that all theology is public discourse and that the principal "public" that the theologian addresses powerfully influences his or her theology. The social location of the theologian also provides "elective affinities" for a particular emphasis in the theology.[2]

The "academy" is the social locus where the scholarly study of theology most often occurs. Tracy includes within the academy the distinct settings of the seminary, where professional training for ministry is the primary responsibility; departments of religion and/or theology in major church-related colleges and universities; divinity schools of older secular universities; and departments of religious studies in other private or state colleges and universities.[3]

Curran employs Tracy's framework of the three publics to illustrate the dramatic changes in Roman Catholic moral theology during the twentieth century.[4] Under "academic aspects," Curran describes the shift from seminaries to colleges and universities as the primary home of moral theology, the more scholarly training of professors, the founding of journals for theological publication, the initiation of doctoral programs in theology, the organization of professional societies, the development of moral writing from purely pastoral to more academic in nature, the change in instruction from quasi-catechetical classes to serious university courses, the increased autonomy of Catholic institutions of higher education, the recognition of theology as a legitimate discipline within them, and the active professional engagement of Catholic moralists with their ecumenical colleagues.[5] These academic changes were sweeping and radical; in Curran's judgment, the result is that "both the quality and quantity of professors of moral theology has increased dramatically, . . . there are more moral theologians in this country than in any other, . . . quality is shown in the many articles and books that have been published."[6]

Curran has carefully chronicled these academic developments in the story of American Catholic moral theology, and there is no reason to doubt his conclusions. Is there another view of the scene, however? The reality, for example, of a new public in seminaries in particular highlights a qualitatively different educational dynamic that will force changes on how theology is understood and taught. Thus, in addition to a new public there is a changing social location.

A New Educational Dynamic

Curran, following Tracy, focuses on the "academic public" for the discipline of moral theology as principally the colleague group of professors, the guild for which one writes and converses professionally. This "public" is better trained, more numerous, more productive, and more scholarly than ever before. Because the "academy" is the social locus where the scholarly study of theology most often occurs, we need to focus on the changing nature of this locus.

"Academe" is the place where teaching and learning takes place. The academic dimension of moral theology must include the dynamics of the educational process, in addition to the qualities of the professoriate. Who are the conversation partners in the teacher-learner dialogue? Who are the participants in the academic discussion within the classroom? Who sits around the seminar table? The changes in this theological academic scene are even more radical than the ones listed above, and they may have more sweeping consequences for the discipline.

Before the 1960s, almost everyone who studied Roman Catholic moral theology in the United States did so in a seminary setting. They were either clerics or candidates for the clergy. They were all males. They were almost exclusively young, white, Catholic, from the middle or blue-collar classes, celibate, and self-described as heterosexual. These people were on both sides of the desk, with the exception that the teacher was older.

Now the academic context is very different. Most people now study moral theology in colleges and universities where a pluralistic social and intellectual context is a given. Even the seminary classroom contains a diverse ethnic and ideological mix. As with students in undergraduate and graduate programs, even in seminaries we now have large numbers of lay persons—many of whom are male but more of whom are women, married and single, of all ages, with a wide range of experience, from all socioeconomic groups, gays and lesbians, some African Americans, many Hispanics and international students, as well as some from other faith traditions. The instructors are nearly as diverse.[7] This is a very different academic conversation. One can only guess at its outcome and eventual impact, but the slice of humanity engaged in theological education is very different than it was before.

Teaching and learning methods also have changed greatly, even in very traditional academic settings. The same is true in seminaries. Memorization of moral and dogmatic manuals is long gone—as are the manuals themselves. Even when lectures still predominate, there is a wider range of assigned readings, more dialogue, seminar-style exchanges, reflection and research papers, and never-ending Internet searches. Case studies are frequent; experience—personal and social—weighs heavier.

A Welcome Separation: Moral Theology and Canon Law

Sometimes silent departures receive scant attention but are very welcome all the same. Such was the case with the academic disjuncture of canon law and moral theology after the Second Vatican Council. The two had been long closely associated, even intertwined, and their separation was healthy for both. In an era that purports to celebrate interdisciplinary effort, this example of disciplinary distancing deserves special mention particularly because of the disciplinary implications.

Canon law came of age as an organized academic specialization in the twelfth century, whereas moral theology began to be studied as a distinct field of theology only after the Council of Trent, in the late sixteenth and seventeenth centuries. The dominant deontological (morality as obedience to laws) tendency in early moral theology[8] caused it to be overly influenced by canon law. On the other hand, the church's rules of order and discipline (the essence of canon law) became overly moralized, that is, its rules were regarded as norms of goodness or sinfulness when in reality they are prudent guides for action, safeguards for good order in the church.

The two disciplines were remarkably interlinked in the manuals, and this linkage was reflected in the seminary curriculum. Large portions of moral theology courses were devoted to an exegesis of the canons.[9] Whole sections—on the sacraments, for example—were omitted from canon law textbooks and treated in moral theology manuals because those large topics were treated in moral courses rather than in canon law classes.[10] The two disciplines were so overlaid and interpenetrated that at many points they were nearly indistinguishable. Both suffered distortions as a result.[11]

Moral theology and canon law separated quietly after the Council, almost without a word, like uncomfortable traveling companions. Both were happier for it; neither ever looked back. Moral theology still respects law but has many other guides besides, and canon law, though not amoral, devotes itself to the common good of the individuals and communities that make up the communion called church. Both are moving ahead on more solid ground and with clearer vision.

We have, then, changing publics, radically altered academic settings, and an establishment of moral theology as its own discipline, shaped by its separation from canon law and by internal efforts at renewal. Such changes are even more important as we turn to one specific problem that shapes and is shaped by these changes: academic freedom.

ACADEMIC FREEDOM AND CATHOLIC COLLEGES AND UNIVERSITIES

No Catholic theologian has contributed more to the discussion of academic freedom in American Catholic higher education than Charles Curran. In the preface to his 1990 *Catholic Higher Education, Theology, and Academic Freedom* he wrote:

> For almost twenty-five years I have been immersed in the issue of academic freedom in Catholic higher education in the United States. I have co-authored two books, and written a number of articles on this issue. In addition I have been practically involved in some significant struggles centered on academic freedom.[12]

Curran did not seek out these struggles, but neither has he been one to run from a fight. His contributions have been neither disinterested nor dispassionate, but they have been remarkably objective, especially in that painstakingly researched, historical, and balanced 1990 book.

Academic freedom has been a rallying cry and cherished principle for most of the twentieth century in American higher education.[13] George Marsden has written that "the ideal of academic freedom . . . emerged as the most sacred of all principles within the new academic professions."[14] Curran reminds us, however, that the principle of academic freedom is severely limited in practice: It protects faculty far more than students, tenured faculty more effectively than nontenured faculty or those in doctoral studies; it protects faculty from administrations, governing boards, and external authorities but not from the prejudices of other faculty or from sponsors of research (e.g., government or industry); it functions well in tranquil times but limps badly in time of war, political unrest (e.g., the "Communist menace" of the 1950s), or economic distress; it has not always served the interests of women or minorities.[15] In sum, academic freedom is extremely important, but its practice has produced mixed results.

Although Catholic universities and colleges generally resisted the principal of academic freedom prior to the mid-1960s, they strongly endorsed it suddenly in the late 1960s—but without much published debate or public reflection.[16] A blue ribbon group of distinguished Catholic educational leaders[17] met for three days in June 1967 at the resort town of Land O'Lakes, Wisconsin, and adopted a position paper that has had extraordinary influence. Its first paragraph read as follows:

> The Catholic university today must be a university in the full modern sense of the word, with a strong commitment to and concern for

> academic excellence. To perform its teaching and research functions effectively the Catholic university must have a true autonomy and academic freedom in the face of authority of whatever kind, lay or clerical, external to the academic community itself. To say this is simply to assert that institutional autonomy and academic freedom are essential conditions of life and growth and indeed of survival for Catholic universities as for all universities.[18]

The signers simply asserted that academic freedom is essential for the survival, life, and growth of the university. Is it possible to give a better rationale, a fuller justification, for academic freedom?

The 1940 American Association of University Professors (AAUP) Statement of Principles on Academic Freedom and Tenure stated, "The common good depends upon the free search for truth and its free exposition."[19] In other words, academic freedom promotes the common good. Its purpose within the university is to enable that institution to serve the larger society. Curran finds this "pragmatic justification" for academic freedom more satisfying than "doctrinaire or metaphysical" justifications. "Academic freedom for institutions of higher learning is ultimately for the good of society itself."[20]

Curran braces this rationale with John Courtney Murray's argument for the right to religious liberty in a pluralistic society—an argument that simultaneously grounds the First Amendment to the U.S. Constitution. Such a right follows from the dignity of the human person existing in specific historical, social, and cultural circumstances. It is a juridic requirement for peaceful living, not an article of faith. Academic freedom, as protected speech, has been prudently judged to be necessary for the university to serve the common good of society, just as religious liberty was regarded as a practical necessity for Americans to live at peace with one another.[21]

Is it possible to sink the foundations of academic freedom deeper than this pragmatic justification? From a Catholic perspective, is there a more solid grounding for academic freedom than this social contract about the function of the university in society?

Christian Freedom as a Ground for Academic Freedom

Although often obscured and partially submerged,[22] imbedded in the Catholic tradition is a "fundamental option for freedom." This value is fully authentic and eventually always finds its way to the surface. Freedom in Christ is a fundamental New Testament theme: In John's gospel, in

Paul's letters, in James, and in Acts, the "glorious freedom of the children of God," guaranteed by the active presence of the Holy Spirit, epitomizes the Christian calling.[23] This basic conviction about Christian freedom reemerged and found powerful expression at the Second Vatican Council:

> The right to religious freedom is firmly based on the dignity of the human person as this is known from the revealed word of God and from reason itself. . . . In accordance with their dignity as persons, equipped with reason and free will and endowed with personal responsibility, all are impelled by their own nature and are bound by a moral obligation to seek truth, above all religious truth. . . . [24]
>
> It is only in freedom . . . that human beings can turn to what is good, and our contemporaries are right in their evaluation and assiduous pursuit of such freedom. . . . Genuine freedom is an outstanding manifestation of the divine image in humans. . . . Their human dignity therefore requires them to act through conscious and free choice, as motivated and prompted personally from within, and not through blind internal impulse or merely external pressure.[25]
>
> Since culture flows immediately from the rational and social nature of human beings, it continually requires the just freedom to develop and the legitimate opportunity to exercise independence according to its own principles. . . . All this also demands that, while observing the moral order and the common benefit, people should be able to seek the truth freely, to express and publicize their views. . . . [26]

Speaking specifically about the aims of Christian education, the Council included the pursuit of true freedom as a principal goal.[27] Such an emphasis also is highlighted by becoming one of the central themes of the theology of Karl Rahner,[28] the most highly regarded and influential Catholic theologian of the past half-century. Rahner witnesses convincingly to the rehabilitation of the theme of Christian freedom.

Although one cannot claim that the "fundamental option for human freedom" of the Catholic tradition leads inevitably to the principle of academic freedom in American Catholic universities, one does find in this rich source a profound resonance, a justifying rationale, and an appropriate context for legitimate and responsible academic freedom. Freedom in Christ, like our cherished First Amendment guarantee of freedom of speech in the United States, creates and maintains a congenial climate for academic freedom in our colleges and universities. Curran probably would concur.

Academic Freedom and the Mandatum

One of the most pressing questions regarding academic freedom in Catholic colleges and universities is the requirement of the "mandatum" for teachers of theological disciplines. This requirement is being newly urged in the United States by the application of the norms of the 1990 apostolic constitution on Catholic higher education, *Ex corde ecclesiae*.[29] The mandatum requirement was an innovation in the 1983 *Code of Canon Law*. It had been entirely unobserved in the United States (and the rest of the world) since that time by teachers of theological disciplines, by bishops, and by the administrators and boards of trustees of Catholic colleges and universities. All of these parties regarded the mandatum as an unsuitable requirement.[30]

Ex corde ecclesiae mentioned the canonical obligation of the mandatum in passing in its normative section.[31] The American bishops tried for a decade to fashion norms of application that would avoid imposition of this juridical instrument.[32] The Congregation for Catholic Education would not approve an application that did not require the mandatum, however, so in November 1999 the bishops approved a version, heavily edited by the Congregation, that included it.[33]

Naturally this requirement of a mandatum issued by an ecclesiastical authority outside the normal academic process for faculty appointments is regarded as a grave threat to academic freedom, in principle and in practice. Teachers of theology in Catholic colleges and universities should be treated no differently than teachers of any other discipline—a fact that *Ex corde ecclesiae* itself explicitly acknowledged, ironically enough:

> The church, accepting "the legitimate autonomy of human culture and especially of the sciences," recognizes the academic freedom of scholars in each discipline in accordance with its own principles and proper methods (*Gaudium et spes* 59), and within the confines of the truth and the common good.
>
> Theology has its legitimate place in the university alongside other disciplines. It has proper principles and methods which define it as a branch of knowledge. Theologians enjoy this same freedom so long as they are faithful to these principles and methods.[34]

What, then, is the justification for singling out teachers of theology for special scrutiny and approval before or during their college or seminary faculty assignments? It remains to be seen how this reiterated canonical requirement will be actualized in the United States. At minimum, its application could cause the serious erosion of the principle of academic freedom that now is fully accepted and well established in American Catholic higher education.[35]

INSTITUTIONAL AUTONOMY AND CATHOLIC IDENTITY

As important and sensitive as the issue of academic freedom is, the question of the autonomy and identity of Catholic colleges and universities is much greater. Its long-term implications raise issues of critical urgency. It would not be an exaggeration to claim that the integrity of a meaningful Catholic presence and influence in American higher education hangs in the balance.

In the past ten years, several thoughtful studies have illumined this problem. Some focus on the long-term "secularizing" trend among American church-related institutions of higher learning in general,[36] some center on the situation of Catholic schools in particular,[37] and still others cluster around the apostolic constitution *Ex corde ecclesiae* (and related ecclesial documents) and Catholic colleges.[38]

The larger movement away from direct connections with sponsoring churches and towards the schools' own self-determination among American church-related institutions has been in process for many decades. Harvard, Yale, Princeton, Columbia, Michigan, Johns Hopkins, Chicago, Southern California, and many other colleges and universities that were founded under religious auspices moved completely away from their founding churches. The contemporary allegation is that Catholic schools are speeding down the same path.

The Catholic trend is much more recent, taking place almost exactly in the final third of the twentieth century. The causes are more identifiable; they include the empowerment of the laity by the teachings of the Second Vatican Council, the consequent "laicization" of boards of trustees, the growth and professionalization of the schools, the lack of vocations in the religious teaching orders of women and men that sponsor many of the schools, financial and competitive pressures, fear of exclusion from government funding if the schools are perceived to be too closely affiliated with the church, and a desire to be mainstream like the best American schools, with full autonomy and academic freedom. The ensemble of these and other developments has led to a different and, in some cases, diminished Catholic identity.

The range of terms used to describe the changed relationship between the colleges and the church is rich and varied (and worrisome):

disestablishment, disengagement, estrangement, alienation, separation, secession, breakaway, withdrawal, turn away, draw beyond arm's length, unraveling of the bond, cleavage, divergence, emancipation, liberation. Regardless of the rhetoric, there is an underlying reality that has caused many to raise the cry of "secularization."[39]

Even Charles Curran, long a champion of freedom and autonomy, admitted that there is a danger of secularization in Catholic institutions of higher education. He said that it is a challenge to be resolutely faced: The internal forces of each academic community, especially the faculty and trustees, must come to grips with the identity issue, clearly articulate their position, and remain steadfastly committed to it.[40]

A Theological Vision

A theological vision of the nature of the church and of the relationship between faith and reason in the university is essential to help guide this critical on-campus discussion of Catholic identity. A theological view that equates church with hierarchy or expects doctrines of faith to dictate answers to scientific questions is seriously deficient and will not contribute to a satisfactory articulation of the authentic relationship between the church and the academy. Nor will it address the needs of the various publics identified above.

Each Catholic college or university exists within the church (unless or until it decides not to remain), as *Ex corde ecclesiae* reminds us. Most important, however, "church" must be understood "in the integral sense recovered by the Second Vatican Council: It refers to the whole assembly of Christian believers *(congregatio fidelium)* gathered into a communion of faith, hope, and love, served and governed by the apostolic ministry of the pope and bishops, and sent by Christ to be his redemptive sign and instrument in the world."[41] Every institution of higher learning lives and finds its role within this people. It has a particular mission: By virtue of its catholicity, the church strives to integrate the whole human community, with all its varied gifts, under Christ and in the unity of his Holy Spirit.[42] This is not a narrow space in which to dwell, nor is it a confining context within which to carry on the school's educational task. It offers distinctive direction and perspective to each school's mission.

Catholics operate out of a conviction that faith and reason are in harmony. Ultimately the truths of revealed faith and of human understanding will not contradict one another but will be reconciled and found to be mutually supportive.[43]

> The very foundation for the idea *Catholic university* is that faith does not present itself as opposed to reason, but rather presupposes and completes it.
>
> The immediate implication is that the Catholic university is always more or less in a state of crisis, and it has to be: If faith and reason are two entranceways to the one truth and only come together behind the horizon, then it is obvious that in the foreground both—faith and reason—must be engaged in dialectical dialogue. . . . The "crisis" is imprinted . . . in the very "genes" of the idea of a Catholic university. . . .
>
> The Catholic university has a unique and irreplaceable role to play precisely because it is a beacon of trust in the power of reason and in the compatibility and harmony between the two entranceways—faith and reason—in the midst of a skeptical and pragmatically oriented world.[44]

This theological stance affords a vision of the college or university within the church that is challenging, but hardly confining:

> to be an intellectual community where in utter academic freedom the variant lines of Catholic tradition and thought can intersect with all forms of human culture . . . and can move toward a reflective unity . . . between human culture and the self-revelation of God.
>
> These do not simply intersect; one brings the other to its completion. The experiences and practices of faith reach a new completion as faith advances into human understanding; the human dynamic to understand, found in whatever field of inquiry, reaches a new completion in the ultimacy of the self-disclosure of God.[45]

Practical Actions

The delicate balance of institutional autonomy and Catholic identity is not reached by theological reflection alone. It must begin there, however, and this is where *Ex corde ecclesiae* brings real assistance. In his personalized introduction, Pope John Paul II affirms the theological vision of the organic integrity of faith and knowledge, the dynamic integration of the academic and the religious. Then the apostolic constitution goes on to state solidly the principle of academic autonomy:

> Every Catholic university . . . possesses that institutional autonomy necessary to perform its functions effectively and guarantees its members academic freedom, so long as the rights of the individual person

> and of the community are preserved with the confines of the truth and the common good.[46]

Having clearly declared the legitimate autonomy and self-determination of Catholic universities, the papal statement then urges each of them to articulate and make known its Catholic identity in a mission statement or other document and to provide means that will guarantee the expression and preservation of this identity.[47] In other words, the document invites each school to work out its self-description, tell the world what it is, and structure itself to reflect and preserve that identity. It invites the whole academic community to move beyond theory and rhetoric to practical action.

Ex corde ecclesiae itself suggests several practical matters, such as recruiting trustees, administrators, and faculty who are Catholics and/or are firmly committed to the school's identity and mission, providing pastoral ministry for the whole university community, and relating to church authorities in "mutual trust, close and consistent cooperation and continuing dialogue."[48]

Several writers on this complex topic of identity have put forth more practical actions: maintaining a critical mass or even predominance of Catholic faculty and trustees, searching out Catholic intellectuals, organizing structured discussions of identity-related issues, providing access to the Catholic tradition in the curriculum, involving students in experiences related to justice and peace, celebrating the community's worship in a vital manner, having a trustees' committee regularly ask departments about promoting Catholic identity, and enhancing the quality of theological reflection and teaching.[49] Symbols reinforce identity. The visual and aural reminders afforded by architecture, inscriptions, statues, music, theater, lectures, and commemorations must not be overlooked.

None of these "practical matters" is easy to resolve, but the institutions must address them. Catholic identity will not be preserved (or re-achieved) by thinking and wishing. It will take determined and sustained action.

Moral Theology in the Balance

Curran has averred: "Because of the large number of Catholic colleges and universities in the United States, there are more moral theologians in this country than in any other country in the world."[50] Their quality increased dramatically over the last thirty years of the twentieth century. Although Curran's claims are true, these achievements in moral theology are in jeopardy. If those Catholic colleges and universities "go secular," or even if many of the biggest and best of them do, where will Catholic moral theology be forty years from now? More important, where will the Catholic moral tradition and its influence in this country and in the world be?

Moral theology and ethical issues are at the heart of the matter. *Ex corde ecclesiae* affirms this point.[51] Cardinal Daneels put it vividly:

> Discoveries create problems that the single individual can no longer handle. This is especially true in the medical sector. Here big questions confront us: It is no longer can we? But may we? Just about all faculties today call upon the ethicist. And not only in the sphere of medicine. Other faculties have reached the point of having to establish ethical committees in order to deal with their own problems.[52]

Moralists do far more than advise on newly emerging discoveries. Indeed, one hopes that their formative influence as Christian educators and mentors surpasses their role as problem-solvers. Without teaching positions and the incentives to devote themselves to the difficult task, however, the profession is bound to decline. Moral theology, in sum, has a large stake in the Catholic identity issue.

Formula for the Future

John Mahoney has reminded us of two powerful themes from two of Catholic moral theology's most influential sources: Paul's idea of *koinonia,* the fellowship of the Holy Spirit, and Thomas Aquinas' notion of the law of the gospel, the primary element of which is the presence of the Holy Spirit within us.[53]

These two central themes, in combination, offer a formula for the pursuit of a healthy Catholic moral theology in its academic dimension. Academe is one sector of the communion that is the church, a locus of moral theologizing, a matrix for a continually renewed moral theology. A consciousness of the Christian community theologizing together on campus could deliver us from the rugged individualism that is so prevalent in Catholicism's past and in American culture.[54] The community, aware of the Spirit's presence and guidance as it reflects together on the difficult applications of the new law of the gospel, could lead us beyond casuistry and deontology in pursuit of the truth. An ethics of communion led by the Spirit may be a successful formula for the future of moral theology in academe.

NOTES

1. The particular factors in this chapter's purview seem to require this variation on the format that is followed elsewhere in this volume.
2. David Tracy, *The Analogical Imagination: Christian Theology and the Culture of Pluralism* (New York: Crossroad, 1981), 3–5.
3. Ibid., 14–15.
4. Charles Curran, "Moral Theology at the End of the Century," in *The Pere Marquette Lecture in Theology* (Milwaukee, Wisc.: Marquette University Press, 1999).
5. Ibid., 25–41. Curran also treated this academic context of moral theology in "Moral Theology in the United States: An Analysis of the Last Twenty Years (1965–1985)," in *Toward an American Catholic Moral Theology* (Notre Dame, Ind.: Notre Dame University Press, 1987), 35–39, and in "The Academic Nature of (Moral) Theology," *Horizons* 26:2 (fall 1999): 282–85.
6. Curran, "Moral Theology at the End of the Century," 39.
7. There now are many women members in the Catholic Theological Society of America; there were none in the early 1960s. The College Theology Society has a larger percentage of women members. Both societies are ethnically diverse.
8. See, for example, Charles Curran, *The Catholic Moral Tradition Today: A Synthesis* (Washington, D.C.: Georgetown University Press, 1999), 61–66.
9. Curran, who admitted that he was attracted to the study of canon law before he embarked on his career as a moralist (*Ongoing Revision: Studies in Moral Theology* [Notre Dame, Ind.: Fides, 1975], 263), taught canon law when he began his teaching at St. Bernard's Seminary in Rochester (*Faithful Dissent* [Kansas City, Mo.: Sheed & Ward, 1986], 80). "In the pre–Vatican II church, moral theology was heavily intertwined with canon law. Often the same person taught both disciplines"; ibid.
10. T. Lincoln Bouscaren and Adam C. Ellis, *Canon Law: A Text and Commentary* (Milwaukee, Wisc.: Bruce, 1946), perhaps the most widely used canonical textbook in the United States from the time of its publication until after the Council, is one example.
11. This is part of what John Mahoney describes as moral theology's "obsession with law." "Moreover, the casting of moral theology as the handmaid of canon law has only reinforced the predominantly legal approach to morality which has dominated the making of moral theology." *The Making of Moral Theology: A Study of the Roman Catholic Tradition* (Oxford: Clarendon, 1987), 35.
12. Charles Curran, *Catholic Higher Education, Theology, and Academic Freedom* (Notre Dame, Ind.: University of Notre Dame, Press, 1990), ix.

13. The widely accepted formulation of academic freedom that originated with the American Association of University Professors in 1915 was accepted by the Association of American Colleges in 1925. It was further refined in 1940, 1958, 1961, and 1966 and continues to be clarified by the AAUP. It refers to freedom of faculty members in research and publication, in teaching within the institution, and in extramural utterances. See *Academic Freedom and Tenure: A Handbook of the American Association of University Professors,* ed. Louis Joughin (Madison: University of Wisconsin Press, 1967).

14. "The Soul of the American University: An Historical Overview," in *The Secularization of the Academy,* eds. George Marsden and Bradley Longfield (New York: Oxford University Press, 1992), 9–45, at 18.

15. Curran, *Catholic Higher Education,* 13–21.

16. Ibid., 73–78. The abrupt acceptance of academic freedom took place, however, within a welter of developments in American Catholicism as well as in Catholic higher education; ibid., 85–104; David O'Brien, *From the Heart of the American Church: Catholic Higher Education and American Culture* (New York: Orbis, 1994), 51–81; James Annarelli, *Academic Freedom and Catholic Higher Education* (New York: Greenwood, 1987), 27–55; and, with a telling title, Andrew Greeley, *From Backwater to Mainstream: A Profile of Catholic Higher Education* (New York: McGraw-Hill, 1969).

17. It was a regional meeting of the International Federation of Catholic Universities held to describe the role of the Catholic university in the modern world (in harmony with the Vatican II constitution, "The Church in the Modern World"). The group included representatives of Boston College, the Catholic University of America, Fordham, Georgetown, Notre Dame, Saint Louis University, and Seton Hall, among others.

18. "Land O'Lakes Statement: The Nature of the Contemporary University," in *American Catholic Higher Education: Essential Documents, 1967–1990,* ed. Alice Gallin. (Notre Dame, Ind.: University of Notre Dame Press, 1992), 7–12, at 7.

19. *AAUP Bulletin* 45 (March 1959): 110–11.

20. Curran, *Catholic Higher Education,* 157. In addition to Curran's discussion of "Rationale in Defense of Academic Freedom for Catholic Higher Education," ibid., 154–91, see Annarelli, *Academic Freedom and Catholic Higher Education,* 107–18 and 196–217, as well as the lawyer-like arguments in John Hunt and Terrence Connelly, *The Responsibility of Dissent: The Church and Academic Freedom* (New York: Sheed & Ward, 1969), 52–128.

21. Curran, *Catholic Higher Education,* 160–62.

22. Curran offers several examples of Catholic suspicions about the dangers of freedom; ibid. 58–59. The prior censorship of books and the index of prohibited

books (from 1487 and 1564 until 1975 and 1966, respectively) is another illustration.

23. Rom. 8:21; 2 Cor. 3:17, Gal. 5:13. I have developed this theme of Christian freedom somewhat in *Canon Law as Ministry: Freedom and Good Order for the Church* (New York: Paulist Press, 2000), 79–105.

24. *Dignitatis humanae,* Declaration on religious freedom, Second Vatican Council (December 7, 1965), para. 2, in Norman Tanner, ed., *Decrees of the Ecumenical Council,* vol. 2 (Washington, D.C.: Georgetown University Press, 1990), 1002–3.

25. *Gaudium et spes,* Pastoral constitution on the church in the world of today, Second Vatican Council (December 7, 1965), para. 17, in Tanner, *Decrees,* 1078.

26. Ibid., para. 59, in Tanner, *Decrees,* 1109–10.

27. *Gravissimum educationis,* Declaration on Christian education, Second Vatican Council (October 28, 1965), para. 1, in Tanner, *Decrees,* 960

28. For example, "The Dignity and Freedom of Man," in *Theological Investigations II* (Baltimore: Helicon, 1963), 235–63; "Theology of Freedom," in *Theological Investigations VI* (Baltimore; Helicon, 1969), 178–96; *Grace in Freedom* (New York: Herder & Herder, 1969); "Institution and Freedom," in *Theological Investigations XIII* (New York: Seabury, 1975), 105–21.

29. The apostolic constitution can be found in *Origins* 20:17 (October 4, 1990): 265–76; the norms of American application in *Origins* 30:5 (June 15, 2000): 68–75; the guidelines for granting or withdrawing the mandatum in *Origins* 31:7 (June 28, 2001): 128–31. The norms of application went into effect on May 3, 2001.

30. The reasons for its unsuitability are summarized in *The Code of Canon Law: A Text and Commentary,* ed. J. Coriden, T. Green, and D. Heintschel (New York: Paulist Press, 1985), 571–72, 575–77.

31. II. General Norms, Art. 4. The University Community, n. 3; *Origins* 20:17 (October 4, 1990): 274.

32. For instance, the bishops approved norms of application that did not include the "juridical instrument" of the mandatum on November 13, 1996, by a vote of 224 to 6.

33. See *Origins* 30:27 (December 14, 2000): 425–29.

34. *Ex corde ecclesiae,* n. 29; *Origins* 20:17 (October 4, 1990): 271.

35. For a discussion of this issue, see the Catholic Theological Society of America (CTSA), "Report of the Ad Hoc Committee on the Mandatum" (University Heights, Ohio: John Carroll University, September 2000). One is compelled to wonder why this almost meaningless juridical element, the mandatum, should not be relinquished entirely in favor of a much more authentic usage:

"Mandatum novum do vobis, ut diligatis invicem, sicut dilexi vos" ("I give you a new commandment: love one another as I have loved you"; Jn. 13:34).

36. *The Secularization of the Academy,* ed. George Marsden and Bradley Longfield (New York: Oxford University Press, 1992); George Marsden, *The Soul of the American University* (New York: Oxford University Press, 1994); Douglas Sloan, *Faith and Knowledge: Mainline Protestantism and American Higher Education* (Louisville, Ky.: Westminster/John Knox, 1994); James Burtchaell, *The Dying of the Light: The Disengagement of Colleges and Universities from Their Christian Churches* (Grand Rapids, Mich.: Eerdmans, 1998).
37. William Leahy, *Adapting to America: Catholics, Jesuits, and Higher Education in the Twentieth Century* (Washington, D.C.: Georgetown University Press, 1991); Theodore Hesburgh, ed., *The Challenge and Promise of a Catholic University* (Notre Dame, Ind.: University of Notre Dame Press, 1994); David O'Brien, *From the Heart of the American Church: Catholic Higher Education and American Culture* (Maryknoll, N.Y.: Orbis, 1994); Philip Gleason, *Contending With Modernity: Catholic Higher Education in the Twentieth Century* (New York: Oxford University Press, 1995); Alice Gallin, *Independence and a New Partnership in Catholic Higher Education* (Notre Dame, Ind.: University of Notre Dame Press, 1996); Joseph O'Keefe, ed., *Catholic Education at the Turn of the New Century* (New York: Garland, 1997); Michael Buckley, *The Catholic University as Promise and Project: Reflections in a Jesuit Idiom* (Washington, D.C.: Georgetown University Press, 1998); John Wilcox, *Enhancing Religious Identity: Best Practices from Catholic Campuses* (Washington, D.C.: Georgetown University Press, 2001); Robert Sullivan, *Higher Education and Catholic Traditions* (Notre Dame, Ind.: University of Notre Dame Press, 2001).
38. Alice Gallin, ed., *American Catholic Higher Education: Essential Documents, 1967–1990* (Notre Dame, Ind.: University of Notre Dame Press, 1992); John Langan, ed., *Catholic Universities in Church and in Society: A Dialogue on* Ex Corde Ecclesiae (Washington, D.C.: Georgetown University Press, 1993).
39. George Marsden is careful to describe what he means by secularization: "Our subject is the transformation from an era when organized Christianity and explicitly Christian ideals had a major role in the leading institutions of higher education to an era when they have almost none." (*The Secularization of the Academy,* 5). He goes on to say that not all secularization represents a decline. Although many people would say that the change in the role of religion is in some ways a loss, there is no doubt that the earlier Christian schools had a great many faults that deserved to be corrected.
40. Charles Curran, "The Catholic Identity of Catholic Institutions," *Theological Studies* 58 (1997): 105–08; idem., "What is a Catholic College?" in *History and Contemporary Issues: Studies in Moral Theology* (New York: Continuum, 1996), 212–14.

41. Joseph Komonchak, "The Catholic University in the Church," in Langan, *Catholic Universities in Church and in Society,* 35.
42. *Lumen gentium,* Dogmatic constitution on the church, Second Vatican Council (November 21, 1964), para. 13, in Tanner, *Decrees,* 859.
43. *Dei Filius,* Dogmatic constitution, First Vatican Council (April 24, 1870), in Tanner, *Decrees,* vol. 2, 808–09.
44. Cardinal Godfried Daneels, who is chancellor of Leuven and Louvain, speaking to Association of Catholic Colleges and Universities in Washington, January 27, 2001; *Origins* 30:35 (February 15, 2001): 559.
45. Michael Buckley, *The Catholic University as Promise and Project,* 20.
46. *Ex corde ecclesiae,* I, A. The Identity of a Catholic University, n. 12; also in II. Norms, art. 2, n. 5; *Origins* 20:17 (October 4, 1990): 268, 274.
47. Ibid., II, art. 2, n. 3; 20:17 (October 4, 1990): 274.
48. Ibid., I, A, 3, n. 28; 20:17 (October 4, 1990): 271.
49. Curran has urged several of these items; see *History and Contemporary Issues,* 211–12, and "The Catholic Identity of Catholic Institutions," 107–08. Others were suggested by Brian Hehir, Michael Buckley, David O'Brien, Philip Gleason, James Burtchaell, and Ladislas Örsy in works already mentioned.
50. Curran, *Moral Theology at the End of the Century,* 39.
51. *Ex corde ecclesiae,* I, nos. 18, 32–34; *Origins,* 269, 271–72.
52. Daneels, "The Dynamics of a Catholic University," 560.
53. *The Making of Moral Theology,* 343–47, 254–55.
54. "Truth is wrought out by many minds, working together freely." John Henry Newman, *Letters and Diaries XX* (London: Nelson, 1970), 426.

PART II

Sexual and Medical Ethics

CHAPTER 5

Divorce and Remarriage

Kevin T. Kelly

The second half of the twentieth century saw a steady rise in the number of marriages breaking down, at least in the West, and this trend has continued to the present day. Various reasons have been suggested for this phenomenon.

A cultural shift has led many people to regard marriage primarily as an interpersonal relationship rather than a relationship that is entered for the sake of children. Although this relationship model of marriage brings higher expectations, there are economic and social pressures militating against the interpersonal needs of such a relationship. An individualist interpretation of human freedom also sometimes leads to the view that lifelong commitments are humanly impossible, as well as undesirable. In addition, the simultaneous breakdown of the extended family means that the support system it provides is no longer available. Finally, longer life expectancy imposes further demands on a couple's relationship after their children have left home and the couple is left to rely mainly on their own emotional resources.

Christians have not been untouched by the cultural changes affecting people's understanding and experience of marriage. Consequently, Christian marriages have not been immune from the increase in divorce. Not surprisingly, therefore, the issue of divorce and remarriage has steadily crept into the church's pastoral and doctrinal agenda.

The pastoral impact is the first to be felt. Everyone who is involved in parish ministry knows this from their own experience. The pain felt by a couple and their children when a marriage is breaking down often is extremely traumatic, and the emotions triggered by the couple's separation often are compared to the bereavement experience. Individuals can feel extremely vulnerable at such a time. They may even rebound into a new relationship that, instead of bringing healing, merely compounds their problems and exacerbates their pain. Happily, such "rebound" second marriages are not the only scenario—and they certainly are not the kind of "divorce and remarriage" situations with which this chapter is mainly concerned.

Despite cautionary statistics about the failure of second marriages after divorce, most priests and others who are engaged in pastoral ministry encounter a fair number of instances in which a second marriage appears to have been a deeply healing experience and has brought the kind of mutual love and shared happiness that had been the unfulfilled dream of the previous marriage. Even when a second marriage does not satisfy such high expectations, it may bring sufficient healing and emotional security to enable a person at least to cope with the wounds of breakdown and live a life of tolerable peace and harmony.

This cultural sea change was already well under way when the bishops met at Vatican II, keen to read the "signs of the times" of our modern age. Their project involved listening to what was going on in people's lives, tuning in to the way people had a deeper knowledge and understanding of themselves as sexual persons and how this was affecting the way they were experiencing marriage. The bishops were trying to discern how far this new understanding was enriching our self-knowledge and how far it was impoverishing the way we shared our lives together.

In the Pastoral Constitution, *Gaudium et spes*, nn.47–52, the Council Fathers clearly accepted a personalist approach to marriage as helping us to appreciate much more positively the gift of human sexuality and its important role within the marriage relationship. They moved away from a predominantly functional view that regarded procreation as the primary purpose of marriage. Instead they used the language of "relationship" (covenant) to speak of marriage. The bishops were prepared to recognize that the sexual expression of a couple's love reflects and communicates God's own love for us. They even went so far as to warn couples that sexual abstinence could threaten their faithfulness to each other and thus pose a danger to the stable home life needed by their children. All of this was light years away from St. Augustine's insistence that sexual acts were sinful because they disturbed the calmness of mind demanded by rational self-control and needed to be "excused" by the reasonable purpose of procreation. In contrast, Vatican II's personalist approach spoke of children as the "fruit" of married love, not its purpose. It also left the church feeling uncomfortable about describing marriage in terms of a legal "contract," even though that kind of language was not entirely discarded.

This paradigm shift regarding marriage is very much in line with the way people feel about marriage today. Nowadays most people marry for love, even though they may also long for children. Consequently, a loveless marriage is regarded as a contradiction; even more so a marriage that is experienced as mutually destructive by both partners. Being faithful to a loveless marriage can hardly be said to be a reflection of God's faithfulness because it is precisely the faithfulness of God's love that marriage is supposed to reflect.

In this view of marriage, divorce is regarded as a tragedy rather than as a sin. Divorce is a sign that a couple has failed to achieve the mutual love that constitutes the very heart of marriage. In fact, their relationship may have deteriorated to such an extent that living together creates a potentially explosive environment that might range from scarcely being able to tolerate each other, through outright hostility, right up to having a mutually destructive effect on each other. In such circumstances, divorce may well be experienced as liberating and redemptive, despite all of its accompanying problems for the couple and especially for their children. It has brought healing in place of wounding and pain. To a person who has felt emotionally dead, experiences no meaning in life, and perhaps sees life at an end, divorce might even have a touch of a resurrection experience about it.

CHARLES CURRAN ON DIVORCE AND REMARRIAGE

Charles Curran has always been a moral theologian with very sensitive pastoral antennae. He has always personified John Mahoney's description of theology as "making faith-sense of experience and experience-sense of faith."[1] As we might expect, Curran was alert to the momentous sea change that was taking place in how people were experiencing and interpreting marriage in their lives. He was aware of the pastoral benefits this change brought—but also the personal hurt and pain that came in its wake. He was early in the field among moral theologians, looking at what was happening to people in the midst of the upheaval in the field of marriage and sexuality.

Not surprisingly for such a sensitive person, what first attracted Curran's attention was where people were hurting and being hurt: the area of divorce and second marriage. Hence, he was soon off the starting block, writing an early article in 1974 surveying pastoral theory and practice in the United States with regard to divorce and second marriage.[2] The tone of practical and positive pastoral concern combined with rigorous and courageous theological reflection in this article carries over to his subsequent writings on this topic, most prominently articles published in 1975[3] and 1978.[4]

In the first of his major writings on divorce and remarriage, Curran reports the widely accepted practice in the United States of admission of divorced-remarried people to the Eucharist, provided certain conditions were verified. A few years later, in *Divorce and Second Marriage: Facing the Challenge,*[5] I report that similar practice is common in Europe and the United Kingdom. In his 1975 book, Curran forecast that this would soon become regular practice throughout the church, with or without official approval:

> If the above reading of the signs of the times is accurate, there will soon be a change in the pastoral practice of the Catholic Church concerning the participation of divorced and remarried Catholics in the sacramental life of the Church. Even without any hierarchical sanction, today many Catholics in this situation are participating in the sacramental life of the Church. It seems that this will become the regular practice whether it is officially sanctioned by the hierarchical Church or not.[6]

Curran also reported a growing acceptance among priests of the grace-filled character of many second marriages. He found that sometimes such situations could be handled through the traditional means of resorting to the marriage tribunal for a nullity decision. In other instances, even when there were good grounds for believing the first marriage to be null, recourse to the tribunal was deemed impossible (lack of the caliber of evidence required by a tribunal) or pastorally inadvisable (harmfully opening up old wounds). In such cases, Curran felt that priests were becoming more confident in applying the "pastoral solution"—according to which, under certain generally agreed conditions, they would respect what they deemed to be the conscientious judgment of one partner about the nullity of his or her first marriage and therefore would accept the consequent pastoral applications for their living together and receiving the sacraments. In fact, Curran saw this practice becoming so widely accepted that he was prepared to state:

> In my estimation this practice is now so well entrenched that it not only exists side by side with the tribunal system but is becoming the

> primary way in which marriage cases are handled in practice because of the inherent weaknesses and cumbersome procedures of the existing legal system.[7]

Even when the validity of the first marriage did not seem to be in doubt, however, priests were encountering second marriages in which they felt the workings of God's grace was evident. Although Curran could not justify any official church celebration of such a marriage, he reported that priests often were prepared to have a more private celebration. He even describes his own practice:

> I do not think that now I can officially witness such a marriage in the eyes of the Church, for such a witness would say in the external forum that the Church recognizes such a marriage as valid, but in reality this is not the position of the Church at the present time. After explaining this to the couple I propose a somewhat small but not totally private celebration involving a Eucharist and an exchange of vows which in conscience we are convinced is a true marriage in the eyes of God.[8]

By 1975 Curran had developed the stance on divorce and remarriage that was to cause him so many difficulties with the Congregation for the Doctrine of the Faith (CDF). No longer content merely to advocate a new pastoral practice, he was prepared to state very bluntly, "I believe that the Catholic Church should change its teaching on the indissolubility of marriage."[9] Curran could see that the change of pastoral practice that was taking place had implicit within it a more fundamental change of teaching.

Curran realized that theologians often were inclined to shy away from admitting this implication because their main concern was to offer pastoral relief to people in difficult marriage situations. He felt unhappy with such evasion of the truth. For him such pastoral relief, by itself, might come at an unacceptable price. It might involve couples having to accept that what they have done is sinful, while they know in their heart of hearts that this is not true. (Certain pastoral approaches to contraception are open to a similar objection.) This is the cost of any pastoral policy that appeals solely to God's compassion and loving forgiveness.

Although Curran recognized that many couples whose marriages have broken down are in need of forgiveness, he denied that this is necessarily the case. Experience shows that there can be instances in which a couple's marriage has broken down without sin on the part of either partner. For Curran, such experience is an important *locus theologicus*. It is one of the reasons he felt convinced of the need for a change in the church's teaching. After going through all these reasons in his 1974 article, he reached the following conclusion:

> On the basis of all the foregoing evidence I conclude that the Roman Catholic Church should change its teaching and practice on divorce. Divorce and remarriage must be accepted as a reality in our world that at times can take place even without personal guilt on the part of the individuals involved. Indissolubility or permanency is a radical demand of the gospel that is seen as a goal but not an absolute norm.[10]

This final sentence encapsulates the position that Curran defends in his subsequent writings, a position that brings him into conflict with the CDF. For Curran, maintaining that the indissolubility of marriage is a radical demand of the gospel, a goal but not an absolute norm, does not involve any watering down of the radical teaching of the gospel. In fact, most New Testament scholars insist that the radical demands of the gospel have to be interpreted and lived out in the midst of all the change and moral ambiguity of existence this side of the *eschaton*. Thus, Curran concludes:

> In the case of the indissolubility of marriage it is precisely the eschatological fullness of love which is not always able to be had in this pilgrim existence. Human limitation and finitude also play a role. Some people will obviously fall short in their marital commitment because of personal sin—a point which can never be forgotten; but even without personal sin it is not always possible for pilgrim Christians to live up to the fullness of love. . . . This limitation of the present affects the objective understanding of marriage in the only world we know. Indissolubility of marriage in such a perspective can only be the goal which is imperative for all and which the couple promises to each other in hope; but which without their own fault, might at times be unobtainable.[11]

This viewpoint coheres with the usual way New Testament scholars interpret the radical demands of Jesus in the gospel. Hence, Curran writes:

> I opt for the opinion that one can partially understand some of the strenuous ethical teachings of Jesus in the Sermon on the Mount as a goal or ideal toward which the Christian must strive without always being able to attain the ideal. In the light of these and other reasons, I propose that indissolubility remains a goal and ideal for Christian marriage; but Christians, sometimes without any personal fault, are not always able to live up to that ideal. Thus the Roman Catholic Church should change its teaching on divorce.[12]

The CDF specifically quotes this passage against Curran. As we have seen, Curran prefers to use the terms "ideal," "goal," or "radical demand" instead of "absolute norm." This is not because he denies that every marriage carries within it an imperative to indissolubility. It is because, for him, "absolute norm" seems to bind everyone absolutely, and no violation of an absolute norm is defensible. This point comes out in his 1982 reply to the CDF:

> I do look upon the indissolubility of marriage "as a radical demand of the Gospel that is seen as a goal but not as an absolute norm" (*New Perspectives in Moral Theology,* 272). I do not contrast normative and ideal, for I see a normative character to the ideal. "Indissolubility of marriage in such a perspective can only be the goal which is imperative for all and which the couple promises to each other in hope; but which, without their own fault, might at times be unobtainable" (*Ongoing Revision in Moral Theology,* 105).[13]

The cutting edge of Curran's position is his constant assertion that the church needs to change its teaching that the indissolubility of marriage has absolute binding force.

So many marriages are breaking down these days that some people are arguing that the church needs to accommodate itself to modern life and admit, sadly, that marriage as we know it today is no longer indissoluble. Although the CDF never says so explicitly, this assertion seems to be how it interprets Curran's position. By arguing that marriage is not absolutely indissoluble, he seems to be implicitly throwing in the towel and conceding that marriage is dissoluble. This is one of the main reasons the CDF has ruled that he can no longer be recognized as a Catholic theologian.

Curran, on the other hand, regards himself as believing firmly in the indissolubility of marriage. He recognizes that this is a clear teaching of the New Testament that has been sustained throughout the whole of the church's history. All Christians who marry are bound by this teaching. He claims that nothing he has ever said actually denies the indissolubility of marriage. It is simply untrue to assert that he is compromising with the modern spirit and climbing down on this essential piece of Christian teaching. He is simply arguing that the CDF's presentation of this teaching does not adequately do justice to what has come down to us from scripture and tradition. Moreover, its philosophical basis sits uneasily with the personalist approach to marriage embraced by Vatican II.

I have tried to explore this point in *Divorce and Second Marriage: Facing the Challenge.*[14] In the remainder of this section, I interpret what

Curran says about marriage and marriage breakdown through the lens of the personalist approach in that volume.

The question behind Curran's disagreement with the CDF's presentation of the church's teaching on the indissolubility of marriage seems to be the following: Does indissolubility mean that when a couple marries, an ontological reality comes into existence that is distinct from their marriage relationship, that continues to exist regardless of the existential state of their relationship, and that is dissolved only by death? Or does it mean that when a couple marries, they embark on a relationship which, of its very nature, brings with it a moral obligation to be faithful to each other for life?

The CDF claims that its position is simply being true to the objective order of reality. Marriage is indissoluble. The teaching of Jesus rejects the compromising divorce laws permitted by Moses: "It was not so from the beginning." Indissolubility belongs to the very nature of marriage. It is objectively indissoluble.

Although the CDF teaching might seem to occupy the moral higher ground, Curran's position, seen through the lens of personalism, is much more open to the action of God's grace in human life. For the CDF, indissolubility is not of our doing. It is simply part of objective reality. Hence, if a couple exchanges marriage vows, their marriage is indissoluble, regardless of how they live out their marriage vows.

There is nothing "wonderful" about this indissolubility. It is equally present in a faithful, loving marriage as in one in which the couple have long ago separated and gone their separate ways and now look on each other with indifference, if not downright hostility. The latter case is hardly an inspiring reflection of the relationship between Christ and his church!

For Curran there is something much more creative and redemptive about indissolubility. It grows out of a couple's shared struggle to be faithful to the God-given obligation they have undertaken in making their marriage vows. The bringing into being and nurturing of the indissolubility of their marriage has been, and perhaps continues to be, a long and hard shared undertaking. The indissoluble relationship of faithful, life-giving love they have brought to fruition between them is a gift they are both proud of and immensely grateful for. It has come about through the working of God's unifying, healing, and affirming grace acting between them and within them. It is much more than an ontological reality existing independently of the quality of the marriage relationship. It belongs to the spiritual dimension of being human. As such, it touches a much more profound level of human objectivity—the realm of the spirit. It is a miracle of grace.

Curran maintains that indissolubility regarded as a radical demand (or ideal or goal) makes much better sense of the way tradition has handled indissolubility in pastoral practice through the centuries. The eastern church, for instance, throughout its long history has consistently held that after the tragedy of marriage breakdown, a second or even third marriage might be acceptable. This does not mean that the first marriage carried no obligation to indissolubility. Instead, the teaching is based on the comforting belief in God's compassionate understanding, forgiveness, and healing in the face of human failure. This whole approach is embraced within the eastern concept of "divine economy." Obviously, this approach is very different from what is found in the Roman Catholic Church. Nevertheless, at the Council of Trent, when the Council fathers reaffirmed that western discipline, they worded that particular canon with extreme care to ensure that it would not be interpreted as expressing any disapproval of the eastern approach.

Moreover, even within the Roman Catholic Church certain dissolutions of marriage have been allowed that sit much more easily with an interpretation of the indissolubility of marriage as a radical moral obligation than as an absolutely binding ontological reality (e.g., the Pauline and Petrine privilege).

In our own day, despite repeated attempts by the CDF to stamp out the practice, increasing use by priests—and even some bishops—of the "pastoral solution," broadly interpreted, seems to indicate a move toward an understanding of indissolubility that appears to be more in tune with Curran's basic approach. In other words, in many cases remarriage after divorce no longer is spoken of as "living in sin" (not even objectively). Instead, a remarried person often is regarded as moving beyond the wounding and sin-infected context of the first marriage and finding healing and a profoundly grace-filled relationship within the second marriage.

In the Curran-CDF exchange of correspondence, the CDF seems to be interpreting Curran as saying that the indissolubility of marriage is only external—it comes from a command of God, of Christ, of the church. It does not flow from the very nature of marriage itself. On the contrary, the CDF insists strongly on the ontological character of indissolubility. It flows from the very nature of marriage. It is intrinsic to it. The church's teaching does not create this indissolubility; it merely points to its undeniable existence.

Although I favor Curran's position, I do not think he adequately faces this CDF objection. He could have done more to help the CDF understand that his position does not threaten the internal indissolubility of marriage and that, paradoxically, its own position fails to do justice to the intrinsic indissolubility of marriage as we are better able to understand it today. The Vatican II paradigm shift regarding marriage from contract to covenant-relationship brings with it a richer, person-centered understanding of marriage. In other words, the heart of the reality of marriage lies in the persons themselves rather than in some legal contract. A couple's exchange of marriage vows binds them to a shared commitment to build their existing relationship into something much more profound, lasting, and irrevocable. It is as though this commitment contains the seeds of this lifelong fidelity that they are jointly promising to each other. That is to be the foundational quality of the interpersonal relationship to which they are committing themselves. This lifelong fidelity is intrinsic to the covenant-relationship that is their marriage. It is an obligation flowing from the very nature of their covenant-relationship. Admittedly, some people deliberately commit themselves to a relationship that is only temporary—even calling it marriage. That is essentially different to the notion of marriage we are discussing here, however.

The nature of this kind of interpersonal marriage relationship is that its quality, and even its continued existence, depends on the persons themselves—both of them together. There can come a point when the relationship is no longer that to which the couple committed themselves. It has ceased to be precisely a marriage relationship. When this happens, the intrinsic foundation for the obligation of lifelong fidelity also has ceased to be. Perhaps, for a time at least, one or the other partner—especially the one claiming to be "innocent"—might still feel bound by the commitment. This deeply felt obligation might be based on a variety of subjective reasons. Especially it might be that one partner is clinging to the hope that the marriage relationship might still have some life in it—and therefore some chance of revival. If the marriage relationship is truly dead, however, such hope lacks any basis in objective reality because, from a personalist point of view, the intrinsic foundation for the obligation—the marriage relationship itself—has ceased to exist.

FUTURE AGENDA

Recently a couple came to see me to arrange their marriage. They had been living together for the past eighteen years. The youngest of their four children had made her first communion the previous year. The woman, who was not a Catholic, had been previously married in a Registry Office wedding more than twenty years before and had been divorced a couple of years later. She mentioned this first marriage only because she thought it was something I would want to know about. To her, that first marriage meant nothing; it was just an act of folly between two teenagers that she now regarded as a passing phase of early development—like a booster rocket discarded as waste once its temporary role was complete. This couple's visit suggested to me some items that might well feature on our agenda for the future.

First was the fact that they had been living together for more than eighteen years and were only now coming to ask to be married! As I look at how life, at least in the West, has been developing in recent years, it seems that remarriage after divorce is becoming less and less of a pastoral problem because fewer people are getting married at all—certainly not at the beginning of their living together. Most young couples seem to be living together for a considerable period of time before they even start to contemplate the possibility of getting married.

Officially their cohabiting relationship lacks any formal standing in the eyes of the church—apart from being described as "living in sin"! Based on conversations with many priests, however, I get the impression that most, if asked to celebrate the wedding of such a couple, would see themselves as presiding at some kind of public, religious recognition and celebration of their existing relationship. They are not "putting right" something that is wrong; they are "completing" the formal side to something that is already full of goodness and grace. Some couples go so far as to suggest that their living together for some years prior to their getting married has lessened the chance that their marriage will end in breakdown. Though none of them have used the analogy, it is as though they regard it as somewhat akin to the novitiate in preparation to entering the religious life or the long period of seminary training prior to ordination and acceptance of a commitment to lifelong celibacy.

This item must surely rank high on the church's agenda. It poses the question: Given the variety of ways couples have entered marriage through history and the plurality of marriage customs in different cultures and religions, is there any possibility that the church might be able to see its way to responding officially in a more positive way to this modern phenomenon? For instance, if marriage is regarded essentially as a relationship that is open to growth, perhaps entry into marriage might include some kind of preparatory or initial phases and hence be regarded less as a contractual moment and more as a key stage in an ongoing process.

Second, how do couples like the one who came to visit me see their forthcoming marriage affecting the stability of their relationship? Do cohabiting couples believe they are committing themselves to a much firmer form of fidelity through their marriage vows? In this respect, has the church anything to learn from its earlier practice of *sponsalia* (formalized engagement with certain legal implications)—a custom originating from a view of entry into marriage as a process rather than a single act—or even from some imaginative thinking linked to the heated medieval debate about whether coitus or consent gives rise to marriage?

Third, the woman's first marriage meant virtually nothing to her. She described it as an act of two foolish teenagers belonging to the dim and distant past. Does her attitude force us to face some important questions? Since Vatican II, a personalist approach to marriage has raised major—as yet unanswered—questions for the notion of nullity as applied to marriage. Nullity has its natural home in the contract paradigm of marriage. It sits uncomfortably in the relationship paradigm. Relationships can be healthy, they may grow and develop, they may diminish and even die away—but they are never null! Even allowing for the continuation of the nullity process in the church, the relationship paradigm introduces a different feel to the nullity investigation. The focus is less on the contractual moment and much more on the capacity of the couple to undertake or sustain the marriage relationship—or even on whether they are sufficiently mature to appreciate the special kind of relationship involved. All of this has been increasingly recognized since Vatican II. With the new phenomenon of couples living together for many years prior to marriage, however, are teenage marriages (probably more the exception than the rule these days!) something to be rejoiced at—a young couple standing out against the advancing tide of decadence? Or are teenage marriages today more likely to be a cause for concern? In other words, in a personalist understanding of marriage in which the quality of the relationship is crucially important, are such teenage marriages somewhat analogous to a novice entering into final vows without a proper period of testing and preparation?

Fourth, other factors that are likely to appear on a future agenda arise from the perspectives of ecumenism. I have mentioned the all-encompassing theme of "divine economy" in the Eastern Orthodox churches. Various pleas have been made that the Roman Catholic Church should open itself to this dispensation. Interestingly, Charles Curran has not joined his voice to this chorus, even though his late and good friend Bernard Häring was a strong advocate of this position.

In recent years, most other Christian churches also have turned their attention to the issue of divorce and remarriage. In 2000, for instance, a working party commissioned by the House of Bishops of the Church of England published a major discussion document titled *Marriage in Church after Divorce.*[15] This document came in the wake of a whole series of Church of England documents on the topic: *Putting Asunder* (1966); *Marriage, Divorce, and the Church* (1971); and *Marriage and the Church's Task* (1978).

In its summary, the 2000 document accepts the possibility of remarriage in church after divorce. This position clearly is based on the kind of personalist approach to marriage:

> We hold steadfastly to the view that marriage is a gift of God in creation and a means of grace and that it should always be undertaken as a lifelong commitment. Nothing in this report should therefore be taken to imply any change in the Church of England's teaching on marriage. We nevertheless believe that it can be said of two living people that they were married and are no longer married. We therefore concur with the General Synod's view (as expressed in 1981) that there are circumstances in which a divorced person may be married in church during the lifetime of a former spouse.[16]

This document also includes a chapter summarizing the positions of the other major Christian churches in the United Kingdom—Roman Catholic, Methodist, United Reform, Church in Wales, Church of Scotland, and Orthodox—as well as several other churches in Europe. Despite minor variations, most seem to allow remarriage of divorcees in church, while recognizing the right in conscience of clergy not to be involved.

The position of the Roman Catholic Church obviously is out of step with the other Christian churches. Given that many Roman Catholic theologians, laity, clergy, and even bishops favor a change in the church's discipline, this divergence raises questions that the church must face up to urgently. Unless the moral integrity of the other Christian churches is to be questioned, it would seem that Roman Catholic Church authorities need to ask themselves in all humility whether they should be more open to learn from other Christian churches on this pastoral issue that touches the lives of so many people so intimately. For instance, writing from within the United Kingdom, I suggest that the carefully researched and well-argued reports of the Church of England cannot easily be dismissed. They are based on serious scholarship in the field of New Testament studies and church tradition, and the authors' work is highly respected by most of their Roman Catholic colleagues. Yet these reports have been able to reach, with integrity, a conclusion that is different from that embraced by the hierarchical magisterium of the Roman Catholic Church!

Fifth, perhaps reflections on marriage in other cultures and other faiths—including the way they handle divorce and remarriage—should be part of our future agenda. Linked to this item on the agenda should be that of recognition of the full and equal dignity of women. In some cultures and in some interpretations of other faiths, the position of women within marriage would seem to violate their basic humanity. If that is the case, the liberation and empowerment of women might involve enabling them to challenge the institution of marriage as currently accepted and practiced in their culture. In such a culture, divorce often might be experienced as a form of liberation. (Sadly, this is sometimes true even in "more enlightened" cultures.) Although the church normally should be a champion of the indissolubility of marriage, in cases such as this the church's obligation is to stand up for the dignity of women rather than defend a form of marriage that is oppressive to them. A divorce that frees a woman from an oppressive marriage and allows her to enter a second marriage in which her dignity is respected should be a cause of celebration for the church!

CONCLUSION

One final item must be on the church's future agenda. Charles Curran has written very forcefully about this issue in the second half of his 1978 essay, "The Gospel and Culture: Divorce and Christian Marriage Today."

If the indissolubility of marriage is not some abstract ontological entity but a task couples solemnly commit themselves to through their marriage vows, the rest of the church must not leave them to carry out this task unaided. In other words, high on any future agenda must be the practical help that the local church community gives to married couples as they embark on their journey in faith to build a marriage revelatory of the faithfulness of God himself.

> The Church must expend its pastoral efforts to create an ethos somewhat opposed to the prevailing cultural ethos, so that the ideal of Christian marriage remains a possibility. Yes, Christian theory and practice must accept the possibility of divorce, but an even greater source of challenge focuses on the need to create an atmosphere in which Christian marriage may be both understood in theory and lived in practice.[17]

This practical help should begin in early school years, be there through the teens, and be around when the arrival of children enriches but also puts a strain on their relationship; it should entail offering sound help as couples prepare for the marriage (or even during the years they may be sharing together before marriage), making available good parenting courses, and offering counseling when the going gets rough. Moreover, couples do not just need practical help. They need to feel valued. Couples should experience the parish liturgy as a celebration of God's presence in the nitty-gritty of their everyday lives.

Thus, pastoral care is the final item, and perhaps the most important. This challenge, like so many others, is beautifully articulated in the work of Charles Curran. Let his words be the last: "Yes, the Catholic Church must accept divorce, but even more importantly the Church must strive in every way possible to make the ideal of Christian marriage a reality for Christian people today."[18]

NOTES

1. John Mahoney, *Bioethics and Belief* (London: Sheed & Ward, 1984), 112.
2. "Divorce: Catholic Theory and Practice in the United States," in *New Perspectives in Moral Theology* (Notre Dame, Ind.: University of Notre Dame Press, 1974), 212–76.
3. "Divorce in the Light of a Revised Moral Theology," in *On-going Revision in Moral Theology* (Notre Dame, Ind.: University of Notre Dame Press, 1975), 66–106.
4. "The Gospel and Culture: Divorce and Christian Marriage Today," in *Issues in Sexual and Medical Ethics* (Notre Dame, Ind.: University of Notre Dame Press, 1978), 3–29. Curran also refers to divorce and remarriage in one of his earlier books: *A New Look at Christian Morality* (London & Sydney: Sheed & Ward, 1969), 16–21 and 226–31. The issue also comes up in his exchanges with the Congregation for the Doctrine of the Faith: *Faithful Dissent* (Kansas City: Sheed & Ward, 1986), 129–33, 187–88, 190–93, 204, 207–08, 240–41, 250, 257–58, and 272.
5. Kevin T. Kelly, *Divorce and Second Marriage: Facing the Challenge* (London: Collins, 1982).
6. Curran, "Divorce in the Light of a Revised Moral Theology," 75.
7. Curran, "Divorce: Catholic Theory and Practice in the United States," 249.
8. Ibid., 246.
9. Curran, "Divorce in the Light of a Revised Moral Theology," 75.
10. Curran, "Divorce: Catholic Theory and Practice in the United States," 271–72.
11. Curran, "Divorce in the Light of a Revised Moral Theology," 105–06.

12. Curran, *Issues in Sexual and Medical Ethics,* 15–16.
13. Curran, *Faithful Dissent,* 187–88.
14. Kevin T. Kelly, *Divorce and Second Marriage: Facing the Challenge,* new and expanded ed. (London: Continuum, 1996).
15. *Marriage in Church after Divorce* (London, Church House Publishing, 2000).
16. Ibid., xi.
17. “The Gospel and Culture: Divorce and Christian Marriage Today,” 27.
18. Ibid., 25.

CHAPTER 6

Sexual Ethics

Lisa Sowle Cahill

The publication of *Humanae vitae* and Charles Curran's reaction to it was perhaps the defining event of Curran's theological career. Curran developed not only his distinctive moral agenda affirming freedom and conscience but also more fundamental categories, such as historical consciousness and the difference between social and personal ethics in relation to the ecclesial controversy over birth control.[1] Paul VI's encyclical on birth control, of course, also precipitated Curran's self-defined stance as a "dissenting" theologian and his forced departure from the Catholic University of America, under pressure from the Vatican Congregation for the Doctrine of the Faith.[2]

Curran has consistently portrayed dissent as a form of loyal opposition that moves doctrine ahead. Yet to define new ideas as dissent may enshrine received notions in a way that vitiates bona fide testing of the former and critical reinvigoration of the latter. Although Curran's position on birth control has been roundly rejected by the magisterium, he raised questions about the meaning of sexual love that found a hearing in the experience and concerns of many other Catholics who experienced Vatican II.

In my view, Curran's efforts to renew Catholic sexual teaching by returning to its sources in scripture, tradition, and experience are not best termed dissent but participation in the development of doctrine. This categorization does not mean that all of his ideas have been accurate. They have been a salient factor, however, in driving the Vatican II church toward an ethic for sexual behavior and relationships that is positive and constructive, respectful of long-standing Catholic moral values, sensitive to the complexities of human experience, and inclusive of many different constituencies within Catholicism. Curran is conservative of traditional values in that he holds love and permanent commitment as the normative context of sex; regards heterosexual unions as ideal; and assumes that married couples will become parents, barring exceptional circumstances. His writings typify Vatican II Catholicism by bringing a personalist perspective to interpretation of natural law, seeking flexibility at the level of individual behavior, and referring to concrete experiences of sexual relationship (from the perspectives of married people and increasingly of women specifically and of gays and lesbians). They also reflect the Council's call for a renewal of the scriptural foundations of theology. In Curran's work, like that of many others, this new note can be difficult to integrate with the more traditional grounding of moral theology in natural law.

Above all, Curran's writings on sexual morality exemplify the moral mindset of the Vatican II generation by focusing on the defense of specific moral norms. Norms for individual behavior are the decisive battleground for "liberals" and "conservatives," although both sides accept with little question the Catholic view that sex belongs in marriage (or its functional equivalent), expresses conjugal love, and has some normative moral relation to parenthood. Like other moral theologians of the decades immediately following the Council, Curran tends to rely on manipulation of the standard categories of moral theology (e.g., double effect, toleration) to enlarge the arena of freedom for the consciences of individuals within this traditional framework.[3] Although Curran is a champion of "historical consciousness," he does not seriously question whether the whole system of reasoned casuistry that was pervasively ensconced in eighteenth- and nineteenth-century Catholic tradition through the seminary use of moral "manuals" should be rejected in a postmodern era. Nonetheless, we can find even in some of Curran's earlier writings a surprising and commendable sensitivity to what later were much more strongly recognized by feminists and other critics of race, class, and gender to be the social determinants and consequences of sexual ideology, identity, and behavior.[4]

After a brief review of the situation of Catholic moral theology and sexual issues in the latter half of the twentieth century,[5] I explore Curran's role in the development of sexual ethics by examining two topics that display his particular concerns and their development over four decades: birth control and homosexuality. In each case, exemplary writings from three different time periods focus the discussion. Among the many other topics in sexual ethics that Curran has treated over the years are masturbation,[6] premarital sex,[7] divorce and remarriage (treated in this volume by Kevin Kelly), in vitro fertilization,[8] and abortion.[9] My concluding remarks suggest future paths of development in this area of Catholic scholarship.

CATHOLIC SEXUAL ETHICS AND THE VATICAN II TRAJECTORY

Many of the stresses and strains in Catholic life and thought over the past fifty years have been caused by the inevitable difficulty of bringing into alignment an ancient, worldwide institution that is also Eurocentric and hierarchical with an increasingly powerful and global awareness of the contingency of cultural traditions—a recognition that makes it difficult for any moral authority to command broad and popular support. In moral theology, the dialectic of the universal and the particular has taken place along the axis of interpretation of natural law—that supposedly universal orientation of all creatures to their proper goods and ends, knowable by reason and unfailingly attractive to the properly ordered will.

The twentieth-century adaptation of natural law thinking that has been most important to Catholic sexual ethics is personalism—the attempt to lend abstract claims about human (sexual) nature and its norms a basis in relationships and personal, intersubjective experience. Defenders of past teaching have asserted that all traditional sexual norms can still be verified by using new personalistic criteria; critics of that teaching have argued to the contrary, that full appreciation of the realities of personal life and moral responsibility relativizes the authority of many traditional norms. Thus, the language of personal dignity has been used to advance very different understandings of sexuality. On one side the fully human, personal nature of sex still is deemed to include an unfailing openness to procreation as well as the love of spouses. On the other, the freedom of the person and the priority of love in sexual morality are invoked to make the quality of the interpersonal sexual relationship normative and to make procreation and sexual orientation secondary considerations.

The Roman Catholic birth control debate gained momentum after the Anglican Church's 1930 Lambeth Conference accepted artificial birth control. Pope Pius XI's *Casti connubii* (1930) staked out an opposed position reaffirming the prohibition. Even though Pius's encyclical acknowledged that love, as a "mutual and intimate harmony," is "the elemental cause and reason for matrimony,"[10] however, he ranked procreation and mutual help as primary and secondary ends of marriage and of sexual acts.[11]

Expressing currents of thought that were becoming more prevalent in philosophy generally, Catholic theologians such as Dietrich von Hildebrand[12] and Herbert Doms[13] turned explicitly to the marital relationship as a resource for further moral reflection on the problem. Their emphasis on the personal and intersubjective relationship of spouses in defining sexual morality brought a gradual shift in the way the ends of sexual intercourse (procreation and union) were understood, so that love of partners came to be identified as the foundation of the whole relationship and the ultimate determinant of the moral quality of all actions within it, including sexual intercourse and procreation. Even though the view that love of spouses is foundational to marriage was not inconsistent with *Casti connubii,* the Sacred Congregation for the Doctrine of the Faith ordered Doms's book withdrawn from publication for recommending that the language of primary and secondary ends be abandoned altogether.[14] The Congregation then issued a decree condemning such ideas.[15] Ironically, two decades later Vatican II's *Gaudium et spes* followed Doms's example by identifying two ostensibly equal purposes as requiring "harmonization" in marital sexuality: "conjugal love" and "the responsible transmission of life."[16] So much for lack of historical change in magisterial teaching on sex.

The specific teaching on artificial birth control was not destined to undergo a similar transition so rapidly. The development of the contraceptive pill in the 1960s had stimulated a broad cultural and religious debate about birth control because the pill made the ability to separate procreation from sex more predictable and reliable, avoided barrier methods that made the act of intercourse seem less "natural," and in the process raised questions about how to determine the "nature" of sexuality in the first place. In 1963, three much-discussed essays were published by Catholics—one by the archbishop of Mainz (J. M. Reuss). These essays argued the acceptability of contraception in experiential and personalist terms.[17] These writers and others proposed that sex as an expression of mutual love is a value beyond the times when procreation is appropriate, that sexual intercourse in humans is not always naturally fertile in any event, that the church has long accepted intercourse between sterile spouses, that sometimes it is morally valid to intend to avoid procreation, that the use of infertile periods to space births is a good but insufficient means, and that a change on the specific question of contraceptive use could be undertaken without threatening the fundamental values on which Catholic sexual teaching is based or the consistency and authority of the church.[18]

The Council itself took no position on artificial birth control. Paul VI had delayed a decision on this matter, pending his own review after the recommendations of the *Pontifical Commission for the Study of Population, Family and Birth,* constituted by John XIII before his death. The commission's majority report (rebutted by a small but vocal and ultimately victorious minority) concluded that the marital relationship is the proper context for evaluating sexual morality.[19] Within that context, the morality of sexual intercourse and procreation depends on the totality of a marriage—furthering, expressing, and fulfilling the love relationship. Although procreation is important to the whole relationship, it need not be a part of each and every sexual act. Deliberately avoiding conception, the report concluded, even by artificial means, is acceptable if it is necessary to protect the other important goods of marriage.

These arguments represented the perceptions of many people in the church at the time—people were well aware that the moral acceptability of artificial contraception was highly contested and that changes in attitude were emerging not only in the culture but at the level of religious institutions such as the Church of England. Many Catholics anticipated a more flexible Roman Catholic response to contraception as well, at least for married couples with good reason to limit or space their children. *Humanae vitae* (1968) disappointed these hopes. It rewarded defenders of the magisterium who insisted that its authority would be undermined by any loosening of so long-held a prohibition, even though in return for loyalty it had greatly burdened the lives of many Catholics.

Reaffirming procreation was one way for the Catholic Church to stave off change, which it did with *Humanae vitae.* The encyclical's heightened affirmation of love co-opted the growing emphasis on interpersonal relationship that had prompted the criticism that church teaching on sexuality and marriage was inadequate in the first place. In an effort to unite the idea that contraception violates natural sexual biology with the new emphasis on personal love, the immorality of artificial means of birth control was restated in terms of the requirements of marital love itself. Preventing conception artificially was said to violate the meaning of sex as an expression of love as self-gift. Paul VI abandons hierarchical language when he stipulates the meanings of "the conjugal act," the unitive and procreative.[20] Yet he insists that the personal nature of "true mutual love" demands that both ends be represented in every sex act, not merely along the continuum of a marriage.

In what on one level is an accommodation to the needs of families and on another a logical inconsistency, Paul VI also defines respect for the procreative end as adequately represented when a couple, though rightly intending to avoid conception in respect of their duty of "responsible parenthood," refrains from interfering in the physical or biological structure of the act of intercourse. Paradoxically, this provision makes it possible for couples to fulfill what is their admitted obligation to avoid pregnancy, yet remain "open to the transmission of life."[21]

Needless to say, this intervention hardly ended the theological debate, much less noncompliance on the part of married persons who feel that the papal definition of the realities of married love and parenthood is not confirmed in their own lives. Repeated attempts at a more persuasive rendition of *Humanae vitae*'s argument have been ventured by John Paul II, as well as by other theologians. Employing personalist and biblical themes, John Paul II has developed the metaphor of sex as a "language of the body" whose truthfulness depends on forgoing artificial contraception.[22] The ban on artificial contraception is reaffirmed vehemently in *Familiaris consortio* (1981), where we find the following assertion:

> The innate language that expresses the total reciprocal self-giving of husband and wife is overlaid, through contraception, by an objectively contradictory language, namely, that of not giving oneself totally to the other. This leads not only to a positive refusal to be open to life, but also to a falsification of the inner truth of conjugal love, which is called upon to give itself in personal totality.[23]

The crux of the ongoing debate is whether the traditional Catholic value triad of love, sex, and procreation can be in any way broken apart, to what degree, and for what reasons. To answer this question it also is necessary to establish whether these values are absolutely equal or whether they can be prioritized. Although official teaching from Vatican II to John Paul II presents the marital relationship as the most fundamental value, it refuses it status as a primary or controlling value that would justify the occasional exclusion of the procreative aspect of sex (in contraception), or of the sex act itself (as when a loving couple achieves conception through a technology such as in vitro fertilization).[24]

At the level of behavioral rules, magisterial teaching seems to grant procreation practical priority in the evaluation of sex acts because artificial birth control may not be used even to permit the sexual expression of love at times when conception is strongly contraindicated. Recent teachings against the morality of most forms of assisted reproduction also follow from the requirement that all procreation be accomplished through a sexual act. Arguments against same-sex acts derive from the requirement that love be expressed only through sexual acts whose physiological structure is of the type from which conception may follow and from the premise that the love and mutual self-gift that form the context for moral sex must be heterosexual, expressing physiological and psychological male-female complementarity.

Contrary positions have highlighted the quality of affective relation and commitment between sexual partners as the overriding value in sexual morality. They also stress the personal responsibility of individuals to determine their ultimate moral obligations in so intimate and personal a sphere and note the cost in human suffering that has accompanied excessively rigid applications of procreation-oriented norms of the past. Feminist critics and those who are sensitive to matters of race and class also have criticized the heterosexual-couple, two-parent, procreation-focused model of the nuclear family that the current teaching seems to presume. They have asked whether, at a minimum, the ban on artificial birth control contradicts the right and responsibility of women to contribute to the common good through public works and vocations and the equality of women that the pope himself repeatedly has said he supports.[25] The line of critique that is most represented in the writings of Charles Curran focuses on the negative, constraining, and even cruel effects on individual persons and married couples that rigid adherence to the teaching of *Humanae vitae* represents.

CURRAN ON BIRTH CONTROL

Curran's position on birth control can be fruitfully sampled in three different periods: his conversion to the view that contraception can be permissible; some years later, when he assesses the effects of widespread dissent from *Humanae vitae;* and in recent years, as he considers what integrated place sexual ethics has within Catholic moral theology as a whole.

In *Christian Morality Today*[26]—written at the end of the Council and before the appearance of *Humanae vitae*—Curran includes two contrasting essays setting out his own arguments first against and then for contraception. "Christian Marriage and Family Planning" begins with the sort of painful case example one wishes were apocryphal. A young couple living on a single schoolteacher's salary has nine children, having been told by a priest after the fourth that the use of rhythm was unjustified in their case. As an alternative, they have tried to limit their sex life to so-called "incomplete sexual acts," but they experience trauma and guilt because sometimes these intimacies have gone further than they had planned, resulting either in a risk of pregnancy or in the supposedly sinful "wasting of seed." Curran's reply concerns the legitimacy of rhythm; the lack of guilt surrounding involuntary orgasm; and the possibility, which he did not consider all that likely at the time, that the church's teaching on birth control might change. He emphasizes that sexual love is good, the "cornerstone" of marriage—to be enjoyed, not condemned.

Although Curran raises the question of whether the experience of married couples is not the best indicator of marital sexual morality, he finally concurs in the official line on birth control. Catholic teaching opposes contraception "because it destroys the marital act as an expression of the union of love in the service of life," because it "no longer symbolizes the complete surrender of love."[27] In any event, the generative faculty is not intended for the good of the person or couple alone but for the species and thus cannot be violated on behalf of merely personal interests. Nonetheless, Curran continues—somewhat inconsistently—that "the principle of responsible parenthood" requires recognition that in some circumstances risking a pregnancy and endangering "wife and family" can be "a greater evil" than contraception. In such cases, even though contraception is "objectively wrong," it can be counseled by a confessor.[28]

The essay that follows, "Personal Reflections on Birth Control," carries through on this last insight, defending artificial birth control. Curran concludes directly that what is objectively the lesser of two evils is not objectively wrong in practice and that the experience of married couples confirms the importance of sexual union and the inadequacy of church teaching on birth control. Foreshadowing the later evolution of the method of moral analysis known as "proportionalism," Curran says that "in most moral judgments some particular value (not a moral one as such) might have to be sacrificed for the good of the whole."[29] "What if the biological integrity of the marital acts destroys other such considerations as the educational, the love union of the spouses, the psychic and physical health of the spouses? . . . The biological aspect is not an absolute. . . ."[30] On this basis, Curran recommends a change in church teaching as not a "contradiction" but a "development,"[31] based on a truly "objective" but more "personalist" approach.[32]

Paul VI and later John Paul II took personalism in a different direction on this issue, but not without significant protest by Curran and others. The title *Tensions in Moral Theology* indicates the results. In this 1988 work, Curran reflects on the situation, its causes, and its consequences. A basic point is that many—even most—Catholic moral theologians have not accepted the ban of *Humanae vitae* or even the church's later prohibition on homologous artificial fertilization, a position that Curran believes has eroded the authority of the church. Curran calls not only for a reconsideration of the matter at hand but also for acceptance of the fact that dissent or pluralism and unity can coexist in the church. The magisterium would be enhanced, not hindered, were it to acknowledge the value of the "loyal opposition" and grant that "the critical interpretive function of Catholic theologians at times might call for dissent from the teaching of the hierarchical magisterium."[33]

Interestingly, Curran does not recognize the impact that new currents of thought have had on Catholic teaching in the twentieth century. He repeatedly states that Catholic sexual ethics "went through no change or development at Vatican II."[34] Yet this assertion is true only if one considers the norm on contraceptive sex acts alone—the focus and battleground of the immediately post–Vatican II mindset. If one takes a larger view of the meaning of sexuality and marriage, accompanied by an appreciation that shifts at this foundational level ultimately have repercussions at the more specific, practical level of behavior and norms, one can see that significant changes did indeed take place at Vatican II. These changes concerned not the narrow focus (the ban) but the big picture (the ends of sex and marriage and the implicit primacy of love). Mutual love as the essence of marriage and sexual morality set the stage in Catholicism for the entrance of the feminist critique of unequal roles in marriage and the nuclear family—a critique that has even been absorbed to some degree by John Paul II.[35] Indeed, the issue of birth control is much less important in the pope's later writings—such as *Veritatis splendor* and *Evangelium vitae*—than it was even in *Familiaris consortio,* and much less than in the audience talks at the start of his papacy.[36] The pope has given increasing attention to global economic inequities, including their impact on families and on the status of women.

In another essay in *Tensions in Moral Theology,* Curran contrasts the approach official teaching adopts on sexual issues with the approach it takes on social issues. He observes that the consciousness of the historical development of ideas and practices and the need for cultural nuancing of normative proposals has characterized social ethics much more than personal ethics. The modern papal social encyclicals, with their evolving affirmation of democracy and the rights of the working classes, are a key example. Curran proposes a "relationality-responsibility model" for personal and sexual ethics that incorporates a parallel flexibility and makes room for individual conscience.[37] Because of the prominence of birth control in his analytic schema, however, he does not make the point that Catholic teaching about sex did change at Vatican II when *Gaudium et spes* stopped ranking the ends of sex and marriage, affirming that love gives marriage its foundation and moral orientation. Even though Paul VI did not accept artificial contraception, he did follow Vatican II on this important point, upheld "responsible parenthood" in light of it, and stated directly that there can be frequent and legitimate reasons deliberately to intend to avoid conception, even while seeking sexual expression of love.

Although "historical consciousness" might not be a rubric under which papal teaching on sex formally proceeds, Curran could argue with good reason that the facts illustrate its growing functional importance. The dialectical contributions of "dissenters" such as himself, as well as participation of the laity as encouraged by the Council, has made a relationality-responsibility model more pervasive, even in the sexual area. The uneasy combination in Catholic teaching of a "classicist" or "physicalist" analysis of the structural requirements of sex acts and a personalist and relational approach to marriage, family, and even gender makes the former approach increasingly tenuous.

The social and theological dimensions of sexual ethics come more fully into view in a recent book by Curran, *The Catholic Moral Tradition Today: A Synthesis*.[38] Many of the same concerns and criticisms appear in this book: for example, problems with a "classicist" rather than historically conscious method in ethics, the need for a less hierarchical approach to moral teaching, justification of dissent, and the damage the furor over *Humanae vitae* has had on the church. The lens is broadened, however, in three ways. First, a brief section on the family indicates the social setting that is necessary to any complete ethical discussion of sex today. Participants in sexual acts must be understood within the larger social relations and institutions that color those acts with meaning—indeed, make them possible. Here Curran particularly addresses patriarchal family structure, identifying women as wives and mothers in the home and stereotyping "complementary" gender roles. "Today's theology calls for equality and cooperation, for shared parenthood and equal work opportunities for women and men."[39] Second, in a treatment of the virtues, Curran links sexual morality to temperance, connecting sexual ethics to recent interest in the virtues in theological ethics. As in the past, he depicts sex as a good that fulfills human nature. Not just freedom but discipline is now called for, however—a needed reminder, in a time when sex is trivialized and promoted exploitatively, that the category of sexual "sin" is as relevant as ever,[40] particularly in its social manifestations.

Third, this work includes a substantial discussion of the bearing of a distinctively Christian identity and calling on moral behavior.[41] Although it does not address sex specifically, its emphasis on Christ, grace, spirituality, discipleship, and redemption indicates a new set of questions for

Catholic sexual ethics. In what way will the demanding call of the Christian life affect the natural law analysis of sexuality that looks for moral criteria in the truly human? Although the latter seeks minimal criteria or parameters of acceptable behavior, the former confronts all of Christian existence with evangelical demands. Gospel ideals are not the same as absolute norms defining intrinsically evil acts, however. The area of sexual ethics is a good illustration of a task still ahead of Catholicism: reconciling the challenge of the gospel with the clear and specific moral guidance that has been so key to Catholic moral tradition.

CURRAN ON HOMOSEXUALITY

The issue of homosexuality came into its own in Catholic circles well after Vatican II. In 1971 Curran published an article in *The Thomist* that in 1980 became a chapter in a book presenting a wide variety of Christian perspectives on homosexual relationships.[42] Clearly, in writings up to and including this time, Curran is trying to find a way within the methods and terminology of Catholic moral theology to make room for acceptance of gay and lesbian persons (probably having predominantly in mind male homosexuals). Curran is mindful of people who struggle against the burden of condemnatory social and religious judgment, striving to make a meaningful and satisfying life that includes sexual expression. Although the Catholic Church had granted that people with an "innate" same-sex orientation are not to be blamed for their condition, it still maintained that its expression through genital acts was seriously sinful.[43] Curran was among many Catholics who found this solution unsatisfying because it seemed to pass harsh sentence on those who were committed to live a Christian life and form a permanent relationship with a loving partner under strikingly adverse circumstances. Again typifying the Vatican II Catholic mindset, Curran worked to increase compassion for homosexual individuals—and did so within the framework established by Catholic teaching. This approach assumed, no doubt more correctly at that time than now, that gay persons are dependent on church approval within official structures and documents to find the peace and acceptance they seek. Thus, it was crucial for his project to find expression within familiar moral theological categories.

Curran places the problem of homosexuality within what he calls a "theory of compromise" that is designed to permit latitude to human moral behavior, in view of the unavoidable and distorting presence of sin in the world. "In the total Christian horizon, the disrupting influence of sin colors all human reality."[44] On one hand, this theory seems to envision persons who cannot meet their moral obligations as a result of personal moral fault but are struggling nonetheless to improve. "Sin affects the will, but the help of God will strengthen our good will. . . ."[45] On the other hand, sin also is present in humanity's social situation, creating circumstances in which no choice seems perfectly acceptable but in which we are called to act to the best of our ability. "In sin-filled situations . . . the Christian may be forced to adopt a line of action one would abhor if sin were not present."[46] Homosexuals seem to suffer under sin that is not directly imputable to themselves but that nevertheless creates a moral conflict; this is "the sinfulness incarnate in the human situation which in my judgment affects the person who is an irreversible homosexual."[47] Presumably, Curran refers to the effects on the whole creation of the fact of original human sinfulness.

Against the backdrop of the theory of compromise, Curran then invokes the principle of counseling the lesser of two evils, which traditionally respected "the need for moral growth." In other words, although he regards heterosexual relationships as preferable to homosexual ones, all other things being equal, he is compelled by empathy for gay persons to encourage them to choose the best available alternative in their particular situations. He also states, going beyond the traditional "lesser evil" solution, that such a choice is not objectively evil (though less so) but objectively the right choice in the given situation.[48] Although such a tactic might be a useful strategy for alleviating the condemnatory and exclusionary atmosphere in which homosexuality virtually always was discussed in moral theology in the 1970s, it is not as useful as a platform for addressing gay persons themselves. The terminology of sin, evil, and compromise is bound to come across as derogatory once it moves out of the confines of in-house Catholic moral theory and into a more public engagement with the gay community.

In 1992 Curran delivered an address to the Catholic-affiliated New Ways Ministry (to gays and lesbians), after receiving from it the Bridge Building Award. This address represents another step in the evolution of his approach to homosexuality. New Ways Ministry seeks practical inclusion of homosexual persons at the pastoral level. In 1986 the Congregation for the Doctrine of the Faith had published a *Letter to the Bishops of the Catholic Church on the Pastoral Care of Homosexual Persons,* in which homosexual persons were in theory affirmed but in which the homosexual orientation itself also was called "intrinsically disordered."[49] Worse, it even suggests that violence against homosexuals is partly their responsibility because they persist in militating for civil rights.[50] Clearly, the appearance of such a document made it all the more important to express strongly an inclusive Christian attitude toward gays and lesbians in the church.[51]

Curran's opening sentence to New Ways Ministry is, "I maintain, together with many others, that official hierarchical Roman Catholic teaching should accept the moral value and goodness of committed homosexual relationships striving for permanency and including homogenital sexual relations."[52] Without explicitly changing the content of his position of 1980, Curran accomplishes a revolution in tone that sets aside the issue of whether homosexuality and heterosexuality are equivalent in theory. In practice, that question becomes irrelevant because he and his audience recognize or assume that sexual orientation is far from a matter of free individual choice and that all persons who are not called to celibacy should work constructively to channel their sexuality within committed relationships. Affirmation of this goal is the point of departure for Curran's address. He also draws on the sciences (e.g., studies of sexuality, psychology, and sexual orientation) in informing the moral evaluation of homosexuality and employs the sacramental theology of the church to define human fulfillment and happiness as a mediation of the divine.[53] Curran treats the Bible and homosexuality, but primarily to defeat the thesis that scripture clearly condemns homosexual partnerships as we know them today and that the Bible alone is a sufficient norm.[54] He does not venture into the more difficult area of the relation between the call to Christian holiness, "natural law" norms and exceptions, and the different meanings of human sinfulness. Noting that politics and power relations may make change on this and other sexual issues difficult, Curran concludes on a note of hope that even official Catholic teaching may change to accept openly gay and lesbian persons in committed same-sex relationships.[55]

A final touchstone illustrates with the example of sexual orientation Curran's increasing efforts overall to bring Catholic sexual ethics into the sphere of social analysis and take the terms and concerns of Catholic moral theology outside ecclesial debates and into the public realm. In 1998 Curran contributed a chapter to a volume on sexual orientation and civil rights.[56] He does invoke principles of moral theology such as double effect and toleration, but he uses them to address social institutions and policy. He argues that at a minimum Catholics should recognize that encouraging stable gay relationships, perhaps including legal recognition of domestic partnerships, is a lesser evil than promiscuity. He also points out that such laws would hardly undermine heterosexual marriage more than laws permitting divorce and remarriage—especially because, in the

Catholic view, people do not choose their sexual orientation. (This point is debated not only by social conservatives who want to "convert" homosexuals to heterosexuality but by "queer theorists" who see intentional commitment to same-sex, nonmonogamous interactions as a socially subversive political statement.) Joining Catholic social tradition to sexual ethics, Curran adapts the approach of John Courtney Murray, S.J., an architect of Vatican II's position underwriting religious freedom. Key categories applied analogously to policy on sexual orientation are the priority of the free human person and the limitation of government,[57] as well as distinction of the full "common good" from the narrower concepts of "public order," "public peace," and "public morality."[58] Curran concludes that although there may be disagreement about the morality of gay relationships and about whether their protection best serves the common good, it can hardly be maintained that legal protection of civil rights for gay men and lesbians undermines the public order.

FUTURE NEEDS AND DIRECTIONS

I already have offered several indications of the ways Charles Curran's Vatican II revisionist Catholic moral theology of sex could be and ought to be moved ahead in the twenty-first century church. In conclusion, I focus very briefly on four.

From Catholic Equality to Feminist Critique

Curran's advocacy for women's equality within the Catholic Church has been a significant part of his sexual ethics, and all that he says about sexual relationships indeed assumes that gender equality is necessary and possible. Nor has he lost sight of the fact that social and cultural as well as ecclesial changes will be necessary to bring this equality about. Curran certainly supports the contributions of feminist Catholic theologians and other feminists, as evidenced in a collection on the topic coedited with Margaret Farley.[59] When one turns to these critiques, however, one finds a more radical agenda for change than is typical of the ecclesially oriented genre of moral theology Curran represents. The thrust of the feminist critique is to call into question the basic institutions of sex, marriage, and parenthood within which a more moderate form of revisionism seeks reform—namely, heterosexuality, male-female gender stereotypes, the nuclear family, indissoluble marriage, and parenthood as taken up only by a married man and woman.

On the whole, Catholic feminists, such as Curran, still adhere to an ideal of committed, loving partnership as the realm of sexual union and care for children. Like Curran and the magisterium, they deplore the commercialization, exploitation, and trivialization of sex, promiscuity, infidelity to spouse and children, widespread divorce, and above all violence against women. They call into radical question, however, whether these things can be overcome without thorough reconsideration of the institutions within which they are now all too possible. They start from the experience and insights of women and other constituencies that have been marginal to the traditional enterprise of moral theology and sexual ethics and advocate for inclusion as a precondition of adequate reform. Excellent examples are essays by Catholic feminists (Andolsen, Gudorf, Farley) writing alongside or in response to Curran.[60]

From Historical Consciousness to Global Postmodernism

The pluralism of perspective advocated by feminist authors is an indicator of an even more far-reaching trend in ethical thinking: the idea that social location and history are so important in the formulation of moral ideas and practices that they ultimately must be regarded as "socially constructed" from root to branch. Useful as a strategy for dislodging hegemonic cultural and traditional norms for sex, gender, family, and virtually every other kind of human association, the postmodern critical edge can become perniciously counterproductive when it isolates sex and gender practices in one locale from the mutual critique that the premise of "common humanity" can underwrite.

Curran's writings on sexuality take a hidebound version of natural law and subject it to the revisionary demands of "historical consciousness." Curran (like others of his theological background and era) never acknowledges, however, the now philosophically popular idea that the whole idea of a "human nature," historically conscious or not, is a dangerous sham and should be abolished. Many Catholic feminists, including those who write from other cultures, agree with Curran that some convictions about basic humanity, human needs, possibilities, and rights are essential to global solidarity around sex and gender issues. A huge challenge for future thought, however, is to reestablish the essentially realist trajectory of natural law while incorporating a true appreciation of cultural differences, the partiality of perspective, and the dialogical nature of knowledge.

From Natural Law to Scripture and Back

A related issue of universality and particularism involves the special identity and perspective that is provided by a religious community. For Christians, the focus of identity is Christ, the living heart of scripture, mediated through community and tradition and reappropriated in the experience of every new generation. Natural law ethics has always claimed that despite the special character of Christian vocation and spirituality, all humans share some natural determinants of human fulfillment and moral obligation, including the physiological and interpersonal conditions and constituents of sex. Postmodernism and feminism have shown that "human nature" even in so basic and universal an area as human sexuality and reproduction may not be easy to define. Furthermore, some Christian thinkers argue that Christian identity provides a unique perspective on these and other areas of behavior, so that "the human," especially as known under the conditions of sin, can never be an adequate guide for Christian morality. Vatican II made Catholics more aware of the biblical foundations of moral theology, but the task remains to discover the positive dimensions of the biblical narrative for sexual identity and to combine those positive elements with a commitment to shared moral insight among Christians and others, in a productive yet challenging way.

From Vatican II as Experience to Vatican II as History

The Vatican II generation of moral theologians, as well as many other Catholics, grew up in a church and culture that were generally repressive of sex (though qualified by the infamous "double standard"). The Council represented a liberating whirlwind that joined to some extent with cultural forces of the 1960s that were sweeping away constraining rules in general. Despite the fact that most Catholics of the era (certainly including Curran) continued to assume the "sex and kids in marriage" model, the vocal advocacy of some theologians for the goodness of sex, the normativity of personal experience, and changes in moral rules made them seem, at the time, more liberal than they were—and, in the twenty-first century, less relevant to sexual realities. Catholics born after 1960 have no personal experience of the Council or the repressive society before it. As teenagers and adults, they confront a very different sexual culture in which the goodness or even neutral instrumentality of sex is taken for granted, sexual norms are all but destroyed, "permanent" commitments end in divorce more than half of the time, abortion and multidonor procreation are marketed for profit, and sexual exploitation of women continues virtually unabated despite the women's liberation movement. Many younger Catholics are receptive to honest confrontation with the facts of sexual sin, in personal and institutional forms, and may be open to a message of sexual idealism and discipline. Some are even returning to *Humanae vitae*—though, characteristically, within an ethos of personal meaning and choice, not of obedience to authority or negativity toward sex.[61] The answer is not a return to the Vatican II era, with or without *Humanae vitae.* Once again, the challenge is to devise an original response to contemporary realities while remaining true to the best of the past.

In sexual ethics, this attitude means restating attractively and persuasively the Catholic value triad of committed love and partnership, sexual union and pleasure, and mutual responsibility for children who also are their own reward. These values inhere preeminently in relationships, not acts, though acts (not limited to sexual ones) are crucial in defining and furthering relationships. The sphere in which such values are enacted goes beyond individuals to their relationship over time, their children, their extended families, and the communities in which they participate, including the church. In broad terms, sexual responsibility includes attention not only to one's own sexual behavior but also to all of these relationships and the way one's life affects them. The lesson to be learned from social ethics in Catholic tradition and from an evangelical ethic of graced aspiration to eschatological fulfillment is that although specific norms may be vital moral guides in the face of human weakness, they do not capture or sustain the whole of the moral life. It follows that arguments for and against certain specific norms should not be at the center of sexual ethics. Recentering Catholic sexual ethics around long-standing values expressed meaningfully for today's cultural experience and set within appropriate specific behavioral parameters is the daunting challenge for tomorrow.

NOTES

1. On the importance of freedom, the advent of historical consciousness, and the difference in social and personal ethical methodologies, see Charles E. Curran, "Official Catholic Social and Sexual Teachings: A Methodological Comparison," in *Tensions in Moral Theology* (Notre Dame, Ind.: Notre Dame University Press, 1988), 87–109.
2. Charles E. Curran, *Faithful Dissent* (Kansas City, Mo.: Sheed & Ward, 1986). See also Charles E. Curran, ed., *Contraception: Authority and Dissent* (New York: Herder and Herder, 1969).
3. See Charles E. Curran, "Conscience," in *Themes in Fundamental Moral Theology* (Notre Dame, Ind.: Notre Dame University Press, 1977), 191–231.
4. See, for example, two essays in *New Perspectives in Moral Theology* (Notre Dame, Ind.: Fides, 1975): "Sterilization: Exposition, Critique and Refutation of Past Teaching," 209, and "Divorce: Catholic Theory and Practice in the United States" 263–64, 268.

5. For a more detailed treatment up to 1989, see Lisa Sowle Cahill, "Catholic Sexual Ethics and the Dignity of the Person: A Double Message," *Theological Studies* 50 (1989): 120–50. This overview is adapted from that article, with the addition of some more recent works.
6. See "Masturbation and Objectively Grave Matter," in *A New Look at Christian Morality* (Notre Dame, Ind.: Fides, 1970), 201–21.
7. See "The Contraceptive Revolution and the Human Condition," in *Moral Theology: A Continuing Journey* (Notre Dame, Ind.: University of Notre Dame Press, 1982), 142, 144.
8. See "In Vitro Fertilization and Embryo Transfer," in *Moral Theology: A Continuing Journey,* 112–41.
9. See "Abortion: Its Legal and Moral Aspects in Catholic Theology," *New Perspectives,* 163–93; *Politics, Medicine and Christian Ethics: A Dialogue with Paul Ramsey* (Philadelphia: Fortress, 1973), 110–31; and "Civil Law and Christian Morality: Abortion and the Churches," in *Ongoing Revision: Studies in Moral Theology* (Notre Dame, Ind.: Fides, 1975), 107–43.
10. *Pius XI on Christian Marriage: The English Translation* (New York: Barry Vail Corporation, 1931), 12.
11. Ibid., 28.
12. Dietrich von Hildebrand, *Marriage* (New York: Longmans, 1942).
13. Herbert Doms, *The Meaning of Marriage* (New York: Sheed & Ward, 1939); originally *Vom Sinn and Zweck der Ehe* (Breslau, Germany: Ostdeutsche Verlagsanstalt, 1935).
14. Doms, *The Meaning of Marriage,* 88.
15. The decree, dated April 1, 1944, is cited in full by John C. Ford, S.J., and Gerald Kelly, S.J., *Contemporary Moral Theology 2: Marriage Questions* (Westminster, Md.: Newman, 1964), 27–28. Ford and Kelly, the most prominent American moral theologians of their day, also repudiated Doms's suggestion, even though they called marriage's "secondary" ends "essential" (v).
16. *Gaudium et spes* (*The Documents of Vatican II,* ed. Walter M. Abbott, S.J. [New York: America, 1966], no. 51).
17. For an extensive discussion, see Ambrogio Valsecchi, *Controversy: The Birth Control Debate 1958–1968* (Washington, D.C.: Corpus, 1968), 37–71.
18. For two opposing views on these issues, see John T. Noonan, Jr., *Contraception: A History of Its Treatment by the Catholic Theologians and Canonists,* enlarged ed. (Cambridge, Mass.: Harvard University Press, 1986; original ed., 1965), and Germain G. Grisez, *Contraception and the Natural Law* (Milwaukee, Wisc.: Bruce, 1964).
19. For a history of the commission, the authoring of the reports, and the politics thereof, see H. and L. Beulens-Gijsen and Jan Grootaers, *Mariage catholique*

et contraception (Paris: Epi, 1968), and Robert Blair Kaiser, *The Politics of Sex and Religion* (Kansas City, Mo.: Leaven, 1985). The majority report is available in *Official Catholic Teachings: Love and Sexuality,* ed. Odile M. Liebard (Wilmington, N.C.: McGrath, 1978), 314–20.

20. Paul VI, *Humanae vitae* (Paramus, N.J.: Paulist, 1968), no. 12.

21. Ibid., no. 11.

22. This theme was developed in the pope's general audience talks of 1979–81. These are published by the Daughters of St. Paul (Boston) and include *Original Unity of Man and Woman: Catechesis on the Book of Genesis* (1981); *Blessed are the Pure of Heart: Catechesis on the Sermon on the Mount and Writings of St. Paul* (1983); *Reflections on* Humanae Vitae: *Conjugal Morality and Spirituality* (1984).

23. John Paul II, *Familiaris consortio (Apostolic Exhortation on the Family)* (Washington, D.C.: United States Catholic Conference, 1982), no. 32.

24. See Congregation for the Doctrine of the Faith, *Donum vitae (Instruction on Respect for Human Life in Its origin and on the Dignity of Procreation)* (Washington, D.C.: United States Catholic Conference, 1987).

25. See John Paul II, *Mulieris dignitatem (On the Dignity and Vocation of Women)* (Washington, D.C.: United States Catholic Conference, 1988), and "Letter of Pope John Paul II to Women" (Rome: Libreria Editrice Vaticana, 1995).

26. Charles E. Curran, *Christian Morality Today: The Renewal of Moral Theology* (Notre Dame, Ind.: Fides, 1966).

27. Ibid., 51.

28. Ibid., 57.

29. Ibid., 71.

30. Ibid., 72.

31. Ibid., 73.

32. Ibid., 74.

33. Charles E. Curran, "The Development of Sexual Ethics in Contemporary Roman Catholicism," in *Tensions in Moral Theology,* 83.

34. Ibid., 78.

35. John Paul II, *Mulieris dignitatem* and "Letter of Pope John Paul II to Women."

36. John Paul II, *Original Unity of Man and Woman, Blessed are the Pure of Heart, Reflections on* Humanae Vitae.

37. "Official Catholic Social and Sexual Teaching: A Methodological Comparison," in *Tensions in Moral Theology,* 96.

38. Charles E. Curran, *The Catholic Moral Tradition Today: A Synthesis* (Washington, D.C.: Georgetown University Press, 1999).

39. Ibid., 100.
40. See also Charles E. Curran, "Sin and Sexuality," in *Themes in Fundamental Moral Theology,* 178.
41. Examples of earlier discussions are "The Relevancy of the Gospel Ethics," in *Themes in Fundamental Moral Theology,* 5–26, and "Dialogue with the Scriptures: The Role and Function of the Scriptures in Moral Theology," in *Catholic Moral Theology in Dialogue* (Notre Dame, Ind.: University of Notre Dame Press, 1972), 24–64.
42. "Homosexuality and Moral Theology: Methodological and Substantive Considerations," in *Homosexuality and Ethics,* ed. Edward Batchelor, Jr. (New York: Pilgrim Press, 1980), 171–85. The earlier version appeared in *The Thomist* 35 (1971): 447–81. See also "Dialogue with the Homophile Movement: The Morality of Homosexuality," in *Catholic Moral Theology in Dialogue,* 184–221.
43. Sacred Congregation for the Doctrine of the Faith, *Declaration on Certain Questions Concerning Sexual Ethics* (Washington, D.C.: United States Catholic Conference, 1976).
44. Charles E. Curran, "Natural Law," in *Themes in Fundamental Moral Theology,* 31.
45. Ibid.
46. Ibid., 32.
47. "Utilitarianism, Consequentialism, and Moral Theology," in *Themes in Fundamental Moral Theology,* 141.
48. "Homosexuality and Moral Theology," in *Homosexuality and Ethics,* 185.
49. Congregation for the Doctrine of the Faith, *Letter to the Bishops of the Catholic Church on the Pastoral Care of Homosexual Persons* (Washington, D.C.: United States Catholic Conference, 1986), no. 7.
50. Ibid., no. 10.
51. For a more successful statement in this regard, see U.S. Bishops' Committee on Marriage and Family Life Statement, *Always Our Children: A Pastoral Message to Parents of Homosexual Children* (Washington, D.C.: United States Catholic Conference, 1997).
52. "Is There Any Good News in the Recent Documents from the Vatican about Homosexuality?" in *Voices of Hope: A Collection of Positive Catholic Writings on Gay and Lesbian Issues,* ed. Jeannine Gramick and Robert Nugent (New York: Center for Homophobia Education, 1995), 159.
53. Ibid., 166–67.
54. Ibid., 168–69.
55. Ibid., 172.

56. "Sexual Orientation and Human Rights in American Religious Discourse: A Roman Catholic Perspective," in Saul M. Olyan and Martha C. Nussbaum, eds., *Sexual Orientation and Human Rights in American Religious Discourse* (New York: Oxford University Press, 1998), 85–100.

57. Ibid., 90.

58. Ibid., 91.

59. Charles E. Curran, Margaret A. Farley, and Richard A. McCormick, S.J., *Feminist Ethics and the Catholic Moral Tradition: Readings in Moral Theology No. 9* (New York: Paulist, 1996).

60. See Margaret A. Farley, "Response to James Hanigan and Charles Curran," in Nussbaum and Olyan, *Sexual Orientation and Human Rights,* 101–09; two authors were contributors along with Curran to Ronald M. Green, ed., *Religion and Sexual Health: Ethical, Theological and Clinical Perspectives* (Dordrecht, The Netherlands: Kluwer Academic, 1992): See Barbara H. Andolsen, "Whose Sexuality? Whose Tradition? Women, Experience, and Roman Catholic Sexual Ethics," 55–77; Christine Gudorf, "Western Religion and the Patriarchal Family," 99–117; and Charles E. Curran, "Sexual Ethics in the Roman Catholic Tradition," 17–35.

61. Jennifer J. Popiel, "Necessary Connections? Catholicism, Feminism and Contraception," *America* (November 27, 1999): 22–25.

CHAPTER 7

Perspectives on Medical Ethics: Biotechnology and Genetic Medicine

James J. Walter

STATE OF THE QUESTION

The Second Vatican Council opened on October 11, 1962; Francis Crick and James Watson had discovered the double-helical structure of the DNA (deoxyribonucleic acid) molecule only nine years earlier, in 1953. The classical genetics of Gregor Mendel (died 1884)—the Austrian monk who had discovered the laws of heredity by working with garden peas—were beginning to give way to the study and application of the new molecular genetics. In 1962 there was no biotechnology as we currently know it; that area of biology and technology did not begin to develop until almost a decade later. Medical ethics at the time still was basically restricted to the study and application of traditional deontological rules to the physician-patient relationship. The new interdisciplinary field of bioethics, which would supersede but incorporate standard medical ethics, did not develop into an academic discipline for approximately another decade in the United States. This new area of scholarly study, generally understood as the systematic study of the moral dimensions of the life sciences and health care,[1] evolved partially in response to the new genetics and biotechnology.

I study two areas in this chapter: contemporary medical genetics and biotechnology. They certainly are related to one another, and each has had a period of rapid development since the 1970s. Medical genetics is "the aspect of human genetics that is concerned with the relation between heredity and disease."[2] Although the categories of the field overlap, many people would consider medical genetics to comprise the following: diagnosis of genetic disease (e.g., preimplantation diagnosis, prenatal diagnosis, population screening); eugenics as the elimination of disease-related traits (e.g., through selective mating, sterilization); gene therapy on either body cells or germ cells; genetic enhancement of body or germ cells; patenting of human gene sequences or techniques of genetic control; embryo research; cloning; and genetic testing on controlled groups.[3]

Biotechnology, on the other hand, involves "any technique that uses living organisms to make or modify products, to improve plants or animals, or to develop microorganisms for specific uses."[4] It involves using biology to discover, develop, manufacture, market, and sell products and services. Many applications of biotechnology are used in the health care arena, and this is where the linkage to medical genetics is made. As an industry, biotechnology was first developed by about ten to twenty venture-backed companies that were involved in pharmaceuticals.[5] Controversies over biotechnology and its applications to plants, animals, and humans began to arise in the mid-1970s because these powerful techniques allowed dramatically increased control over the design of living organisms.[6]

What are some of the developments in medical genetics and biotechnology—along with the ethical reflection that has accompanied them—that have occurred since the 1970s? Surely, recombinant DNA (rDNA) research that was developed in the mid-1970s is a watershed for much of the work that is being done today in medical genetics and biotechnology. Commonly known as gene splicing, recombinant DNA research is a procedure whereby segments of genetic material from one organism are transferred to another organism or species. The basis of the technique lies in the use of special enzymes (restriction enzymes) that split DNA strands wherever certain sequences of nucleotides occur. These procedures have led to the production of vaccines against several diseases and the introduction of substances such as insulin, interferon, and growth hormone. Pharmaceuticals developed from this technique have substantially improved patient outcome and quality of life, but many people have questioned the wisdom of "playing God" with the very molecules that make up all of life.[7] In 1976 the National Institutes of Health established the Recombinant DNA Advisory Committee (RAC) to study and evaluate various clinical proposals to utilize this new scientific technique.

In the past twenty years, scientists have discovered that DNA is virtually interchangeable among animals, plants, bacteria, and humans. Consequently, biotechnology has been extended to plants and animals; the DNA from one animal or plant can be spliced into the genetic material of another. I focus briefly on the area of plant bioengineering as an example.

Most of the plant genetic engineering projects that are in progress globally fall under one of the following three types: engineering for improved crop production and quality (e.g., herbicide or pest resistance); engineering for improved health (e.g., edible vaccines for disease prevention); and biopharming or engineering of plants for alternative nonfood uses (e.g., rather than building expensive factories, we might be able simply to grow the chemicals needed to make plastics, detergents, and construction materials). In the last case, within the next ten years it is possible that 10 percent of U.S. corn acreage will be devoted to this type of bioengineering.[8] Some of these projects involve insertion of animal genes into plants to create what are called transgenic plants. For example, the DNA Plant Technology Corporation in New Jersey added a gene from the Arctic flounder to make a frost-resistant tomato. Corn and tobacco plants have been engineered to accept human genes as part of their DNA so they can make drugs to fight cancer and osteoporosis.

There have been mixed reactions to these biotechnologies around the world. In the United States, where people tend to be pragmatic and are more willing to take risks with the environment, biotechnology companies are moving forward with great speed to produce these transgenic plants. Things may be moving forward even more rapidly in China—where, in 1986, Chinese scientists already were aggressively pushing for governmental efforts to bioengineer plants to feed the country's 1.2 billion people. On the other hand, the situation has been much different in Europe. People in the United Kingdom and Germany have staged many protests against the introduction of genetically altered foods into their countries, but the Swiss, after many protests, voted decisively in June 1998 to reject a proposal to outlaw the production and patenting of genetically modified plants, ostensibly because they did not want to surrender Swiss leadership in biotechnology.

In October 1990, the publicly funded Human Genome Project was launched in the United States at an estimated cost of $3 billion. Its aim was to map and sequence all of the genetic material of the human person. The project ended approximately five years early in June 2000, and a rough map was unveiled in February 2001. We now know that the human person possesses far fewer genes than previously thought—instead of 80,000 to 100,000 genes, we have 30,000 to 40,000 (maybe as few as 26,000). The knowledge that we have gained from this scientific endeavor, and the biotechnologies that will be developed, will revolutionize clinical medicine over the next twenty to thirty years. Cancer treatments will soon be developed to treat the specific DNA of the patient, personalized pharmaceuticals will be created and marketed by the pharmaceutical industry, and physicians will be able to splice out defective sequences of genes and replace them with proper ones.

The newest scientific venture is concerned with the proteome, or the mapping of all of the human proteins coded by genes. Enormous ethical, social, and legal problems already are being raised about the medical genetics and proteomics that will be developed out of these efforts by "big science." How will we be able to protect the confidentiality of this genetic information? Should we use the new technology involved in gene therapy and apply it to enhancing ourselves? Who owns the rights to the genes and their sequences once they are discovered? Who will have fair access to the new biotechnologies that will be developed? Will we discriminate on the basis of genetic makeup, such that we will deny health insurance or employment to people who possess certain genetic traits or defects? The U.S. Department of Energy has established the Ethical, Legal, and Social Issues Program (ELSI) to study many of these issues, but the questions seem almost endless. Religious groups wonder about the wisdom of "playing God" with DNA,[9] and they are forced many times to rethink their traditional doctrines of creation, divine providence, and redemption.[10]

Two other areas where medical genetics and biotechnology come together to present us with great potential opportunities but also with tremendous ethical questions are human cloning and stem-cell research. Once Dolly the sheep was successfully cloned by Ian Wilmut in Scotland, the expectation by some people has been that we could or should do the same with humans. Wilmut succeeded by taking a body (somatic) cell that contained all of the genetic material to make an exact duplicate of the donor sheep and inserted it into an egg whose own nuclear DNA had been destroyed. Once the full complement of nuclear DNA from the body cell was fused with the egg (using a small electrical charge), the fertilized ovum began to divide and grow. The National Bioethics Advisory Commission (NBAC) was asked to study the scientific and ethical dimensions of human cloning and to make recommendations to the president of the United States and Congress. The NBAC recommended against application of this technology to humans on the basis of its lack of safety.[11]

One need not use this technology to duplicate a whole human person, however; one could use it with stem-cell research to grow organs or tissues for a wide range of diseases (Alzheimer's disease, Parkinson's disease, etc.). Pluripotent stem cells exist as very special cells in the early embryo (ES cells) or in the primordial reproductive cells of the developing fetus (EG cells). Because they have the capacity to become almost any of the 210 cell lines in the mature human body, many researchers believe that the retrieval and differentiation of these special cells could benefit hundreds of thousands of patients. To retrieve these cells, however, one must destroy the early embryo or retrieve them from aborted fetuses, and either of these procedures presents great ethical problems for some people in our society, especially if the research is funded by public monies. Once again, President Clinton asked NBAC to study the scientific, ethical, and religious issues related to this technology. The commission's report was complex, but it did recommend public funding of the derivation and use of pluripotent stem cells from embryos remaining after infertility treatments at in vitro fertilization (IVF) labs and from cadaveric fetal tissue.[12]

If one did pursue this course, the technology could be combined with human cloning for therapeutic purposes. In this case, the scientist would take a body cell from a patient, extract the nuclear DNA from his or her somatic cell, insert its nucleus into a human egg whose own nucleus has been destroyed. Once fused, the fertilized egg would be allowed to develop to the four- to six-cell stage; then the pluripotent stem cells would be removed, destroying the embryo in the process. Then the stem cells would be differentiated into the tissue needed by the patient (e.g., spinal cord tissue or brain tissue). Because the tissue would have been cloned from the patient's own body cells, there would no need for special drugs to suppress the patient's immune system after the transplant. Many researchers believe that there is great promise in this new technology (when combined with medical genetics), but others question the morality of such procedures that rely on the taking of one life to save another.

CRITICAL ASSESSMENT OF CHARLES E. CURRAN'S CONTRIBUTIONS TO MEDICAL GENETICS AND BIOTECHNOLOGY

I develop this section in four parts. First, I present a broad overview of Charles Curran's writings in the general field of bioethics or medical ethics. In the second part I narrow the discussion by briefly presenting Curran's moral positions specifically on genetic medicine and biotechnology. In the third section I analyze what I and others have judged Professor Curran's theological, philosophical, and ethical contributions to be on the topics of genetics and biotechnology. Finally, I undertake a brief critical assessment of Curran's writings on the topics under consideration.

Overview of Curran's Writings in Medical Ethics

Approximately six months after the Kennedy Institute of Ethics at Georgetown University opened its doors on July 1, 1971, Charles Curran took a sabbatical leave from the Catholic University of America and went to the institute as a fellow to complete a book on the writings of Paul Ramsey—a Protestant theologian at Princeton who had already written on issues in medicine and ethics.[13] One of Curran's doctoral dissertations had been in the area of medical ethics,[14] and he had published several additional essays in the field before going to the institute. Though he would not consider himself a "bioethicist" as such, Curran certainly was one of the original group of theological ethicists[15] who had begun to dedicate at least some of their scholarly research to the new field of bioethics in the late 1960s and early 1970s.

More than one-tenth of Curran's published works has been in the general field of medical ethics. He has contributed substantially to the areas of medical genetics and biotechnology, but also he has written on many of the bioethical topics that were confronting society in the 1970s and beyond. He probably is best known for his many essays on birth control, especially in light of the Catholic tradition.[16] His essays also have analyzed issues ranging from abortion[17] and assisted reproductive technologies[18] at the beginnings of life, to topics of experimentation on human subjects[19] and the right to health care[20] in the middle of life, to care for the dying[21] and euthanasia[22] at the end of life. Despite the fact that bioethics has not been one of the central areas of Curran's research, it is clear that he has made some important and lasting contributions to the general field.

Overview of Curran's Writings on Medical Genetics and Biotechnology

A substantial portion of Charles Curran's publications in the field of bioethics has been dedicated to the two areas under consideration in this essay. One reason for his focus on these topics has to do with the proposals that were coming from noted geneticists—such as H. J. Muller, a Nobel Prize winner from the University of Indiana. Curran is interested in these proposals because they contain recommendations about how to overcome the deficiencies of the human genetic code through implementation of eugenic measures. Perhaps more important, the field of medical genetics was beginning to expand enormously in the 1960s, and the biotechnology industry was establishing itself and its research and development programs in the 1970s after the introduction of recombinant DNA technology. An ethical voice amidst these scientific and technological developments was needed—especially a voice that could also address the deep religious and anthropological questions that lay beneath the ethical surface. Yet from Curran's own perspective, writing on these topics gave him the opportunity to place contemporary science and technology in a critical dialogue with his own theological tradition of Roman Catholicism to challenge the methodological and anthropological assumptions of both.[23] This strategy has been one of the distinctive marks of Curran's contributions to bioethics.

Curran recognized early in the development of medical genetics and biotechnology that science had the possibility of improving the human condition around the world. Deleterious genes in the gene pool could be eliminated, and new genes could be added to improve not only individuals but also the human species. Curran regarded these possibilities as potential pluses. He recognized, however, that a scientific mentality could become so predominant that trust in science and technology—and their emphasis on power over the human and nonhuman world—could negate the potential gains. Careful analysis and critique were called for, and Curran was prepared to bring his theological and ethical talents to bear on these topics.

In the area of medical genetics, Curran consistently recognized that there are three issues at stake. First is eugenics: the selection and recombination of genes that already exist in the human gene pool. This issue can be further divided into negative and positive eugenics. Whereas negative eugenics aims at removing deleterious genes from the gene pool, positive eugenics attempts to improve the genes that are in the gene pool.[24] Eugenics can use three technological procedures: artificial insemination with sperm that have been stored, IVF and embryo transfer to a womb, and cloning of human beings.[25]

The second issue in medical genetics for Curran is called genetic engineering, genetic surgery, algeny, or transformationist eugenics as distinct from selectionist eugenics. The aim of genetic engineering is to change the genes to eliminate a certain defective gene (negative) or to improve the genotype (positive).[26] When Curran wrote many of his early essays in this area, he noted that medical science did not have the ability to perform what is now called "human gene transfer"—the process of using restriction enzymes to open the DNA molecule; splice out a defective gene or splice in a new gene sequence; and then, using another enzyme (ligase), close the molecule. The Human Genome Project (1990–2000) had not even been conceived when Curran wrote on eugenics in the late 1960s and early 1970s, so his understandings of the real possibilities of this technology for therapy or enhancement purposes may have been somewhat understated.

The third issue is concerned with euphenics, which for Curran is somewhere between eugenics and euthenics or environmental engineering. It aims at the control and regulation of the phenotype rather than the genotype, and it would involve all efforts at controlling gene expression in the human without changing the genotype.[27]

What are Curran's moral conclusions on the application of these genetic technologies to the human? On the issue of negative eugenics, he is in favor of voluntary efforts to use genetic counseling for couples who are carriers of deleterious genes. More scientific experimentation must go forward, but such experimentation must respect human dignity and not totally subordinate the individual to the goals of scientific advancement.[28] On the issue of positive eugenic interventions, Curran has taken a negative stance. He does not believe that we have enough knowledge or wisdom for such undertakings,[29] and he argues strongly against the use of assisted reproductive technologies (e.g., IVF and embryo transfer) to achieve eugenic ends.[30] Although the technique of cloning mammals (somatic cell nuclear transplant cloning) used by Ian Wilmut was not yet developed when Curran wrote his essays, he does note that, if human cloning were ever available it would create enormous problems.[31] On the issue of gene splicing, Curran takes a positive, though cautious, position. He believes that constant oversight and vigilance are needed, but he does not hold that such interventions necessarily open a Pandora's box or are acts of "playing God."[32]

Curran has focused a good deal of his scholarly analysis in the area of bioethics on the proper role of biotechnology in human life. He understands all technology, including biotechnology, as "applied science by which human beings are able to control and influence human existence."[33] The issue of control is important here because there is always a tendency in the application of technology to manipulate not only the nonhuman world but also the human person. A process of discernment must be in place to distinguish proper from improper forms of control over the world and self, and Curran frequently looks from within his theological tradition to discover this process.

Curran establishes a general framework for understanding and evaluating technology—especially biomedical technology—from the perspective of theological ethics in the Catholic tradition. He develops three theses from this framework. First, we must be open to the data of science and the possibilities of technology. He gives two reasons to support this thesis. The first reason for a basic openness to biotechnology stems from an acceptance of the goodness of human reason and the belief that religious faith and human reason can never contradict one another. The second reason comes from theological recognition of the goodness of the natural and of the human. The Catholic tradition has insisted on the compatibility between grace and nature.[34]

Curran's second thesis is essentially historical. It recognizes that the Catholic theological tradition has not always lived up to its theoretical affirmations about biotechnology and science. History is replete with examples of where the Catholic Church has been suspicious or even hostile to science (e.g., the Galileo case).

The third thesis focuses on the limitations of science and biotechnology and argues that they always must be in the service of the human. There is not an identity between the human and the scientific or technological; thus, three limitations arise on the use and application of science and technology. Because there is no identity between the human and technology, Curran argues that sometimes we must simply say no to what science and technology can offer us. The second source of limitation comes from the limitation that is inherent in any particular science or technology. Other sciences (psychology, sociology, etc.) can add insight into the human, so a total focus on what basic science or technology can offer is inappropriate. The final source of limitation comes from the different opinions within any particular empirical science or applied technology. For Curran these differences of opinion are clear signs that the nature of the human is complex and that no single position can possibly capture the entirety of what it means to be human.[35]

Curran's moral position on the development and application of biotechnology is consistent throughout his writings. First, he holds that biotechnology is an essential good, though it is only a limited good that cannot be identified totally with the human.[36] Second, all medical technology, including biotechnology, must be used in service of the human and in terms of truly human progress in overcoming disease and improving the length and quality of human life.[37] Truly human progress and technological progress are not the same; in fact, they may even be opposed to one another on certain occasions. Whenever human and technological progress do coincide, however, Curran argues that we can view technology as positively related to God's final kingdom.[38] Third, he notes that there may be points of conflict between the scientific/technological worldview and the one espoused by Christianity. When the former focuses on effects and performances and values success and results, conflict will exist with the Christian understandings of reality and the nature of the person. For Christianity, the value of the person is not primarily determined by what he or she does or can do. Instead, value is assessed in terms of what God has first done for us.[39] Finally, Curran argues that there is a constant danger in biotechnology to give such great attention to comparatively esoteric procedures that basic medical care often tends to be neglected. Justice and the right to health care become important moral considerations in this context. For 44 million people under the age of 65 in the United States who have no health insurance, this judgment on biotechnology is particularly poignant. Ultimately, Curran seeks some kind of fair and equitable balance between the needs to develop and apply new biotechnologies and the medical needs of people in our society.

Curran's Contributions to Medical Genetics and Biotechnology

Charles Curran's contributions to the areas of medical genetics and biotechnology are significant, and his writings have had an enduring effect on the way in which Catholic ethicists now approach these and other topics in bioethics. The focus throughout his scholarly essays is to place medical science and biotechnology in a dialogical conversation with his own religious tradition and with the ways in which that tradition has approached bioethical topics in the past. Consequently, I would proffer that Curran's most incisive and lasting contributions are not primarily in his concrete investigations and the particular moral recommendations that he offers on the two topics under consideration. Although these contributions are important and certainly worthy of careful consideration, the lasting contributions he makes can be analyzed under three categories: theological-anthropological issues, philosophical issues, and ethical issues.

When the field of bioethics was coming into existence in the United States in the mid-1960s, many of the founders of the discipline were originally trained in the theological sciences. As they began to tackle the two major concerns of the time—experimentation on humans and the dramatic development of scientific knowledge and technology—most of them brought their theological anthropology to bear on the issues. Perhaps more than others, Curran is convinced that a fully articulated theological anthropology is necessary to meet the challenges of the modern era. He does not believe, however, that one formulates a view of the human and then simply applies it from the top down to contemporary questions of medical genetics and biotechnology. Instead, he argues that the very questions posed by biomedicine help to form his understanding of theological anthropology, and a dialogical relation therefore must exist between the two areas.[40]

As Curran carries on this dialogue over several years, he formulates his theological anthropology in terms of a Christian stance. For Curran, stance or the horizon of meaning forms the way a person interprets reality and structures his or her understanding of the world and reality. Stance is logically the first and primary consideration in any methodology; hence its importance in the analysis of any concrete issue in bioethics.[41] Curran formulates his stance by reference to the fivefold Christian mysteries: creation, sin, incarnation, redemption, and resurrection destiny. Each one of these mysteries is informed by the questions of biomedical science and technology, and each mystery, in turn, plays an important part in critiquing science and technology. One example demonstrates how this dialogical structure operates in Curran's writings on bioethical issues, especially those concerned with medical genetics and biotechnology.

Contemporary developments in genetics and biotechnology raise important questions about the control that humans should have over creation—especially the control they should have over themselves and their genetic future. Modern science also adopts a concept of the universe as unfinished and evolving. From a theological perspective, different views of creation and the special place that humans have in creation need to be sorted out. If creation is entirely completed by the divine and the human serves the principal role of conserving and preserving what the divine has already accomplished, then human control over the genetic future of humanity may not be morally warranted. In this case, theological ethics would critique efforts to engineer humanity's genetic future. If one understands creation to be a process (*reatio continua*) that is not yet completed by the divine, however—a view that is shared by modern science—and if one understands the role of humans to be one of cooperation with the divine in bringing creation to its completion, then one might accord more responsibility and control to humans to intervene into the genetic pool, at least to correct defects. Curran adopts the latter view on the basis of his dialogue with modern science and biotechnology. For him, however, the Christian mystery of the Fall might temper one's emphasis on human control over our genetic future, as would the mystery of eschatology (views of the final times). Each mystery would point to a limitation: The former mystery recognizes limits on our abilities to do good; the latter recognizes a limit on the importance of science as good in relation to the total human good. Curran methodically develops each of the fivefold mysteries in dialogue with modern genetics and biotechnology and then systematically applies these mysteries to the questions, developments, and applications of these sciences.

Curran makes two lasting contributions here. First, his willingness to place modern science and technology in a critical dialogue with Christian ethics has encouraged others in the field to follow in a similar vein. Such a dialogue surely has been one of the forces that has resulted in a revised anthropology in Catholic ethics at least. Though Curran certainly has not accomplished this shift alone, his writings are a model for how to carry on this dialogue. Second, his insistence that theological anthropology must be explicitly brought to bear on all questions of bioethics is important and instructive for others in the field. Some theologians believe that much of the literature in bioethics today devotes little or no attention to this anthropological focus, and they argue that this *lacuna* leads to an impoverishment in the discussion of contemporary bioethical issues.[42]

The second area in which Curran has made lasting contributions is concerned with various philosophical issues. The standard method for ethical analysis in the Roman Catholic tradition, especially by the teaching authority of the church, has been natural law. As a method of ethical analysis, it assumes that there is a range of basic goods or values that all people pursue as part of their nature and that knowledge of these goods is available to all people of good will. The theory of natural law in the manuals of moral theology of the late nineteenth through the mid-twentieth centuries seemed too easily to identify the physical action itself or the physical structure of its effects with the actual moral determination of the human action. In addition, the way this method was applied, especially to issues in bioethics and sexuality, was overly deductive and ahistorical. At the level of epistemology, the theory tended to search for certitude and did not trust human experience as a valid font of knowledge.

From both a methodological and an epistemological point of view, Curran sees multiple problems with the way the natural law theory had been developed and then applied to questions in bioethics. From his vantage point, the received tradition on natural law is inadequate to deal with contemporary issues in genetic medicine and biotechnology thus, a dialogical conversation has to be opened to revise the theory. Much of Curran's early work in bioethics focuses on revision of natural law, not its rejection.[43] He is committed to many of the presuppositions of natural law theory (e.g., its insistence on the ability of all humans to know the good), and his intent is to revise and reformulate the theory to deal with the bioethical issues facing his discipline. Curran's conception of natural law takes on many of the characteristics of modern consciousness: It is more historically minded, it gives a significant role to human experience as a valid font of moral wisdom, it is much more inductive in its approach, and it recognizes limits on the certitude we can have in our moral judgments. Many of these characteristics now regularly inform the analyses of Catholic bioethicists.

The final area of Curran's lasting contributions to the field is concerned with specifically ethical issues. Ethics is the systematic study of morality, and it involves the theoretical component in moral judgments. One of the components of ethics is called normative ethics or simply ethical theory. All ethical theories attempt to articulate objective criteria for judging actions and character to be right/wrong and good/bad and to discern the ways in which we might know whether these criteria are fulfilled. Each ethical theory relies on various models of the moral life and human agency. Historically, the two standard ethical theories have been teleological theories that focus on the goals of the moral life or the ends and consequences of actions and deontological theories that focus on our duties and obligations or the actions we perform.

Curran's contribution to this important discussion—and through it to issues in bioethics—is to offer an alternative to the existing ethical theories. Relying on the previous work of H. Richard Niebuhr,[44] Curran calls his theory a relationality-responsibility model, and he regards it as distinct from the existing theories.[45] His model places much more emphasis on relations between persons and relations between persons and the world. It also focuses on the issue of responsibility that humans have toward themselves, others, and the world. Although Curran certainly needs to fill out more fully the exact criteria that must be used in judging actions, this model of the moral life has attempted to meet the many complex challenges of contemporary biomedicine and technology.

Critical Assessment of Curran's Writings

Before I begin a brief critical assessment of Charles Curran's writings in bioethics, I mention two points. First, bioethics is not an area that Curran regularly worked in, and he never considered himself a bioethicist in the sense this term is used in current academic circles. Second, in many cases he is more interested in the dialogical conversation between contemporary medical genetics and biotechnology, on one hand, and theological ethics, on the other. Thus, Curran's writings in these areas frequently focus more on theological anthropological issues, philosophical presuppositions to ethical methodology, and ethical theory than on concrete bioethical issues themselves.

Briefly, there are three areas for critical assessment. First, because Curran is so deeply concerned with revising many of his own theological tradition's categories (e.g., natural law), some observers may regard his analyses as somewhat parochial. His dialogue with genetic science often is less a deep ethical analysis of contemporary genetics than an analysis of the deficiencies that he sees in Roman Catholic ethics and the way the teaching authority of his church had used various anthropological, philosophical, and ethical concepts.

Second, the theory of compromise that Curran develops to deal with conflict situations that arise as a result of the existence of human sinfulness in the world[46] ultimately is not helpful.[47] Although he applies this theory to a few bioethical topics,[48] he seems to abandon it in his later writings.

Finally—and possibly most important—Curran's corpus may need a more sustained, overarching theory or system that underlies his concrete ethical analyses of bioethical topics. His writings probably are best characterized as eclectic because he borrows from others inside and outside the field of Christian ethics. For example, he clearly borrows from some authors who have employed a personalist theory, such as Bernard Häring, although it may be inaccurate to classify Curran's writings strictly as personalist. In addition, Curran borrows from H. Richard Niebuhr a phenomenology of human agency and applies these insights to the bioethical issues at hand, yet it would be inaccurate to classify Curran's writings as phenomenological. Although his essays on medical genetics and biotechnology are very good and insightful, a general underlying system or theory that unifies his approach to these topics is lacking.

FUTURE AGENDA AND CHALLENGES

Medical genetics and biotechnology will continue to pose enormous challenges, and the pace will only hasten as each of these areas develops and applies its newfound knowledge to human and nonhuman life. Thus, a clear ethical agenda is necessary to confront these challenges. Although the list is not sacrosanct, many people in the field of bioethics probably would agree that there are seven or eight areas that must be included. There is no rank ordering of these priorities, though surely some are more important than others or the urgency of one will take priority over others.

First, there will be a need to put increasing pressure on the scientific community and biotechnology companies to protect the dignity of their research subjects. There is more and more evidence that harms are accruing to human subjects in various research protocols.[49] Part of this agenda also must deal with protection of early embryos in research protocols and with their creation and use to benefit the health of others. Second, we will have to introduce new ethical and legal measures to protect the privacy of genetic information. We will need to sort through who should rightfully have access to this knowledge and who should be excluded. Because genes are inherited within families, do family members also have a right to this knowledge that could adversely affect their health? Genetic discrimination is a real possibility, especially in the workplace or the clinic; it also is a possibility in terms of securing health and life insurance.

Third, now that the human genome is basically mapped and sequenced and the scientific community is moving forward not only with identifying defective genes but also with mapping the proteins that cause disease, what will we do with this knowledge? Because our knowledge will outstrip our clinical abilities to cure many of these genetic diseases, how will we use this knowledge when we counsel patients? Will we simply create the lifetime identity of a "sick person" when we tell an adolescent that she will get adult-onset Alzheimer's disease when she's eighty years old?

Fourth, genetic screening of targeted populations must come under severe scrutiny. The chances for discrimination are enormous, particularly if this type of screening is routine at birth or during a visit to the clinic. Fifth, human gene transfer, either with somatic cells or germline cells, for purposes of therapy or enhancement probably will be introduced on a regular basis within the next twenty or thirty years at the clinical level. This technology could be combined with human cloning techniques and embryonic stem cell research, and different combinations of genetic medicine will develop over the next few decades. The agenda must sort out the differences between therapy and enhancement, and it must decide whether we should ever cross into the germline with any of these technologies.

Sixth, there are huge marketplace issues at stake, especially with multinational pharmaceutical companies that stand to gain enormous profits. Fair pricing of new drugs and therapies that will be developed must be constantly assessed. Ownership of gene sequences must be decided at the ethical and legal levels. Next, and very important, we must ensure that the development and use of these biotechnologies will not simply benefit the few who are rich enough to afford them. We will need to focus our attention on the equity of the delivery of health care in a way that we have not in the past. Not only are there millions of people in the United States who are virtually without any health care, there are millions and millions throughout the world who essentially have no access to the wonders of modern medicine. Just social policies must be forged, not only in the scientific and medicine-rich West but around the world.

Finally, theological ethicists and their communities must continue to develop methodologies and strategies for incorporating religious beliefs and traditions in ethical assessment of these bioethical topics. The goal will be to establish a dialogue between religious traditions and science/technology while avoiding reductionism. We are fortunate that Charles Curran has provided us with one very helpful example of how to carry on this dialogue.

NOTES

1. Warren Thomas Reich, "Introduction," in *Encyclopedia of Bioethics,* rev. ed., vol. 1, ed. Warren T. Reich (New York: Simon & Schuster Macmillan, 1995), xxi. For Reich, the word "bioethics" was introduced in 1971 with the publication of Van Rensselaer Potter's book *Bioethics: Bridge to the Future* (Englewood Cliffs, N.J.: Prentice Hall, 1971), but he also argues that André Hellegers first used the word in an institutional way to designate the focused area of inquiry. See Warren T. Reich, "The Word 'Bioethics': Its Birth and the Legacies of Those Who Shaped It," *Kennedy Institute of Ethics Journal* 4 (December 1994): 319–35, especially 320. In either case, bioethics did not begin as a discipline until around the 1970s.
2. Victor A. McKusick, *Human Genetics,* 2d ed. (Englewood Cliffs, N.J.: Prentice Hall, 1969), 181.
3. Lisa Sowle Cahill, "Genetics, Ethics and Social Policy: The State of the Question," in *Concilium: The Ethics of Genetic Engineering,* ed. Maureen Junker-Kenny and Lisa Sowle Cahill (London: SCM, 1998), vii.
4. Nanette Newell, "Biotechnology," in *Encyclopedia of Bioethics,* rev. ed., vol. 1, ed. Warren T. Reich (New York: Simon & Schuster Macmillan, 1995), 283.
5. Alison Taunton-Rigby, *Bioethics: The New Frontier* (Waltham, Mass.: Bentley College Center for Business Ethics, 2000), 6–8.
6. For the authoritative encyclopedia on this topic, see Thomas H. Murray and Maxwell J. Mehlman, eds., *Encyclopedia of Ethical, Legal, and Policy Issues in Biotechnology,* 2 vols. (New York: John Wiley & Sons, Inc., 2000).
7. For example, see the President's Commission for the Study of Ethical Problems in Medicine and Biomedical and Behavioral Research, *Splicing Life: The Social and Ethical Issues of Genetic Engineering with Human Beings* (Washington, D.C.: U.S. Government Printing Office, 1982).

8. Aaron Zitner, "Fields of Gene Factories," *Los Angeles Times* (June 4, 2001), A7.

9. For a helpful essay on the meaning of the phrase "playing God," see Allen Verhey, "'Playing God and Invoking a Perspective," *Journal of Medicine and Philosophy* 20 (1995): 347–64.

10. For example, see Ronald Cole-Turner, *The New Genesis: Theology and the Genetic Revolution* (Louisville, Ky.: Westminster/John Knox, 1993).

11. National Bioethics Advisory Board, *Cloning Human Beings,* 2 vols. (Rockville, Md.: U.S. Government Printing Office, 1997).

12. National Bioethics Advisory Board, *Ethical Issues in Human Stem Cell Research,* 3 vols. (Rockville, Md.: U.S. Government Printing Office, 2000).

13. At the end of his sabbatical Curran published his *Politics, Medicine, and Christian Ethics: A Dialogue with Paul Ramsey* (Philadelphia: Fortress, 1973).

14. Charles E. Curran, *The Prevention of Conception after Rape* (Rome: Pontifical Gregorian University, 1961).

15. Some of the other theologians, Protestant and Catholic, who belonged to this original group were Joseph Fletcher, Paul Ramsey, William F. May, James M. Gustafson, James F. Childress, Karen Lebacqz, Albert R. Jonsen, Bernard Häring, and Richard A. McCormick.

16. For example, see Charles E. Curran, ed., *Contraception: Authority and Dissent* (New York: Herder & Herder, 1969), especially 151–75.

17. Charles E. Curran, *New Perspectives in Moral Theology* (Notre Dame, Ind.: Fides, 1974), 163–93.

18. Charles E. Curran, *Moral Theology: A Continuing Journey* (Notre Dame, Ind.: University of Notre Dame Press, 1982), 112–40.

19. Charles E. Curran, *Issues in Sexual and Medical Ethics* (Notre Dame, Ind.: University of Notre Dame Press, 1978), 71–102.

20. Charles E. Curran, *Transition and Tradition in Moral Theology* (Notre Dame, Ind.: University of Notre Dame Press, 1979), 139–70.

21. Curran, *Politics, Medicine, and Christian Ethics,* especially 147–63.

22. Charles E. Curran, *Ongoing Revision: Studies in Moral Theology* (Notre Dame, Ind.: Fides, 1975), 144–72, especially 158–61.

23. Charles E. Curran, *Contemporary Problems in Moral Theology* (Notre Dame, Ind.: Fides, 1970), 189–224, especially at 195.

24. Ibid., 192.

25. Curran, *Ongoing Revision,* 166.

26. Ibid., 193–94.

27. Ibid., 194–95.

28. Ibid., 216–17.

29. Curran, *Politics, Medicine, and Christian Ethics,* 218–19.

30. Charles E. Curran, *Moral Theology: A Continuing Journey* (Notre Dame, Ind.: University of Notre Dame Press, 1982), 130.

31. Charles E. Curran, *Critical Concerns in Moral Theology* (Notre Dame, Ind.: University of Notre Dame Press, 1984), 109.

32. Charles E. Curran, *Toward an American Catholic Moral Theology* (Notre Dame, Ind.: University of Notre Dame Press, 1987), 78.

33. Curran, *Critical Concerns in Moral Theology,* 99–100.

34. Ibid., 105–06.

35. Ibid., 107–10.

36. Curran, *Toward an American Catholic Moral Theology,* 77.

37. Curran, *Issues in Sexual and Medical Ethics,* 75–76.

38. Curran, *Politics, Medicine, and Christian Ethics,* 201.

39. Curran, *Contemporary Problems in Moral Theology,* 214.

40. Curran, *Toward an American Catholic Moral Theology,* 78.

41. For his essay on stance, see Curran, *New Perspectives in Moral Theology,* 47–86.

42. See Hubert Doucet, "How Theology Could Contribute to the Redemption of Bioethics From an Individualist Approach to an Anthropological Sensitivity," in *Catholic Theological Society of America Proceedings of the Fifty-Third Annual Convention,* vol. 53 (Camarillo, Calif.: Catholic Theological Society of America, 1998), 53–66, and my response, James J. Walter, "Response to Hubert Doucet," ibid., 67–71.

43. For example, see Charles E. Curran, *Medicine and Morals* (Washington, D.C.: Corpus Books, 1970).

44. H. Richard Niebuhr, *The Responsible Self* (New York: Harper & Row, 1963).

45. Charles E. Curran, *Directions in Fundamental Moral Theology* (Notre Dame, Ind.: University of Notre Dame Press, 1985), 173–96.

46. Curran, *Transition and Tradition in Moral Theology,* 59–80, especially 73–78.

47. For a thorough analysis and critique of Curran's theory of compromise, see Richard Grecco, *A Theology of Compromise: A Study of Method in the Ethics of Charles E. Curran* (New York: Peter Lang, 1991).

48. Curran, *New Perspectives in Moral Theology,* 163–93, especially 191–92.

49. See the National Bioethics Advisory Commission's report, *Ethical and Policy Issues in Research Involving Human Participants* (Bethesda, Md.: National Bioethics Advisory Commission, August 2001).

PART III

Social and Political Ethics

CHAPTER 8

Hierarchical Catholic Social Teaching: Analysis and Interpretation

Kenneth R. Himes, O.F.M.

One of the great strengths of the Catholic social tradition is that despite the popular impression many people have of Catholic teaching—that it is unchanging—it has undergone significant and regular alteration. Upon examination, some developments related to official Catholic social teaching are obvious, others less so. In what follows I first cite some of the reasons for developments in the formal social teaching of the magisterium. Then I discuss the contribution of Charles Curran to the topic of hierarchical Catholic social teaching. Finally, I close by proposing areas where further change and/or development is likely to come in the future.

RECENT CATHOLIC SOCIAL TEACHING

Although change in the content of social teaching can be documented easily, the amount of change is so vast that it will be helpful to group these changes under four subheadings, identified by the causal agent that spurred such developments within the social tradition. These causal agents are not mutually exclusive, and I do not mean to imply that only one factor caused any particular change in the teaching. Given the complexities of history, monocausal theories in any field of human endeavor are almost always wrong. I use the categories merely as an organizational device and have selected an example under each heading in which the causal agent seems prominent.

Theological Developments

It is something of a commonplace to state that ours is an age in which the church itself has become a theological issue. In the patristic era, the great questions focused on Trinitarian and Christological doctrines. In the early and middle scholastic periods, there was a good deal of interest in the meaning of salvation, theories of redemption, and an understanding of the "last things." Many of the debates during the Reformation and Counter-Reformation were occasioned by disputes over the nature and means of grace—justification, sanctification, the place of faith, and the role of the sacraments, as well as good works. More recently, we have seen the church itself become a theological concern. That this is a development becomes apparent when

> we consider that the great medieval texts from which students learned theology—Peter Lombard's *IV Libri sententiarum* and Thomas Aquinas's *Summa Theologiae*—had contained no section specifically devoted to the church. Now it is unthinkable that one could study systematic theology without attending to ecclesiology.[1]

As Catholic theologians began to spend more time and energy considering the nature of the church and its mission, as well as the relation of the church to the key doctrines of the Christian tradition, it was inevitable that attention would be given to articulating a theological rationale for the social mission of the church. Whereas Pope Leo XIII had simply assumed a role for the church in social affairs when he promulgated *Rerum novarum,*[2] by the time of Vatican II it was apparent that the church had to explicate its self-understanding to clarify and defend its social mission as a religious institution: "For the Council yearns to explain to everyone how it conceives of the presence and activity of the Church in the world of today."[3] That explanation proceeds from an anthropological starting point: "The pivotal point of our total presentation will be the human person, whole and entire, body and soul, heart and conscience, mind and will."[4] This anthropological starting point opens up to a theological claim, however, because "only in the mystery of the incarnate Word does the mystery of the human take on light."[5] Thus, the church has something to offer to the quest for building a genuinely human society.

At the same time, the church must act with an awareness of the world's diversity and acknowledge that even societies in the west no longer reflect the customs of Christendom.[6] The Council fathers therefore developed an argument for the religious mission of the church while pointing out how fidelity to that mission will affect politics, economics, culture, and social life. Simultaneously, however, the church recognizes that it is a partner and ally with other forces and institutions, not a dominating and controlling presence, in seeking a truly humanized world.[7]

All of this has led church leaders to develop strategies that are appropriate to the conciliar description of the church's mission and the manner of relating to the world. The assumptions of Leo XIII have been tempered by a willingness to reconsider the ecclesiological premises of the social mission. This development has dramatically affected the renewed emphasis that the church places on its social mission, as well as the limitations and strategies that must be observed as the church enters into dialogue with the modern world.[8]

Encounters with Liberalism

Popes Gregory XVI and Pius IX, predecessors of Leo XIII, largely denounced the liberal movements they saw, although Pius was more open to reforms prior to the revolutions of 1848. Leo's active engagement with liberalism in its various forms—political, economic, cultural—led him to compose several major encyclicals.[9] For Leo and subsequent popes, the Achilles heel of all three variants of liberalism is the exaltation of human autonomy to a degree that challenges the authority of God as it is known through divine revelation and natural law. What later popes have done, however, is demonstrate greater appreciation for the positive elements of liberalism, even as they continue to point out its errors.

Political liberalism supported democracy and limited constitutional states. The church, especially in some quarters, was slow to rally to the cause of democracy. There were excesses of nationalism, anticlericalism, and revolutionary fervor within the ranks of liberal democrats, and the church was particularly sensitive to these errors. Although Leo XIII began the rethinking of democracy, the rise of totalitarianisms on the left and right in the twentieth century further encouraged the popes to note the advantages of democracy.[10]

Economic liberalism exalted the working of free markets and the inviolability of property rights. Economic freedom was understood to be the engine of social progress and a morally superior approach that channeled self-interest into behaviors that ultimately served the good of others. Of course, the suffering of the laboring class in the heyday of the industrial revolution occasioned *Rerum novarum,* but that encyclical also accepted the wisdom of private property, the rights of producers, and the basic conditions of free markets. Popes since Leo have refined the teaching on property rights, highlighting the social obligations that accompany private property. Moreover, Catholic social teaching has never accepted the idea that markets cannot be regulated by the state or that producers are not bound by duties toward workers and the common good. Because the posture of official Catholic social teaching is essentially reformist, it generally has resisted the call for condemnation of capitalism in principle.[11]

Liberalism in its cultural expression promoted civil liberties, the autonomy of reason from the authority of inherited traditions, and freedom of religion. Without endorsing the relativism and antireligious sentiments that Leo and other popes feared lay behind cultural liberalism, Catholicism has come to a deeper appreciation of the connections between human dignity and personal liberty, social equality, and rights of conscience. In *Gaudium et spes* one finds the following statements: "Authentic freedom is an exceptional sign of the divine image within the human";[12] "the basic equality of all must receive increasingly greater recognition";[13] and "conscience is the most secret core and sanctuary of an individual. . . . To obey it is the very dignity of a person."[14]

The church properly objected to much of what was espoused under the guise of liberalism. Liberalism, too, has had to undergo alteration and achieve greater balance in its promotion of certain goods. It can be fairly said, however, that Catholicism, through its contact with liberal theory and practices, has come to a deeper appreciation of certain dimensions of the person that serve human dignity.

Changed Contexts for Old Issues: The Morality of War

There are few issues about which the church has wrestled longer and harder than that of war. It is widely known that in its early decades the community of disciples distanced itself from the idea of military service. As Christianity spread into new territories and reached new populations with new duties and responsibilities within society, the attitude toward war began to evolve.

This new context for thinking about war led to the adoption and refinement of classical civilization's idea of a just war. Early in the life of the church there were competing attitudes toward civil authority; the one that became prevalent regarded the state as a useful instrument to achieve a modicum of justice within the social order. This view necessitated distinguishing between wars that may be accepted as regrettable necessities for preserving the state and wars that serve lesser values.

As time passed, the just war tradition evolved in the west in a context in which wars often were limited. At least since the Napoleonic wars, however, the context for assessing war has been shifting. In the twentieth century the changed situation was dramatically brought home: Whole populations suffered in "world wars," modern weaponry unleashed devastating destruction indiscriminately, the rules of war were strained by the development of new technologies such as submarines and unmanned rockets, terrorism and its civilian supporters muddied distinctions about legitimate targets.

Yet Pope Pius XII could still assert in 1956 that if a duly elected government declared war, "a Catholic citizen cannot invoke his own conscience in order to refuse to serve and fulfill those duties the law imposes."[15] Less than a decade later, however, the bishops at Vatican II stated, "We cannot fail to praise those who renounce the use of violence in the vindication of their rights and who resort to methods of defense which are otherwise available to weaker parties too, provided that this can be done without injury to the rights and duties of others or of the community itself."[16] What helped to bring about this reversal of position in nine short years was the changing context of modern warfare.

Pius XII was aware of the development of weapons of mass destruction; he himself spoke of the terror of atomic/biological/chemical (ABC) warfare. These weapons were still new in the church's experience, however, and their implications were not fully apprehended. By 1965, when the threat of nuclear war among the superpowers was evident, church leaders had to revisit the age-old question of the morality of warfare. The bishops realized that "if the kind of instruments which can now be found in the armories of the great nations were to be employed to their fullest, an almost total and altogether reciprocal slaughter of each side by the other would follow. . . . [Such a prospect] compel[s] us to undertake an evaluation of war with an entirely new attitude."[17]

The reconsideration of war has led to extensive commentary by popes and episcopal conferences on modern warfare. In general, one finds greater reluctance to accept the justice of war and stronger expressions of support for nonviolent strategies in resolving conflict.

New Voices and Realities

Historian David O'Brien wrote that "Leo XIII confronted a Eurocentric world at the height of the Victorian era."[18] Social teachings that came from Rome largely reflected the Eurocentrism of the papacy throughout the early decades of official Catholic social teaching. Indeed, even at Vatican II the predominant voices were those of European bishops.

Although other regions of the Catholic Church needed more time to find their voice, one result of Vatican II was that it provided an impetus for that to happen. By 1967 those new voices were reflected in Pope Paul VI's encyclical *Populorum progressio* and then, powerfully, in the documents issued by the Latin American bishops at their conference in Medellín, Colombia. Paul's statement in *Octogesima adveniens* that it is up to "Christian communities to analyze with objectivity the situation which is proper to their own country"[19] gave strong support and legitimation for bishops to formulate social teaching appropriate for their particular region.

New topics emerged in Catholic social teaching as a result: international trade, neocolonialism, a preferential option for the poor, integral development, land reform, foreign aid, capital investment, and the institutions of the international economic order. The papacies of Paul VI and John Paul II have looked at social questions from a global perspective, attuned to the situation of peoples living outside the European context.[20] The efforts of local episcopacies to address issues of social justice have added richness of experience and perspective to a tradition that was largely the domain of Eurocentric papal teaching until the postconciliar era.[21]

The four causal factors for change in the Catholic tradition—theological developments, encounters with liberalism, changed contexts for old questions, and new voices—have led to a variety of developments in Catholic social teaching. The lesson is that change in the content of hierarchical social teaching is frequent and results from a variety of causes.

THE CONTRIBUTION OF CHARLES E. CURRAN

Because Charles Curran is not a member of the Catholic hierarchy, his contribution to the documents that constitute official Catholic social teaching cannot have been direct. Instead, Curran has contributed a skillful analysis of the literature constituting the social teaching, helping readers to understand the tradition. His attention to methodology permits a deeper appreciation for the changes in content such as noted above.

Curran has lived and worked in a period of great transition within Roman Catholic moral theology and pastoral practice. He once observed that presenting a comprehensive systematic presentation of moral theology in such a climate was difficult.[22] Yet although Curran has been a masterful practitioner of the theological essay, he recently has turned his attention to developing a more extended exposition of his thought in two significant volumes: *The Catholic Moral Tradition Today: A Synthesis* and *Catholic Social Teaching, 1891–Present: A Historical, Theological, and Ethical Analysis.*[23] Because of the systematic and comprehensive nature of his important volume on Catholic social teaching, as well as its presentation of his mature thought, I rely heavily on this source for my comments on Curran's contribution to the topic of this essay.[24]

At the outset of his new book, Curran observes there are three different but overlapping perspectives that one may utilize in examining official Catholic social teaching. The first perspective focuses on the actual teachings: "What are the positions that have been proposed?" The second perspective emphasizes "the historical development of these teachings in the light of the circumstances and times." A third perspective—the one he adopts in the book—is particularly suited to the work of social ethics: "to study the social teachings in a thematic, systematic, and scientific way." Such a perspective "gives great importance to the methodological aspects" of the tradition.[25] The scholarly contribution Curran has bestowed to others is an acute analysis of the methodology employed within official Catholic social teaching.

Elsewhere, in an essay titled "A Methodological Overview of Fundamental Moral Theology," Curran provides a clear schema for understanding his own approach to moral theology. He identifies four essential components of an adequate method in moral theology: stance, ethical model, anthropology, norms, and decision making.[26] In what follows, I present examples of Curran's methodological analysis of Catholic social teaching under two major headings: theological stance and anthropology.

Theological Stance

Curran's commitment to the Roman Catholic tradition is evident in his description of an adequate stance for moral theology. He uses a shorthand way of summarizing his theological stance or fundamental perspective by employing five central mysteries to explain his position: creation, incarnation, sin, redemption, and resurrection destiny.[27] Again and again in his writing Curran employs his understanding of stance to analyze various documents of Catholic social teaching.

In Curran's writing, the proper stance provides a means to correct an imbalance or undue emphasis in a document. He makes a conscious effort to strike a balance among valid but competing perspectives. One of his frequent appeals is to the Catholic "and" in his method: grace *and* sin, universal *and* particular, realized *and* future eschatology, reason *and* revelation, and so forth.[28] Thus, he has criticized *Gaudium et spes* for an overly optimistic reading of the world that allows too easy a reconciliation of church and world. In Curran's view, the reality of sin was not given sufficient weight in such a reading, nor was there appreciation for the unrealized nature of God's reign in history.[29] Curran employs the same need for balance when he discusses the possibilities of peacemaking in our present world and the legitimacy of armed force in settling conflicts.[30]

When Curran has discussed approaches other than that of Catholic social teaching, such as the social gospel or Reinhold Niebuhr's Christian realism, Curran clearly appeals to an interpretation of the fivefold mysteries of his stance—holding them in creative tension, never losing sight of one by stressing another. So he will claim that "the two biggest problems with the Social Gospel as a whole were its failure to take sin seriously . . . and the danger of forgetting resurrection destiny as future and beyond the present world."[31] The consequence was an overly optimistic expectation of social change. In Niebuhr's case, Curran regards the Protestant theologian as employing all aspects of the stance, but, Curran states, he would "give slightly more emphasis to creation, slightly less to sin, and I would be more insistent that true redemption is already present though not fully realized in our world."[32]

A balanced understanding of the mysteries of creation, sin, and redemption shows the correctness in addressing documents of Catholic social teaching to all people of good will. Too much emphasis on the doctrine of creation, however, can lead to overconfidence in reason's ability to grasp the truth in contingent circumstances. This viewpoint would ignore the effects of the mystery of sin. At the same time, appreciation for the nature of our redemption rescues us from despair about progress in societal transformation. Taking the incarnation seriously means the church must respond to the plight of temporal society. Making too much of the incarnation, however, can lead to overvaluing a given historical institution or practice as the embodiment of God's plan. A healthy aspect of resurrection destiny means the present ought not be sacralized.

Curran consistently returns to his stance—the fundamental perspective or worldview that is profoundly shaped by the Catholic theological tradition—to address themes and problems. One might wonder, however, whether Curran has adequately explored in his published work the role that narrative has played in providing the central symbols and the reading of them he provides. He has written, "My own stance developed in an *a posteriori* way based on a critique of other positions."[33] One can ask, in light of the role of narrative in shaping the religious imagination, whether that claim is fully accurate. It would appear that the essential metaphors and symbols that provide one's reading of reality take hold of the imagination earlier than Curran suggests.

A good illustration of how Curran's use of stance provides him with analytical tools to assess Catholic social teaching appears in his comments about the tradition's inability adequately to address conflict and its role in human society. An overemphasis on reason, rooted in the doctrine of creation, ignores the sinful dimension of human existence. The confidence and assumption of Catholic teaching that appeals to reason will always be heeded, even by people who have power over others, ignores the reality that the powerful do not always surrender or even share power willingly. Similarly, maintaining the conviction that reasonable persons will do the right thing allows Catholic social teaching to ignore the hard question of what to do when conflict is not ameliorated simply by providing reasonable alternatives.[34] More attention to incarnational elements of human existence will assist us in understanding additional motives and forces, besides reason, that are at work in the human person.

A second aspect of the issue is that one should not always relate conflict and power to sinfulness. Conflict can be creative, and power can lead to empowerment that enables positive action. Taking seriously the claim that grace and redemption are also linked to power permits a more positive assessment of people who acquire power to bring about social transformation. The exercise of power is not always morally negative.[35]

Taking adequate account of the fivefold mysteries of his stance keeps Curran attentive to methodological concerns such as whether Catholic social teaching adequately employs scripture in its formulation. He notes that a dramatic shift occurred from *Pacem in terris* to *Gaudium et spes* regarding the use of scripture in social teaching.[36] Based on his analysis of how the documents treat scripture, Curran observes that in keeping with the need to balance other aspects of the stance, Catholicism does not rely solely on scripture as a source of moral wisdom, nor are the scriptures employed in any fundamentalistic way.[37] A risk remains, however, that the Bible can be used as a source of proof-texts even in later social documents.[38]

Still to be achieved is a proper ethical method regarding the employment of scripture. Curran himself proposes that one must distinguish between general and specific aspects of biblical morality.[39] He believes that the pastoral letters of the U.S. bishops on peace and the economy more adequately integrate scripture into social teaching than do many of the papal statements.[40] Taking seriously the need to account for all five mysteries of his stance means that Curran will give scripture a more significant place in his method than hierarchical social teaching has often done.

The scriptures will need to be read, however, with a sensitivity to their historical situation and with an awareness of the need to balance that source of wisdom with the insights of human reason and the development of the Christian tradition.

Anthropology

The anthropological aspect of Curran's ethical method is central because so much else is influenced by it. "Anthropology directs and guides the way in which Catholic social teaching understands the origin of the state, its purpose and limits, the opposing systems of Marxism and capitalism, justice, private property, and human rights."[41] Catholic social teaching relies on two fundamental anthropological claims: the dignity of the human person and the social nature of the person.[42] Because of these twin claims, Catholic social teaching is able to steer a course between two mistaken social views—individualism and collectivism. The dignity of the person resists all schemes that would treat the person as a means and not an end, as simply a part of a collective whole. This understanding is part of Catholic social teaching's criticism of Marxism.[43] Acknowledgement of the social nature of the human helps to avoid the pitfalls of individualism that Catholic social teaching understands to be liberalism's downfall.

In his writings on the anthropological dimensions of Catholic social teaching, Curran has helped to clarify the ways in which liberalism has influenced official Catholic teaching, as well as issues that continue to divide the Catholic social tradition from liberalism. Catholicism's longstanding commitment to a natural law philosophy has shaped Catholic social teaching in a variety of ways. One of those ways has been for Catholic social thought to have a strong bias toward order and harmony in social life. This bias, along with other influences, has led Catholic social teaching to operate with an organic view of society: The unity and differentiation of the human body is an analogue for political society. With characteristic balance, Curran suggests positive and negative factors in this social outlook: "The positive aspect of this approach recognizes the social and communitarian aspect of human existence and opposes a one-sided individualism" but, negatively, the organic model "fails to give due importance to the freedom, equality and participation of all citizens."[44]

For Curran, the strongest obstacle to Catholic social teaching simply accepting liberalism as a social theory is the mistaken individualism it promotes. "The anthropology developed in Catholic social teaching opposes an individualism emphasizing the person as a self-made individual."[45] Other emphases in liberal theory deserve greater appreciation, however, than early Catholic social teaching gave them. In particular, more recent teaching has accepted the significance of freedom, equality, and participation in society as crucial elements in the Catholic understanding of the human person.

Commenting on a development that is never explicitly acknowledged by Pope John XXIII, Curran observes that Part Four of *Mater et magistra* was titled "Reconstruction of Social Relationships in Truth, Justice, and Love." These ideals were the "basic goods [that] constitute the values to be found in a just society."[46] Just two years later, in *Pacem in terris,* John "maintains that truth, justice, charity, and freedom make civil society well-ordered, beneficial for all, and in keeping with human dignity."[47] In the space of two years, freedom has gone from being unmentioned to become "one of the four basic values that must be found in a well-ordered political society."[48] Within another two years, *Gaudium et spes* affirms that "authentic freedom is an exceptional sign of the divine image within the human person."[49]

When Pope Leo XIII addressed equality in *Rerum novarum,* he was not gravely troubled by the social and economic inequality he considered to be the natural condition of humankind.[50] By the time of the Second Vatican Council, however, one finds statements such as the following: "Moreover although rightful differences exist between human beings, the equal dignity of persons demands that a more humane and just condition of life be brought about. For excessive economic and social differences between the members of the one human family or population groups cause scandal, and militate against social justice, equity, the dignity of the human person, as well as social and international peace."[51] Curran underlines that Catholic social teaching allows considerably less inequality than it once permitted, as a result of a shift from an organic model of society to a personalist viewpoint.[52] The political, economic, and social implications of the papacy's support for equality in dignity has taken time to absorb and implement.

An additional theme that entered Catholic social teaching through a new anthropology was endorsement of participation in social institutions. As the church moved beyond the legacy of the medieval world, with its paternalistic social arrangements, it came to appreciate the liberal idea of an individual's rightful participation in the institutions that regulate and govern society. Curran notes that *Gaudium et spes* encouraged wide participation in public affairs, especially juridical and political matters—with the consequent realization that for such participation to be responsible, an individual also must participate in educational and cultural matters.

The theme of participation also was included as part of economic life.[53] The theme of participation was given further encouragement by Pope Paul VI's observation that, along with equality, participation is a fundamental aspiration and a form of human dignity.[54]

Curran's analysis of the dynamic of Catholicism's acceptance of certain anthropological premises of liberalism explains how the church's teaching developed.[55] He also has pointed out the continuity of the tradition even as its language and original formulations develop. Thus, even as the older organic model of society has been challenged by the evolving appreciation for the goods of freedom, equality, and participation in promoting human dignity, one still finds the Catholic concern for genuine community in the emergence of solidarity as a key theme. "Thus, solidarity for the common good has replaced the organic human body metaphor as the basis for political community which recognizes the importance of freedom and equality."[56]

Curran concludes that Catholic social teaching "cannot accept an individualistic liberalism" but that "in keeping with its inclusive 'both-and' tendency, Catholic teaching will accept what is good in liberalism and see the need for more."[57] Besides liberalism, Curran has used the angle of theological anthropology to analyze the nature and purpose of the state, private property, human rights, democracy, and other topics that play a large part in Catholic social teaching.

FUTURE DEVELOPMENT OF CATHOLIC SOCIAL TEACHING

Undoubtedly, many issues will require attention in Catholic social teaching. The phenomenon of globalization and the manifold consequences of this multidimensional process of change certainly will merit increased comment in Catholic social teaching. New perspectives—the experience of women, grassroots community organizations, and Catholics from Africa, Asia, and Latin America—will have to be more successfully integrated into the tradition. Curran has helped us understand how dialogue with liberalism has shaped Catholic social teaching. In the future Catholic social thought will have to be in dialogue with the perspectives of the other great world religions. Catholic social teaching will need an interreligious dialogue, just as it has engaged the major political philosophies of the west. Ethical dilemmas of cooperation and appropriation[58] will need to be addressed as we develop more complex, interlocking economies and cultures. More focused attention must be given to the cultural significance of modern communications systems and their role in promoting moral values and practices.

An agenda for future topics of Catholic social teaching resembles an endless list of issues arising from modern life. On the basis of Charles Curran's scholarship, however, we might suggest that the focus of a future agenda might also address the methodological concerns he has examined so incisively. Integration of scripture and theology into what has been a largely philosophically oriented tradition is a large agenda item. Developing a more consistent ethical method with regard to an integrated and holistic sense of the human person remains important.[59] Finding a more adequate approach to formulating and communicating official Roman Catholic social teaching also is necessary if the tradition is to continue to develop in fidelity to the gospel message and contribute to social transformation.

By focusing on methodology, Charles Curran has helped us see tensions and developments in Catholic social teaching.[60] His retrieval of previously overlooked insights of the tradition and his probing analysis will press Catholic social teaching to develop greater coherence and consistency. Curran's work is an invaluable contribution by a Catholic theologian to hierarchical Catholic social teaching.

NOTES

1. Michael J. Himes, "The Development of Ecclesiology: Modernity to the Twentieth Century," in *The Gift of the Church: A Textbook on Ecclesiology,* ed. Peter Phan (Collegeville, Minn.: Liturgical Press, 2000), 45–67, at 45.
2. "We approach the subject [the condition of the worker] with confidence, and in the exercise of the rights which belong to us. For no practical solution to this question will ever be found without the assistance of religion and the Church. . . . Doubtless this most serious question demands the attention and the efforts of others besides ourselves. . . . But we affirm without hesitation that all the striving of humans will be in vain if they leave out the Church." *Rerum novarum,* no.13.
3. *Gaudium et spes,* no. 2.
4. Ibid., no. 3. Where I have been able to revise the official text for inclusive language without changing the meaning, I have done so.
5. Ibid., no. 22.
6. "If by the autonomy of earthly affairs we mean that created things and societies themselves enjoy their own laws and values which must be gradually deciphered, put to use, and regulated by persons, then it is entirely right to demand that autonomy." Ibid., no. 36.

7. Ibid., nos. 40–44.

8. The theological development of the foundation for the social mission is treated at greater length in the essay by J. Bryan Hehir in this volume.

9. *Rerum novarum,* the best-known of Leo's writings, illustrated the papal reaction to economic liberalism and its false remedy, socialism. *Aeterni patris* and *Libertas praestantissimum* are the two encyclicals that respond most directly to the cultural and intellectual currents of liberalism. *Immortale Dei* and *Diuturnum* are the letters that best express the papal answer to political liberalism.

10. For a fine account of the story of Catholicism and democracy, see the essay by Paul Sigmund, "Catholicism and Liberal Democracy," in R. Bruce Douglass and David Hollenbach, *Catholicism and Liberalism* (Cambridge: Cambridge University Press, 1994), 217–41. See also Gregory Baum and John Coleman, eds., *The Church and Christian Democracy, Concilium* 193 (Edinburgh: T. & T. Clark, 1987), for essays that focus on one important part of the story: the evolution of Christian Democratic parties in Europe and Latin America.

11. Although one might argue that Pius XI was particularly skeptical about capitalism, it remains accurate to state that individual Catholics have been far more critical of capitalism than the official teaching, from the perspective of antimodern social theorists such as K. von Vogelsang or socialist sympathists such as P. Buchez.

12. *Gaudium et spes,* no. 17.

13. Ibid., no. 29.

14. Ibid., no.16.

15. Pope Pius XII, "Christmas Radio Message" (December 23, 1956), in *Peace and Disarmament: Documents of the World Council of Churches and the Roman Catholic Church* (Rome: Tipografia Poliglotta Vaticana, 1982), 137–39, at 137.

16. *Gaudium et spes,* no. 78.

17. Ibid., no. 80.

18. David O'Brien, "A Century of Catholic Social Teaching: Contexts and Comments," in *One Hundred Years of Catholic Social Thought,* ed. John Coleman, S.J. (Maryknoll, N.Y.: Orbis, 1991), 13–24, at 13.

19. *Octogesima adveniens,* no. 4.

20. The specific situation of the United States in the development and reception of Catholic social teaching is addressed in the essay by Thomas A. Shannon in this volume; I do not treat it here.

21. A good overview of this episcopal teaching appears in Terence McGoldrick, "Episcopal Conferences Worldwide on Catholic Social Teaching," *Theological Studies* 59 (1998): 22–50.

22. "The need for truly systematic presentations of moral theology remains the greatest challenge for contemporary Catholic moral theologians." Charles E.

Curran, *Transition and Tradition in Moral Theology* (Notre Dame, Ind.: University of Notre Dame Press, 1979), 21.

23. Charles E. Curran, *The Catholic Moral Tradition Today: A Synthesis* (Washington, D.C.: Georgetown University Press, 1999), is a presentation of Curran's fundamental moral theology. *Catholic Social Teaching, 1891–Present: A Historical, Theological, and Ethical Analysis* (Washington, D.C.: Georgetown University Press, 2002), provides his systematic overview of Catholic social teaching.

24. The ample references in this work to his previous publications will also allow the reader to "track" Curran's growing focus on this topic.

25. Curran, *Catholic Social Teaching,* 1–2.

26. Charles Curran, *Moral Theology: A Continuing Journey* (Notre Dame, Ind.: University of Notre Dame Press, 1982), 35–61. This essay, "A Methodological Overview of Fundamental Moral Theology," remains the best brief summary by Curran for understanding his approach to moral theology. In earlier and subsequent writings, he has further explicated his understanding of these components. See especially "The Stance of Moral Theology" in *New Perspectives in Moral Theology* (Notre Dame, Ind.: University of Notre Dame Press, 1974), 47–86, and *Catholic Moral Tradition,* chapter 2, for stance; *Catholic Social Teaching,* 116–22, and *Catholic Moral Tradition,* chapter 3, for ethical model; "The Changing Anthropological Bases of Catholic Social Ethics," in *Catholic Social Teaching: Readings in Moral Theology,* vol. 5, eds. Charles Curran and Richard McCormick (New York: Paulist, 1986), 188–218, *Catholic Social Teaching,* 174–87, and *Catholic Moral Tradition,* chapters 4–5, for anthropology; and "Utilitarianism, Consequentialism, and Moral Theology," in *Themes in Fundamental Moral Theology* (Notre Dame, Ind.: University of Notre Dame Press, 1977), 121–44, and *Catholic Moral Tradition,* chapter 6, for norms.

27. Curran, "The Stance of Moral Theology," 38.

28. Curran, *Catholic Moral Tradition,* 11–12.

29. Curran, *Catholic Social Teaching,* 39.

30. Curran, *Catholic Moral Tradition,* 16.

31. Ibid., 45.

32. Ibid., 45–46.

33. Curran, "The Stance of Moral Theology," 38.

34. Curran, *Catholic Social Teaching,* 88.

35. Ibid., 90.

36. Ibid., 33.

37. Ibid., 43–44.

38. Ibid., 45.
39. Ibid., 44.
40. Ibid.
41. Ibid., 136.
42. Ibid., 131.
43. Human dignity rests on a reading of the mystery of creation, according to Curran: the doctrine of the human as the *imago dei*. Typically, Curran is sensitive to the imbalance an emphasis on human dignity can suggest when "other created realities" are not given importance but are regarded "only as instrumental with regard to the human person" (Curran, *Catholic Social Teaching*, 132). For Curran, however, a significant insight derived from the theological grounding of human dignity is that "the source of human dignity comes from God's free gift and does not depend on human effort, work, or accomplishments. All human beings have a fundamental equal dignity. . . ." Curran, *Catholic Social Teaching*, 132.
44. Ibid., 87.
45. Ibid., 134.
46. Ibid., 74. Curran is citing *Mater et magistra*, no. 212.
47. Ibid. Curran is citing *Pacem in terris*, no. 25.
48. Ibid.
49. *Gaudium et spes*, no. 17.
50. *Rerum novarum*, no. 14.
51. *Gaudium et spes*, no. 29.
52. Curran, *Catholic Social Teaching*, 72.
53. Ibid., 78. The citations are nos. 31, 41, and 75 of *Gaudium et spes*.
54. Paul VI, *Octogesima adveniens*, no. 22.
55. See especially "The Changing Anthropological Bases of Catholic Social Ethics."
56. Curran, *Catholic Social Teaching*, 152.
57. Ibid., 155.
58. Although cooperation is a familiar category in Catholic moral theology, the perplexity of appropriation has not been examined extensively. See the thoughtful essay by M. Cathleen Kaveny, "Appropriation of Evil: Cooperation's Mirror Image," *Theological Studies* 61 (2000): 280–313.
59. A significant thesis that Curran has argued is that there is an inconsistency between the methodology of Catholic social teaching and the methodology employed in certain documents on sexual ethics. See Charles E. Curran, "Catholic Social and Sexual Teaching: A Methodological Comparison," in

Tensions in Moral Theology (Notre Dame, Ind.: University of Notre Dame Press, 1988), 87–109.

60. A fascinating example of the tension within the tradition is over the use of the expression "social doctrine." Curran's knowledge of the tradition allows him to explain what is at stake in the discussion over whether there is a "social doctrine," with the pejorative sense that term had for an author such as Marie-Dominique Chenu and the efforts by John Paul II to rescue the expression from such an understanding. See Curran, *Catholic Social Teaching,* 63–65.

CHAPTER 9

Catholic Social Ethics in the United States

Thomas A. Shannon

STATE OF THE QUESTION

In finding their way in the United States, members of the Catholic Church moved from being an oppressed minority, to immigrants continuing the customs of their countries of origin, to assimilation into the broader society, and finally to a contemporary position of tension between the values of the larger culture and Catholicism. Along the way, many serious issues have been raised and positions taken that have helped to shape the current fact of American Catholicism.

Of concern to many American Catholics was fitting in and incorporating American values and practices—particularly democratic practices—into their church life. Little could be done, however, because of the lingering effects of the repression of modernism by Pope Pius IX in the *Syllabus of Errors,* which was continued by Pius X. Pope Leo XIII continued this trend in *Testem benevolentiae,* which responded to the so-called Americanist heresy. This condemnation had a significant dampening effect on leadership and laity that essentially resulted in a "pray, pay, and obey" attitude and a general feeling of passivity.

American Catholicism gradually came into its own and, though still under the watchful eye of Rome, began to develop a sense of identity and a style of acting. Two early examples are the school controversy and the Knights of Labor. The school controversy related to whether Catholics could attend public schools or should go to parochial schools. The issue was not only fear of the loss of faith—because the public schools had a not-so-hidden curriculum of Protestantism—but also the larger question of assimilation. The parochial model won the day on the elementary and secondary school levels, and the debate was to be rehearsed again as these students reached college age. Many immigrant Catholics were laborers and suffered the common fate of such individuals in the age of the Industrial Revolution. The bishops took the side of the workers and supported the right to organize and to form unions. The larger Catholic social teaching on the labor question was made most relevant in support for a living wage and decent working conditions.

The Great Depression exacted a high price from all levels of American life. A Catholic response was to argue for social reform and, under the leadership of John Ryan, to produce several documents on appropriate measures to improve the lot of American citizens. Such analysis, however, which accepted some elements of the status quo, also generated protest movements such as the Catholic Worker movement. People associated with this movement regarded themselves as prophetic witnesses to the larger society on the basis of fidelity to a somewhat literal reading of the message of the scriptures. This Catholicism was countercultural and indifferent to success—downward mobility, as Dorothy Day phrased it. The tension regarding Catholics and the economy carried over to *Economic Justice for All,* the 1986 pastoral letter of the U.S. bishops—which was more in the tradition of Ryan rather than Day, more reformist than critical. The document was a thorough analysis of the state of the American economy, together with several proposals that were based on a scriptural and ethical analysis that was dependent on the broader social ethical tradition of the whole church but adapted for an American economy and audience.

The reality of war also intruded on American Catholics, and this reality raised two sets of issues: the relation of church and state and the ethics of both declaring a war and fighting in a war. The church-state question was always complex for U.S. Catholics, many of whom were almost uncritical in their efforts to demonstrate their patriotism. The two practical extremes of this tension over patriotism were Cardinal Spellman's affirmation, "My country, right or wrong," during the Vietnam war and the Berrigan brothers leading raids on draft boards during that same war. Which took priority: the demands of the state or the teachings of the church—teachings that some Catholics regarded as differing little from the teachings of the state because of the radical inculturation of the church into the society? The 1983 pastoral letter *The Challenge of Peace* addressed the ethics of war in the context of the nuclear age and brought a fresh analysis to the centuries-old just war theory. The bishops recognized the legitimacy of pacifism and posed a severe challenge to assumptions supporting the use of nuclear weapons and strategic assumptions supporting the conduct of nuclear war.

Intersecting these and other social issues of the day was the reality of racism. Catholic bishops and religious orders had owned slaves, and the church was slow to reject the reality of slavery. Yet even though the church theoretically rejected slavery, the reality of segregation took its place in the church. Although some people might argue that providing African Americans with their own parishes was analogous to establishing ethnic parishes, the analogy fails because the former slaves were not immigrants, and they were not really wanted in other churches. Moreover, the former slaves did not seek their own churches as other groups did but were forced into such a position because of their rejection by those ethnic churches. Ever so slowly, the church came to see the evils of racism and segregation, and many clergy and laity exerted significant leadership to help reverse course. Pastoral letters were written, and the church supported the Civil Rights movement—though many Catholics did so reluctantly. The realization that once more the U.S. church will soon be a church of immigrants—though this time with immigrants of many different colors—is forcing the church to revisit the problem of racism in a new way and to think seriously about what a truly integrated church will be.

A related question is sexism—again not one of the finer aspects of past or present church life. Even though many people point to stunning examples of female leadership within the church, the dominant history is one of oppression and exclusion from leadership roles. Even though the rhetoric—from pope to parish priest—is changing, the practice of exclusion from leadership remains, as does the claim that equality of dignity does not eradicate natural differences from which different social roles can be assigned. The divisiveness of this question in the church is evidenced by the failed attempt of the U.S. bishops to produce a pastoral letter on women in the church. Two drafts were written, but no final text was approved. The issue remains unresolved.

Surrounding these thematic problems in Catholic social thought are overarching issues such as the relation of law and morality, the relation of church and state, the common good and private morality, and appropriate means of social intervention. These and other questions have formed the heart of Catholic social ethics in the past several decades, and a variety of solutions have been proposed. The evaluation is ongoing and critical.

CRITICAL CONTRIBUTIONS OF CHARLES E. CURRAN

Greatly influenced by Bernard Häring, Charles E. Curran has brought critical and constructive insights to the unfolding story of moral theology in the United States. In addition to substantive contributions on the question of methodology, Curran has written on several topics that are at the center of attention of the country in general and the Catholic community in particular. Although Curran will always be remembered for his leadership in understanding the role of conscience and the development of norms for dissent from noninfallible magisterial teachings following the publication of *Humanae vitae,* he also has cast his analytic eye on a multitude of topics of broad concern to the church and society. I examine several issues evaluated by Curran: the relation of Christian morality to common morality, law and morality, strategic interventions, and the relation between church and state.

A Specifically Christian Ethic

The question of a specifically Christian ethic arose out of the traditional natural law perspective in Catholicism. In light of the post–Vatican II renewal of moral theology, much emphasis was given to the role of scripture and to the role of faith and grace in establishing a vibrant Christian morality. "A purely natural law ethic was too minimalist and did not recognize the supernatural aspect of Christian existence."[1] Following the debate over artificial contraception that was based on a natural law argument that many people inside and outside the church did not find convincing, however, the question of the relation of faith and reason was raised again. The new debate suggested that the "material content of normative Christian morality must be communicable to all human beings and faith itself does not add anything to it."[2]

Curran defines a critical context for this discussion by arguing that there is only one order of nature and, consequently, one history. He rejects the traditional distinction between a purely natural order to which a second story of grace is added and argues that there is a single order of reality in which members of the church as well as all other humans live. Thus, "God's self-communication offers to all the fullness of what it means to be human."[3] On the basis of this assertion, Curran argues his position:

> The normative material content of Christian morality is in principle open to and knowable by all other human beings. In terms of the material content of morality (whether it be virtues, goals, dispositions,

> values, or norms), what is proposed for Christian human beings as such and for their life in human society, there is no exclusively Christian content that differs from what is to be required of all others.[4]

With respect to the larger debate, Curran further nuances four positions within that larger framework. First, he affirms the reality of all humans being called to God's self-communication rather than an abstract concept of human nature that exists in an atemporal, ahistorical framework. Second, moral standards should not be reduced to minimal universal norms; they also should include attitudes, values, goals, and so forth. Third, the Christian scriptures cannot be reduced simply to moral exhortation; they contain normative moral content. Yet although Christians will use these scriptures and other Christian symbols to learn this content, others will use their resources and religious language and can arrive at the same moral understanding. Finally, Curran is opposed to the term *autonomous morality* that is used in some aspects of the debate because it strikes him as too individualistic and can suggest a misunderstanding of the human-divine relation.[5]

Curran concludes by stating:

> My position can be described as "in-principled." In principle all other human beings can arrive at the same moral norms governing human action and the same values, virtues, dispositions, and goals that should characterize our moral selves. This in-principled statement does not in any way claim that all people do arrive at the same material content. Obviously, many people do not. Historicity affects all.[6]

What, then, of Christian ethics? "The proper function of Christian ethics is to address all questions concerning morality, including normative moral content, in the light of the Christian self-understanding and of all the distinctively Christian sources."[7]

Christians also can understand the resolution of moral problems as open in principle to all, however, as the U.S. bishops did in their pastoral letters on peace and the economy. On one hand, these letters brought the best of the Christian tradition to the question; on the other hand, they developed arguments that all could engage on common ethical ground. The critical point of this discussion is that because Christians live in the same historical order that is common to all people, they can join in the discussion of questions of concern to the larger society on grounds that are common to that society as well as on grounds that are proper to their own belief system. Moreover, although the members of the larger society might not accept Christian sources for an argument as such, in principle the heart of the argument will be open to all.

Curran's critical contribution is his continued argument that humans can reason and that such arguments cannot simply be refuted by fiat, whether ideological or ecclesiastical. Clearly this position winds up in the middle of critical arguments over the relation of faith and reason and the role and scope of ecclesiastical authority. The continuing example is that of artificial contraception. Few theologians and even fewer lay Catholics are persuaded by the natural law argument developed by the hierarchy that rejects artificial contraception. The arguments are not convincing, and the experience of married couples does not conform to the dire predictions of the magisterium about those who use contraception. The strength of Curran's contribution is that he continues to hold the torch for the legitimacy of reason and experience. He recognizes that reason is fallible and that mistakes will be made, but the way to respond to that problem is through critical and continual examination of the arguments, not through fiats of various sorts that do not respond to the arguments. The Catholic tradition is rich with resources, but these resources are framed within particular cultures, particular historical contexts, and particular theological and philosophical frameworks. Because part of the tradition is the use of reason in constructing arguments, Curran's affirmation of the role of reason, its centrality in human culture, and its capacity to come to valid and trustworthy conclusions is a critical contribution to moral theology.

The Relation of Law and Morality

The discussion of the reality of an ethic that is common to Christians and people of other traditions leads to the issue of the relation of law and morality. Curran begins this discussion by setting out the two extremes. The first extreme is a traditional Catholic position that argues that because all of reality is governed by eternal law, "the primary function of civil law is to apply the natural law to these particular circumstances, for human law is really only an extension of natural law in the changing circumstances of different cultural and historical situations."[8] At the other extreme is a more pragmatic approach that regards the law as simply reflecting the mores of a particular time and culture. The law does not determine what is good or bad; it tries "to bring about a social equilibrium which permits each one to live according to his convictions and ethic while safeguarding as well as possible the general interest."[9]

In contrast to these positions, Curran develops a position derived from Vatican II and the writings of John Courtney Murray. Some juridical limits are necessary because society must "protect itself against possible abuses. Society must safeguard a genuine public peace, a public morality, and the rights of all citizens."[10] The public order, rather than the natural law, is the controlling factor in establishing legal norms. Following Murray, Curran notes a threefold content to public order: an order of justice, an order of public peace, and an order of morality. The order of morality does not mean, however, that all people have or share the same morality. It refers to "that fundamental public morality which is necessary for men to live together in society with the realization that there may be great differences of opinion and of action existing within society on specific moral questions."[11]

Qualities of such laws are that they be good, equitable, and enforceable. This last point is critical because if the law is not enforceable, the consequence will be disrespect for the law, even though many people might argue that it is a good and needed law (e.g., Prohibition).

The critical conclusion that Curran draws is that many possible laws can be promulgated about even a topic such as abortion: absolute prohibition, regulation on the basis of specific criteria, or no law at all. One must examine the society in which the law is to be promulgated and decide prudently, keeping in mind that although morality cannot be totally distinguished from law, neither can morality be totally identified with law.

Curran complements this position with his views of the relation between religion and the political process. Thus, he identifies three principles to help resolve the question of whether proposed legislation has a truly political purpose. First, freedom is to be respected as much as possible and restrained only when necessary. Second, the only basis for state restriction of freedom is public order—a narrower concept than the common good but one that includes justice, public morality, and public peace. Third, laws that restrict freedom must be equitable and enforceable.[12]

Questions about the relation between law and morality and between religion and government are at the center of national attention. Curran's framework will help us sort through policy proposals currently under discussion (e.g., federal money subsidizing social service programs sponsored by religious organizations).

Strategic Interventions in Society

How might Catholics respond to social issues particularly in light of their complexity and our pluralistic culture? Answers to this question can be found in Curran's studies of several figures in American Catholicism.

"The Right Reverend New Dealer," as Msgr. John A. Ryan sometimes was known, was a social reformer who argued that the social question extended beyond economics to include moral and religious issues that cannot be adequately resolved without the church's help. To this end he proposed three ways that the teachings of popes and bishops can help solve social problems. First, their teachings can lay down moral principles that can guide industrial relations, such as support for a living wage and the state's power to remedy abuses. Second, the church can declare some methods or systems unlawful (as it did with socialism). Finally, the church can advocate certain methods. Although Ryan clearly wanted the laity fully and actively involved in social reform, the clergy in particular "should become involved in assisting and directing cooperative associations of all sorts, settlement houses, and consumer leagues, and not only orphan asylums and schools."[13]

Ryan used the traditional natural law approach as the basis for his social analysis, but in his economic analysis he used an inductive approach that led him to develop his principle of expediency, which argues good ethics is good economics. As a social reformer Ryan asked two questions: "I ask myself, first, 'is this measure in conformity with right reason and Catholic Teaching?' Second, 'is it wise and prudent to advocate the reform at this time?'"[14] Curran notes that although this principle leads Ryan to attack several critical social problems, it also blinds him to other problems, such as race.

Another approach to social intervention is discussed in the context of German immigrants, particularly with regard to the *Central-Verein,* a national federation of German-American Catholic associations that was formed to protect group members' interests (such as national parishes and cultural identity). The issue was whether there could be compatibility between the American ethos and the inculturation of immigrants. German Catholics identified maintaining their customs and language with keeping their faith. This attitude led to the development of parallel organizations such as Catholic schools, benevolent organizations, and labor organizations. This orientation, which developed more directly under the directions of William J. Engelen, S.J., argued the incompatibility of Catholicism and American culture. The model proposed, in opposition to the enemy of liberalism, was a romanticized, organic model of medieval society. Although this movement used this orientation to critique the existing economic structure of the United States, ultimately the movement disappeared because the model was not a viable alternative to American society and because of its essentially isolationist stance. Curran notes, however, that by virtue of the *Central-Verein*'s "insisting that social reform involves both a change of heart and a change of structures, they made a lasting contribution to the ongoing dialogue about Christian social ethics in the United States."[15]

The Catholic Worker movement and priest-sociologist Paul Hanley Furfey provide another approach to social reform that is countercultural in nature but with a different foundation. Rather than using a natural law approach, Furfey used the ideals of Christian life as found in a literal reading of the New Testament as the basis for his Christian radicalism. Furfey rejected the liberalism of the day as represented by Ryan, but eventually he abandoned his own radicalism in favor of Christian revolution. Furfey rejected a society based on specific goals to which members of the society should strive, as well as a society based on truths about humans that are accessible to our reason. Instead, he called for a society "founded on faith in the divinely revealed truth."[16] This position naturally leads to radical incompatibility between Christianity and American society. We are not simply to avoid sin; we are called to holiness on the basis of New Testament ideals. This calling, in turn, leads to two basic strategies: separation and nonparticipation, on one hand, and bearing witness on the other.[17] Thus, for Furfey, "The radical Christian primarily looks to the gospel to determine what is to be done; efficacy and the effects of one's actions are left in God's hands. We do what God requires of us and God will take care of the rest."[18]

The social strategy of John Courtney Murray represents a return to the natural law tradition of Ryan, but with different emphases and orientations. Murray argued that Catholics can accept the American consensus that is based on natural law—articulated in society as the truths we hold. In Murray's judgment, this consensus is unraveling at the very time we need it, and the task is to rebuild it on the basis of natural law. Murray's concept of natural law, according to Curran, "gives us, not a blueprint for all of society, but rather a skeletal law to which flesh and blood must be added by competent, rational political activity."[19] This approach will lead to a public order in which all people of good will can cooperate to bring about the common good. Curran notes that, although this vision of the natural law is optimistic and somewhat elitist, a more critical problem is Murray's tendency to forget "the sinful and to accept the existing reality as an expression of the natural which is not infected by sin."[20] Moreover, Murray's overly rational approach neglects the need for change of heart and the reality of power and conflict.

In one of his most interesting essays, Curran argues that "support of Alinsky-style community organizations is the most distinctive practical approach taken to social justice by the Catholic Church in the United

States."[21] The points of contact are threefold: the Campaign for Human Development, liberation theology, and Catholic social teaching.

In the Campaign for Human Development, the emphasis is on "the struggle for social justice by means of community organizations using conflict approaches."[22] Obviously some Catholics are concerned by such uses of conflict, and some are unaware of the closeness of Saul Alinsky's model to this organization. Nonetheless, Curran argues that there is a significant area of overlap.

Although there are differences, there also are some critical overlaps between Alinsky and liberation theology. Both argue against a value-free understanding of reality and operate within a hermeneutic of suspicion. Both make an option for the poor. Both seek to raise the consciousness of the poor. Finally, both have conflict modes of analysis and practice. Alinsky has fundamental disagreements with three aspects of liberation theology: commitment to work within the system, rejection of single-issue community organization, and willingness to compromise. The connection to the larger tradition of Catholic social thought comes from Alinsky's relationships with then Archbishop Montini of Milan and Jacques Maritain. In particular, there is a closeness between Alinsky and Maritain with respect to common themes: democracy as the "best form of government; education and trust in people are necessary to make democracy truly work; democracy must be built from the bottom up."[23] On the important issue of the relationship between means and ends in politics, Alinsky cites Maritain: "The fear of soiling ourselves by entering the context of history is not virtue but a way of escaping virtue."[24] Alinsky shares with Maritain a sense that means are related to values that limit them, particularly in terms of values that commit us to a democratic form of government. Moreover, the commitment to equality and participation in *Octagesima adveniens* echoes Alinsky's commitment to the core values of freedom, equality, and participation. As Curran notes, "Thus, the papal tradition has come to accept and articulate human dignity in a way which was defended earlier by Saul David Alinsky."[25]

The important lesson that we learn from Curran's studies of these particular individuals is that within Catholicism there is the possibility of a plurality of approaches to social interventions as well as the bases of social analysis. There also is a plurality of values and sources for these values, whether scripture or natural law or some synthesis of the two. Curran does well to remind us of this critical lesson from the history of America.

AGENDA FOR THE FUTURE

In this concluding section I want to extend Charles Curran's thought by discussing several problems. The first is primarily an internal issue, but one with significant consequences: Who are the teachers of moral theology? The second issue is feminism within Catholicism. The third issue is the question of the methodology of the moral theology of the future.

Curran notes in several places that two major issues in the current development of moral theology are its move from the seminary to the college or university setting and the concomitant emergence of a greater number of laity teaching moral theology—as well as other disciplines of theology.[26] The primary implication of this shift of locus is that the formation and academic training of most theologians will not occur within a prescribed ecclesial framework or within the culture of the seminary. In addition, the methods and questions of the students will be broader than those of the past not only because of, for example, rapid advances in technologies such as biotechnology or weapon systems but also because of the university's need to consider a larger range of issues. Furthermore, individuals in graduate schools will be mentored by a large and diverse number of individuals rather than being formed within a common tradition. Diversity of method and interests will be the outcome. Finally, the life situation of these theologians will be very different than that of earlier theologians; many, if not most, will be in partnered sexual relations, and many will raise families and balance the realities and responsibilities of a two-career family.

Various outcomes follow from these changed circumstances. Contemporary theologians are not necessarily socialized with a disposition to conformity. A plurality of methods will be a given. One's knowledge of the traditions of Catholicism will depend on the school one attends, the faculty of that school, and the research one pursues in coursework and dissertation. This plurality will result in different reactions to various documents issued by the hierarchy, as well as different ways of evaluating them. Some theologians might have difficulty, for example, in understanding experientially the teaching on artificial contraception as well as accepting on theoretical grounds the form of natural law argument on which that ban is based.

Practical questions of employment that will follow implementation of *Ex corde ecclesiae* have yet to receive realistic consideration by the hierarchy. *Ex corde* means one thing if the intended audience is clerical or religious. If they are denied a *mandatum,* although they might not have a teaching job they will be supported in some way by the institution or their community. A lay person has no such security. One can already make a strong anecdotal case that few theologians in Catholic academic settings write on issues of sexual morality or marriage because of fear of not obtaining or losing tenure. What will happen when the stakes are even higher?

Finally, the topics such lay theologians are interested in might not be the same as those that are of concern to the hierarchy. Such theologians might have a variety of interests that do not focus on the internal life of the church or on issues discussed in documents from the hierarchy. The loss of the clerical culture in which moral theology historically was undertaken has profound implications for what people perceive as problems, how they perceive them, and the methodology they bring to bear on the analysis of those problems. In my judgment, for example, the Pontifical Academy for Life's "Declaration on the Production and the Scientific Therapeutic Use of Human Embryonic Stem Cells"[27] represents a major step forward. Fifteen of the seventeen footnotes in that document refer to the scientific literature—as opposed to *Donum vitae,* which had no footnotes to any scientific literature. Yet in the last two pages of the declaration, the ethical problems are resolved on the basis of authority—with little, if any, dialogue or interaction with the scientific material presented in the preceding pages. I do not argue that one should base one's morals on science alone; I argue that many readers find insufficient an argument that first presents a scientific description of the issue and then resolves the issue on the basis of authority, with no dialogue between the two traditions. Many theologians will find such a resolution inadequate even for internal church use. Passing on the tradition means not only reporting the teaching of documents but also evaluating the basis of the teaching, its method, and the adequacy of the method in responding to the issue.

A second issue is feminism, of which Curran has noted, "In practice, I think that the most crucial, and unfortunately divisive, issue facing the Catholic Church in the United States is the role of women in church and society."[28] Although many Catholics might consider this statement extreme, a sizeable majority would consider it a fair assessment of the problem. On an institutional level, many women are ignored, underappreciated, unwanted, and institutionally prevented from seeking what they consider to be their calling within the ecclesial community. It is no exaggeration to say that women in the church are—and, if the present course is followed, will remain—second-class citizens.

Women are now taking a part in public life. Pope John XXIII in *Pacem in terris* explicitly recognized this trend as a critical sign of the times. This shift is happening more rapidly perhaps in the industrial world and, more slowly but widely, among peoples who have inherited other traditions or cultures. Because women are becoming more conscious of their human dignity, they will not tolerate being treated as mere material instruments; they will demand rights befitting a human person in domestic and public life.[29]

One problem is the tradition's continued insistence on the position that equality of human dignity does not eliminate or cancel policies that are based on social or gender differences. The tradition argues that such differences are a part of the "natural" endowment of men or women, rather than social constructs. Clearly there are differences between males and females, but these differences are primarily biological. Even these differences, however, may represent more of a continuum than sharp differences. A major challenge for social ethics is to convince members of the church that role differences are not a fact of nature and that setting policy on the basis of such differences is a great injustice.

A second reality is that many more women are going to college, and many more continuing on to some form of graduate education. Many Catholic seminaries rely on the presence of lay women and men to keep themselves fiscally stable. More women than ever—lay as well as religious—are becoming theologians (as is obvious to anyone who attends professional meetings). We have a critical mass of extremely skilled and deeply dedicated women in the church, but many are not yet fully valued. One senior cleric in an eastern diocese said to me that the biggest problem in the diocese was the activities of women who were educated in seminaries that are perceived as progressive. One can only hope that such an anachronistic view is idiosyncratic. Part of the cause of the failure to complete the draft of the pastoral on women was the reality that some questions were simply removed from the discussion. Remember too, the critique of Archbishop Weekland, who held "listening sessions" with the women of his diocese. He was told that he should be teaching them, not merely listening to them. As if the testimony of the lived religious experience of women doing their best to be faithful participants in the church was irrelevant! Should anyone be surprised that many women perceived their very presence—much less their words and experiences—to be unwanted?

The supreme irony, of course, is that were it not for women the institutional dimension of the church in the United States simply would not function. Consider the vast number of women—lay and religious—who are administrators of parishes, chaplains (though they may no longer be called that!) in hospitals and prisons, directors of various religious education programs, and administrators of numerous other programs provided by the local diocese or parish. The list goes on and on. How long can such commitment and dedication continue? Although Curran's general assessment is correct, he vastly understates the reality of the situation of women in the church today. Serious work must be done here.

The third problem relates to the question of methodology in social ethics. Curran identifies the problem this way:

> In my judgment a lack of consistency exists between the positions taken by the American Catholic bishops and the universal hierarchical teaching office in the sexual and medical areas and the approaches taken in social ethic, for two different methodologies appear to be at work in official hierarchical teaching. In the social area official church documents strongly recognize the importance of historical consciousness, and they turn to the subject with an emphasis on the person. These emphases with all their logical conclusions are missing in contemporary hierarchical approaches in the areas of sexual and medical ethics.[30]

In the two most significant pastoral letters of the U.S. bishops—*The Challenge of Peace* and *Economic Justice for All*—one discovers an elegant methodology at work. The bishops begin with a very broad process of consultation with all perspectives of experts and individuals who are concerned about the problem. Data are gathered and examined to help set out the empirical parameters of the problem. Then the bishops turn to the scriptures for an identification of core beliefs, values, and narratives that would begin to formulate a set of priorities. The next step is an ethical analysis of the issues that emerge from the empirical examination, in conjunction with scriptural priorities and in dialogue with the empirical context as determined by the consultation process. A series of conclusions are developed and set forth in order of certitude, from most certain and on which the bishops expect unanimity—for example, protection of noncombatants—to less certain issues, on which disagreement was possible—use of nuclear weapons as part of an overall strategic defense, for example. In the economic pastoral, the bishops set forth several broad values, then propose a set of middle axioms and then policy suggestions that translate the values into actions. Again, the bishops expect broad agreement on the values and general agreement on the middle axioms and accept disagreement on the specifics. Both documents recognize a "hierarchy of truths" and a corresponding diminishment of certitude as one develops increasingly specific policies.

This method engendered broad debate about the topics of the letters from all levels of society and the church. Although the debate was lively and sharp lines of opposition were drawn, one important element throughout the debate was a common sense of ownership of the process and outcome by the Catholic community. Even though many critics of the pastorals rejected several of the specific conclusions and provided specific arguments for their position, this criticism was not regarded as invalidating the documents or the process. The bishops affirmed the reality of disagreement with specific conclusions precisely because of the complexity of the situation and the fact that common sharing of a particular value did not automatically translate into a specific conclusion or policy with which everyone would necessarily agree.

Now the obvious question is: Why can't this process and method be generalized? Pope Paul VI in *Octagesima adveniens* set the tone by saying:

> In the face of such widely varying situations it is difficult for us to utter a unified message and to put forward a solution which has universal validity. Such is not our ambition, nor is it our mission. It is up to the Christian communities to analyze with objectivity the situation that is proper to their own country, to shed on it the light of the Gospel's unalterable words and to draw principles, norms of judgment and directives for action from the social teaching of the Church.[31]

This statement seems to describe the U.S. bishops' approach in these pastoral letters. If anything, the authority of the bishops was enhanced because of the openness of the process, the seriousness with which they took all viewpoints, and their recognition that complex problems have complex solutions and that people of good will can differ on specifics without betraying their common values.

The pastorals also model the dialogue that must occur between values and the empirical situation if the conclusions are to have any credibility. The bishops modeled how to hold one's core values while recognizing that several different social policies could be compatible with those values. The bishops recognized that the strength of their conclusions depended on the strength of their argument. The authority with which they spoke was an authority grounded in their authority of office as well as an authority grounded in the soundness of their argument. This process engaged members of the church and recognized the integrity of each member's conscience in coming to a moral conclusion about the issues under discussion. This process did not reject the traditions of the church or the authority of the hierarchy. Instead, the process regarded the church as bringing the best of its tradition to bear on complicated issues of the day through a wide-ranging dialogue that seeks to respond to these issues with the nuanced arguments required by the situation.

The issues of who future theologians will be, the status of women within the church, and methodology are complex and will not be easy to resolve. Although many Catholics would argue that the current climate in the American Catholic church is not amenable to resolution of these issues, Charles E. Curran—through the example of his life and the testimony of his writings—has shown us the joys and burdens of faithful discipleship as well as an example of how to develop an ethic that is faithful to the traditions of the church as well as responsive to the signs of the times.

NOTES

1. Charles E. Curran, "The Uses and Limitations of Philosophical Ethics in Doing Theological Ethics: Some Reflections from a Roman Catholic Perspective," in *Annual of the Society of Christian Ethics* (Waterloo, Ontario: Council on the Study of Religion, 1984), 125. See also Charles E. Curran, "Dialogue with Humanism: Is There a Distinctively Christian Ethic?" in *Catholic Moral Theology in Dialogue* (Notre Dame, Ind.: University of Notre Dame Press, 1972), 1–23.
2. Curran, "Uses and Limitations of Philosophical Ethics," 128.
3. Ibid., 128–29.
4. Ibid., 129–30.
5. Ibid., 132.
6. Ibid., 133.
7. Ibid.
8. Charles E. Curran, "Abortion: Its Legal and Moral Aspects in Catholic Theology," in *New Perspectives in Moral Theology* (Notre Dame, Ind.: University of Notre Dame Press, 1974), 165.
9. Ibid., 167.
10. Ibid.
11. Ibid., 168.
12. Charles E. Curran, "Religion, Law and Public Policy in America," in *Directions in Catholic Social Ethics* (Notre Dame, Ind.: University of Notre Dame Press, 1985), 132–33.
13. Charles E. Curran, *American Catholic Social Ethics: Twentieth-Century Approaches* (Notre Dame, Ind.: University of Notre Dame Press, 1982), 66.

14. Ibid., 89.
15. Ibid., 129.
16. Ibid., 136.
17. Ibid., 151.
18. Ibid., 161.
19. Ibid., 181.
20. Ibid., 231.
21. Charles E. Curran, *Directions in Catholic Social Ethics* (Notre Dame, Ind.: University of Notre Dame Press, 1985), 148.
22. Ibid., 151.
23. Ibid., 168.
24. Ibid., 170.
25. Ibid., 168.
26. Charles E. Curran, *Catholic Moral Theology in Dialogue* (Notre Dame, Ind.: University of Notre Dame Press, 1972), 246. See also Charles E. Curran, *Moral Theology at the End of the Century* (Milwaukee, Wisc.: Marquette University Press, 1999), 34.
27. Pontifical Academy for Life, 25 August 2000.
28. Charles E. Curran, "Moral Theology in the United States: An Analysis of the Last Twenty Years (1965–85)," in *Readings in Moral Theology No. 11: The Historical Development of Fundamental Moral Theology in the United States,* eds. Charles E. Curran and Richard A. McCormick (Mahwah, N.J.: Paulist Press, 1999).
29. Pope John XXIII, *Pacem in terris,* no. 41.
30. Curran, "Moral Theology in the United States," 41.
31. Pope Paul VI, *Octagesima adveniens,* no. 4.

CHAPTER 10

A Catholic Troeltsch? Curran on the Social Ministry of the Church

J. Bryan Hehir

The contribution of Charles Curran to Catholic moral theology is rooted in the content of his work and the context in which he has written. The content of his thought, which is explored in detail in this volume, would be intrinsically important at any stage of the church's life because it combines a sense of history, a sure grasp of the structure of Catholic thought, and a pastoral drive to relate the "living tradition" to a broad range of contemporary issues facing individuals, the church itself, and American society. In addition to these characteristics, however, there is another dimension to his work. Curran began his professional theological work just as Vatican II was ending. As he and others have noted, moral theology was not a central concern of the Council, but the consequences of the conciliar texts and the debates that led to them opened a host of questions that moral theology and the episcopal magisterium could not ignore. Curran's contribution of systematic scholarly commitment and his concern for the pastoral and public life of the Catholic Church have placed him in the center of the theological debate for the past forty years. From theologians to pastoral ministers to lay members of the church, we have all benefited from his reflection and scholarship.

This essay focuses on a dimension of Curran's work in social ethics; I concentrate on his analysis of the social mission of the church—the line where ecclesiology engages social ethics. Curran has been more attentive to this intersection than any other author in the United States.

ECCLESIOLOGY AND SOCIAL ETHICS: BACKGROUND

Charles Curran's work on the ecclesial foundation of the church's social ministry is a contribution to and reflection of a changed theological agenda in the Catholic community since Vatican II. There is no question that there always was an implicit ecclesiological component for the social ministry of the church, but prior to the Council there was sparse explicit attention given to the themes. The major social encyclicals from *Rerum novarum* (1891) through *Pacem in terris* (1963) were tightly written documents of social philosophy and social ethics, but they lacked any systematic statement of how the presuppositions of Catholic ecclesiology found expression in the social ministry. Clearly these social texts were the product of the authoritative teaching office of the church, and some attention, in the style of apologetics, was given at the outset of these encyclicals to the right and duty of the church to address social issues. However, this narrow theme basically exhausted the ecclesiology and social teaching relationship. This situation changed substantially with the appearance of the final document of Vatican II, *Gaudium et spes* (the Pastoral Constitution on the Church in the Modern World).[1] The text itself provided a distinct break with the style and substance of the social encyclicals, and the promulgation of the document initiated an ecclesial discussion that continues into this century. Curran's writing on the ecclesial basis of social ministry fits into this broader framework. To assess his work, it is necessary to provide a sense of this transformed framework of Catholic social teaching and social ethics.

Gaudium et spes was the product of two streams of Catholic theology. The encyclical tradition sought to renew the natural law social ethic and relate it to a world that was dramatically different from its classical or medieval context. The other source was less magisterial; it was the product of a generation of European theologians working from the 1930s through the 1950s.[2] They sought to make Catholic theology a constructive and relevant voice in a European setting traumatized by two global wars and the holocaust. They wanted to ground the social teaching in a broad, rich synthesis of history, ecclesiology, Christology, and eschatology that would justify the conviction that in seeking to build a just, humane, and peaceful world Christians and all others were collaborating in the work of the Kingdom of God.[3] The theologians sought to demonstrate that these efforts had a meaning and purpose that transcended history even as they concretely changed the sociopolitical order. This theological source of

Gaudium et spes found expression in one of the conciliar text's central paragraphs:

> That the earthly and heavenly city penetrate each other is a fact accessible to faith alone. It remains a mystery of human history, which sin will keep in great disarray until the splendor of God's son is fully revealed. Pursuing the saving purpose which is proper to her, the Church not only communicates divine life to men, but in some way casts the reflected light of that life over the entire earth.[4]

The achievement of *Gaudium et spes* was that it drew on the social teaching and the incarnational theology of postwar Europe yet was not simply a summary of either. The conciliar document had its own distinctive tone and themes, not least of which was the firm bond it established between the moral effort to humanize the world and the ecclesial identity of Catholicism.[5]

Exegesis of the text is not possible here; what is possible is to chart the ecclesiological legacy of *Gaudium et spes* as found in the magisterial and theological debates it catalyzed and inspired. Three moments in the ongoing discussion illustrate the document's lasting significance. The first step is from the council to the 1971 and 1974 Synods of Bishops. Embedded in *Justitia in mundo* (1971) and *Evangelii nuntiandi* (1975) is the search for a precise understanding and articulation of the role social ministry should have in the total work of the church. *Gaudium et spes* had been welcomed in the theological community and in the wider church as a clear statement that the social dimension of ministry was essential to the work of the church. Its intrinsic importance for human dignity and its extrinsic significance for the role of the church in history demanded that the social dimension be central, not peripheral, for an understanding of the church.

The 1971 synodal text provided structural and substantive content for this conviction, describing social engagement as "constitutive" for the preaching of the gospel.[6] The impact of this move was evident in the 1974 Synod, which made efforts to limit the theological thrust of the previous decade; the final text reflects this concern but also provides a powerful social dimension for the understanding of the church's work of evangelization.

Parallel with this magisterial explanation of the meaning of the church's social ministry were multiple theological movements, some initiated by *Gaudium et spes,* that focused on the broad question of the social responsibility of the church. The most visible contribution arose in Latin

America through the theology of liberation, but Europeans produced political theology, and the United States led the way in feminist theologies. Although none of these developments was confined to the textual debates that absorbed much of the magisterial documents, all were influenced by and sought to deepen the conviction of *Gaudium et spes:* "They are mistaken who, knowing that they have here no abiding city but seek one which is to come, think that they may therefore shirk their earthly responsibilities."[7]

The third contribution to the post–*Gaudium et spes* era has been the pontificate of John Paul II, a pope who has been determined to shape the social ministry of the church by word and deed. Rooted securely in the incarnational convictions of the conciliar text, he combines its positive social imperative with its expressed restraints that Christ "gave his church no proper mission in the political, economic or social order."[8] The essence of John Paul II's ecclesial view seems to be that the church should be nonpolitical but socially activist.[9] A certain reading of *Dignitatis humanae* and *Gaudium et spes* sustains this perspective. Such a view leaves open, however, where the line of nonpolitical/activist can be clearly drawn or whether John Paul II adheres to it himself. It is in this context, sketched but not painted here, that Charles Curran has addressed the ecclesial and the social dimension of Catholic theology.

CHARLES CURRAN'S CONTRIBUTION TO THE SOCIAL MISSION OF THE CHURCH

At the outset, a general comment can be made about Curran's work in social ethics. He refers to the work of Ernst Troeltsch—the German philosopher-historian whose typology of the social ethics of different Christian churches continues to define much of Christian social theory today. In a sense, Curran has fulfilled a Troeltschian role within Catholic social ethics, in the emphasis he has given to the relationship of ecclesiology and ethics and in the focus of his writing, where he seeks to frame issues in social ethics rather than argue them in detail. In my judgment, Curran's dominant influence has been methodological, not casuistic.[10]

Fundamental Moral and Social Ethics

Although Curran's work in the past twenty years has moved steadily in the direction of social ethics, there is some value in noting the fact that his lifelong professional work in fundamental moral theology has substantially influenced his choice of topics in social ethics and his style of addressing them. In terms of social ethics, the most evident impact of fundamental moral theology is the way in which Curran situates social ethics and the social ministry of the church in a clearly defined architecture. The question of where the social ministry "fits" in the broader ecclesial ministry has been a much-analyzed topic since Vatican II. Curran's work engages this debate but also broadens it. The impetus provided by *Gaudium et spes* focused the discussion on the necessity of social ministry in any integral conception of ecclesiology; hence, much of the theological commentary has been about the relative weight, importance, or emphasis to be accorded social ministry alongside the teaching and sacramental work of the church.

Curran has a position on this question, but he wants to ground the social dimension in a more expansive theological framework. He describes this framework as a "stance." Curran's stance is a basic perspective for understanding moral theology; it systematically relates the doctrines of creation, sin, incarnation, redemption, and resurrection destiny.[11] Although this stance functions throughout his moral analysis, the role it plays in social ethics and social ministry is to protect the church and Christians from a simplistic understanding of the social context that the church is called to heal, sanctify, and shape. An adequate theological framework is protection against theological versions of Hobbesian realism or Enlightenment optimism. One of Curran's earliest essays on social ministry, "Theological Reflections on the Social Mission of the Church," invokes broad theological arguments to critique views that fail to address the fact of sin in human history or the irreducibly eschatological dimensions of Christian hope:

> There is a widespread theological disease, at times of epic proportions, which I call a case of collapsed eschatology. Such a theological approach thinks that the fullness of the Kingdom is here and now present, forgetting the limitations and sinfulness of the present.[12]

Although this passage highlights one dimension of a theological connection, Curran is never one-dimensional; at other times he highlights the danger of failing to use an eschatological vision to criticize and change existing social institutions.[13] The principal point is the consistency with which Curran uses his stance; from the 1972 essay through his writings in the 1990s, Curran tests proposals for how the church should analyze social reality and how it should act within the social arena against this complex grid of Christian doctrines.

Curran's stance is not confined in its influence to how the church analyzes society; it also shapes how the church understands its own identity. Reflecting Troeltsch's earlier assessment, Curran argues that Roman Catholicism will always be a "big church." This phrase is shorthand for a view of the church that includes saints and sinners, that will be home to individuals of diverse political persuasions and a wide range of racial, ethnic, and cultural heritages. The significance of holding to the inclusive vision of a big church is not simply what political commentators call a "big tent" (often a mix of incoherent pragmatic compromises). The ecclesial reality contains deep and fundamental truths about the social ministry. A big church regards the human (the person, society, human institutions, and academic disciplines) as the raw material from which the Kingdom of God is being fashioned here, even though ultimate fulfillment will be the work of the Spirit. Such an ecclesial perspective is reflected in the statement of *Gaudium et spes:* "On this earth the Kingdom is already present in mystery. When the Lord returns, it will be brought into full flower."[14]

The human is destined for the Kingdom because "the human person deserves to be preserved; human society deserves to be renewed."[15] Therefore, a big church also is an engaged church—one that assumes responsibility for the world, one that sees its role as distinct from the state and other secular actors but understands collaboration with them as part of its religious vocation. In multiple ways, a big church is not only a home to diversity, it also is a large visible actor in human society. As history has shown, there are inherent risks in this conception of the church, but Curran is accurate when he identifies it as the dominant theological view of Catholicism.

A big church in Curran's view also will be a pluralistic community, holding in tension diverse conceptions of theological and social issues. Again, this topic has broader ramifications than social ministry. It constitutes a bridge between Curran's work in bioethics and sexual ethics and his work in social ethics. Curran notes often the difference in teaching style in Catholic theology between these distinct areas of human affairs.[16] In social ethics, Catholic teaching authority invites a degree of pluralism:

> Often enough the Christian view of things will suggest some specific solution in certain circumstances. Yet it happens rather frequently, and legitimately so, that with equal sincerity some of the faithful will disagree with others on a given matter.[17]

This clearly is a limited view of permissible pluralism; it focuses on pluralism among "the faithful" and does not really address the neuralgic issue of the past thirty years, in which Curran has been a major voice, concerning pluralism between theologians and the episcopal magisterium or tensions between the Catholic conscience and magisterial teaching itself.

Curran's argument is that a big church—in social or sexual ethics—must be able to live with a certain degree of pluralism. He grounds this view in the need for church teaching to address complexity and specificity in moral judgment. Because of complexity—in social issues, in science, in medicine—the church inevitably will have to integrate in its moral judgment a vast array of data that lie outside the fields of philosophy, theology, and revelation. As it does so, it inevitably loses the kind of certainty one expects when one is invoking general theological or philosophical principles. The answer is not to stay in the stratosphere of principles, however; moral teaching in the Catholic tradition has always descended to the particular and the specific. Curran supports this willingness to engage the concrete reality of complex questions. The necessary corollary, however, is to expect and admit the legitimacy of a certain arena of pluralism in the Catholic community, particularly for issues that are not at the core of faith. Hence, Curran finds particularly appropriate for a big and engaged church the style of teaching in the two pastoral letters of the U.S. bishops, *The Challenge of Peace* and *Economic Justice for All.*[18] Rather than retaining the general language of Vatican II that the faithful may disagree on social issues, the pastoral letters lay out a structure for distinguishing levels of Catholic teaching; basically, they seek to create consensus at the level of general values or principles and to acknowledge the legitimacy of pluralism on policy choices. Curran supports this view and argues that it should be extended beyond the social teaching.

In summary, Curran's work of locating a place for social ministry in the life of the church yields a set of criteria for assessing the possibilities of social reform, a mandate for church involvement in public life, an inclusive conception of the ecclesial community, a pluralist understanding of how social teaching will be heard and received, and a proposal for how recent social teaching could enhance other dimensions of Catholic moral theology.

The Role of the Church in Society

The two primary ecclesiological conclusions that Curran derives from his broad theological "stance" are the essential role of the social ministry in the life of the church and the conviction that such a role should never be reduced to regarding the church simply as an opposition movement, a bearer of negative critique directed at other institutions and their policies.

These conclusions lead to a discussion of how the church should fulfill its social role. Defining this role requires a mix of theological principles and a sense of strategy.

Theologically, Curran's premises of a big and engaged church that values social ministry and assumes responsibility for the wider society are then joined to a set of subordinate theological criteria. These criteria include recognition that the church cannot claim unique wisdom in the social arena, that the church must avoid a triumphalist posture that disregards the appropriate role of other institutions, and that the church should not exhaust the social responsibilities of its members who should play other social roles as citizens in society.[19] These principles are not unique to Curran, but he often has a specific approach to them. For example, the principle that denies the church a unique perspective on moral wisdom is cognate to the affirmation in *Gaudium et spes:* "Christ, to be sure, gave his Church no proper mission in the political, economic or social order."[20] Curran presses beyond this ecclesial assertion, however, to the broader ethical affirmation that there is no specifically Christian content in material norms of morality.[21] This proposition is contested by some theologians who would agree with the limit established by Vatican II.

Curran gives more attention to establishing the theological limits for the church's social role than he does to specifying a strategy of engagement. He does set out principles, however, to support his position of a socially activist ministry for the church. In his 1972 article, he warned against self-interested policies of engagement and against duplication by the church of what other institutions were doing in social policy.[22] He moved beyond these prudential guidelines in 1993 in *The Church and Morality.* In that work he set out five roles for an engaged church: teacher and learner, provider for the needy, empowerer and enabler, advocate, and model for society.[23] As in other writings on this topic, Curran is not primarily breaking new ground but summarizing a broadly shared consensus. There are supporters for each of these positions in the wider church; often they do not have Curran's systematic perspective, so they press one or two of these roles for the church and ignore or dismiss the others.

The advantage of Curran's writing is that it emphasizes the multiple ways in which the church can engage society; it does not address the potential for conflict or even the incompatibility of some of these positions. There is a complexity of roles involved in being provider for the needy and advocate of deeper social change, as there is in providing service for the poor and being an effective enabler. These roles are not contradictory, but

Curran's commendable desire to see the church fulfill each of these roles requires a more detailed strategic discussion than he usually attempts.

A 1994 article in *Theological Studies* takes Curran to the cusp of strategic choices. He discusses the role of Catholic social institutions—education, social service and health care—particularly as they struggle with issues of Catholic identity. This valuable survey is more descriptive than prescriptive, but it does cut across the provider-advocate-model linkage that many of these institutions face.[24] Although Curran clearly is appreciative of the role these institutions have played, he has a more modest view of their potential than I argue for later.

Addressing Social Issues

How does Curran envision a "big" church exercising its teaching role in a democratic, pluralistic society such as the United States? The cornerstone of his position is a theme that has run through his theology for four decades. Curran sees the idea of mediation as the distinctive mark of Catholic theology and of theological and social ethics. Mediation in essence means that we encounter God in and through the human.[25] From the concept of mediation Curran moves to an endorsement of the traditional Catholic claim that two distinct sources of moral wisdom are available to human beings: reason and revelation. Curran has consistently supported the role of natural law in Catholic ethics. He has often disputed how natural law has been interpreted and some of the conclusions that have been drawn from it. Yet he has upheld the need for a big church to be able to address social issues and civil society in terms that draw on a common conception of morality.

Two qualifications of Curran's position must be noted. First, he has been more critical of natural law conclusions in bioethics and sexual ethics than in social ethics. Second, in recent years he has argued that even in social ethics the conception of natural law in church teaching was artificially divorced from the theological context that should frame the understanding of natural law. Here Curran's stance reappears as he emphasizes the need for both a theological connection to natural law ethics that can account for the impact of sin and the understanding of Christian eschatology.[26] A big church must use the full range of theological resources in developing its understanding of the demands of natural law, and it can and should blend the two sources of moral wisdom when it addresses the believing community. The address to civil society should and can be developed in a way that is not explicitly religious, however. The two sources of wisdom yield two modes of address to social questions; again, Curran supports the efforts of the U.S. bishops to speak to diverse communities in distinct ways.

Beyond the mode of address lies the question of how, specifically, a big church should pursue its response to complex social questions. In the background to Curran's answer to this question is his position that the Christian church does not have unique moral wisdom regarding the content of complex problems; it can and should share its wisdom, but with an awareness that others can and do pursue similar paths of moral reasoning.

The issue of how the church can and should teach on moral questions arose often in the debates surrounding the U.S. pastoral letters. The Catholic discussion had been previewed in the 1960s and 1970s, however, when Paul Ramsey turned his formidable analytical powers on Protestant churches and their social advocacy. Curran engaged Ramsey in his 1973 book, *Politics, Medicine and Christian Ethics.* [27]

Ramsey's critique of Protestant social teaching had an ethical component and an ecclesiological component. Curran's 1973 article on the social mission of the church also had warned against ethical arguments that closed too quickly on a conclusion in the name of the church, and he had warned on ecclesiological grounds against a posture that disregarded the proper autonomy of other institutions in the social arena. He criticized Ramsey's position, however (rightly, in my view) as being far too restrictive about the church's social role. In Curran's judgment, Ramsey legitimates only a "minimalistic" role for the church on political matters.[28] Curran opposes Ramsey's arguments on ethical and ecclesial grounds. Ethically, he finds Ramsey's position that the church can ground its ethic only in terms of Christian warrants (particularly in terms of Christian love) too narrowly conceived; here Curran's commitment to natural law as found in Catholic theology and magisterial teaching surfaces. Curran also is typically Catholic in seeking to protect the right and ability of the church to descend from principles to specific judgments if appropriate criteria are observed. Ecclesiologically, Curran is not prepared to observe the rigid distinction between magistrates (in the political order) and magisterium (in the ecclesial order); without entering the discussion at length, he clearly seeks to guarantee the church a voice at all levels of moral decision making, from principles through motives to specific "prudential" judgments that are never to be understood as devoid of moral content.

Commentary and Critique

I find myself in much agreement with Curran's writing on the ecclesial dimensions of social ministry, taken in its totality. In his persistent commitment to the Troeltschian argument that Catholicism has been and should be a big church, Curran accurately describes the Catholic posture in society and defends its continuing validity. His general position on a carefully defined but multidimensional role for the church in civil society corresponds to the theological logic of a big church, and his defense of the church's teaching role in social policy is congruent with Catholic practice and appropriate in meeting the challenges of American society today. My critique, therefore, lies in the area of specification, refinement, and difference about concrete judgments in each of the three dimensions of Curran's teaching that I have presented.

Having agreed with Curran's defense of a big-church posture for Catholicism, my commentary lies in the direction of the challenge we both face in sustaining this position for the church in the United States. We are in the classically difficult position of defending the *via media,* open to being criticized from left and right. One version of this critique of the *via media* pits left against right. The left finds the *via media* insufficiently prophetic in its negative critique of society, whereas the right sees it legitimizing the church's role in the world in a fashion that secularizes the church.

A different critique—more likely today—is one in which the ecclesial left and right are jointly aligned, in spite of themselves, against the big-church posture. Both find it insufficiently "countercultural"; they differ primarily in terms of which issues pose the test cases for authentic Christian witness. For the ecclesial left the issues are war, capitalism, and consumerism; for the right the issues are abortion, sexual mores, and secularism. In each instance, left and right want a more decisive critique of and practical opposition to their range of issues than the big church often provides. The big church in its Catholic mode has a critique of each of these issues, but its critique allows for distinctions—always the bane of prophets. At times the distinctions of a big church lie in ethical theory (some killing is justified, some not); at other times they rest with prudential calculation (this jurisprudential objective is feasible, another is not, so some things must be tolerated). A big church is willing to move society gradually, even if radical conversion is not likely.

The added complexity of the moment for *via media* advocates is the role John Paul II plays in word and action. In his United Nations addresses; in his trips abroad; and in his teaching on the market economy, international relations, and social policy, John Paul II has represented the posture of a big church, securely in the *via media* between total confrontation with the state and simply collapsing before the state. He also often has struck the prophetic note in word and deed, however, and Catholics in search of a more prophetic church rightly have found support from him. The pope's continuing emphasis on the need to oppose a "culture of death," his reminder that witness even to the point of martyrdom is a potential part of the Christian vocation, and his call to personal discipleship in opposition to much of modern consumer culture parallel his big-church posture.[29]

Curran has creatively reshaped the Troeltschian description of how Catholicism resolved the church-sect tensions within the ecclesial community. For Troeltsch the answer was the religious life—monastic or other forms—that channeled the sectarian choices within an organized sector of the larger church. Curran rightly understands that the religious versus laity distinction implied by this pattern will not hold today. Many Catholics—on the left and the right—who are committed to a prophetic posture are lay people in organizations such as Pax Christi, the Catholic Worker, and some of the pro-life movement. Curran invokes a phrase from Jacques Maritain, "prophetic shock minorities," which Maritain used to describe certain groups in civil society;[30] Curran transfers the term to the ecclesial community, arguing that some Christians will feel a special call to witness to peace or to voluntary poverty or to life itself. They will help keep the larger church honest and faithful even though by definition they will be minorities.

This model is creative and functional; a big church needs pluralistic choices for vocation and witness. The Curran proposal fails to acknowledge, however, that, unlike classical sectarians, the prophetic voices of left and right within Catholicism often define their position as the minimum the church should adopt. They seek not simply a seat at the table but a chance to define the agenda of the meeting. Although papal calls for countercultural witness can be interpreted in diverse ways, one way is to strengthen the sense among prophetic voices that neither Troeltsch nor Maritain captures their aspirations or intentions.

Those invoking a big-church model will need repeatedly to defend its posture in the world and the reasons for the ethical theory that complements it. The argument cannot be purely sociological (i.e., the majority of members will not adopt this position); it must have normative content about why the ecclesial and ethical styles of a big church are grounded in the gospel and in a Christian moral logic.

More briefly, my principal comment on Curran's work on how the church should fulfill its role in society focuses on the role of Catholic institutions. As I indicate above, Curran has fairly and accurately described the history and role of these institutions in American society and in the church. At the level of social strategy, however, I would emphasize and weigh the future of these institutions more heavily. Curran's principle that Catholic institutions should not duplicate what others are doing stands behind a too-stringent definition of the need for and possibilities of these institutions. Even in a highly organized welfare state such as the United States, the fact that some provision is made for education, health care, and social needs does not ipso facto argue against the existence of other actors. In health care, for example, the existence of a Catholic system is strategically important on the grounds of social justice considerations and bioethical imperatives.[31] No doubt how the system functions is one of the tests of its validity and utility, but I would argue for an expansive conception of Catholic social institutions to complement and critique existing institutions in the public and for-profit sectors of American society.

Finally, regarding how a big church should teach about social issues, my differences with Curran again lie at the margin, not with his central position. Like him, I believe a teaching style that distinguishes between the believing community and civil society and approaches them via distinct but complementary ways clearly is the method to be used. His recasting of how a natural law ethic fits into a theological framework is altogether necessary.

On two points I would press the position Curran employs in his writing. First, although I advocate the dual discourse for distinct audiences, I am more skeptical than Curran regarding how much of a theological position can be carried over and recast in a public ethic. The issue here is public intelligibility of religious discourse. Pacifism has a prima facie moral attractiveness; for state leaders it is virtually unintelligible as a strategic posture. In debates about assisted suicide, Christian eschatological hope and convictions about the ultimate meaningfulness of suffering are intrinsic to the Catholic position; can they be shared as reasons in a societal debate? What can we ask others to accept as reasons for legitimating policy and law in civil society? Even if certain theological convictions can be made somewhat intelligible, should they be the basis for law and policy? Here I would distinguish discourse in civil society and discourse that is designed to shape the specifics of law and policy. In this society the former can be as explicitly theological or religious as any citizen or group wishes to employ; public argument should have broad parameters. The latter—actions that will invoke the coercive power of the state and touch the lives of all citizens—should be cast in terms of a public philosophy.

Second, given all that Curran has written and accomplished in his productive career, I raise a final point with a good deal of diffidence. Yet it bears on how the church should teach on complex social issues, and Curran has recognized its saliency in his own writing. His emphasis on method, on precise use of ethical theory, and on careful analysis of the mode of argumentation in church documents and the writings of other theologians give much of Curran's work an abstract quality. When he addresses issues in the social arena, he often stays at a high level of generality or formal discourse. This approach is of great help in structuring questions, defining positions, and mapping the terrain of current theological concerns. It sometimes lacks, however, the specificity that is the product of engaging the dense empirical data of problems. His treatment of the nuclear debate criticized and clarified the ethical reasoning of various episcopal conferences, but one does not find in his work the grappling with the details of deterrence that Ramsey exemplifies or the specificity of policy judgment that Reinhold Niebuhr invoked in his writing. No one does everything, and Curran has done more than enough, but when I am unclear about his position it usually is because the density of casuistic analysis is not in the essay.

THE FUTURE: A BASIC THEME

The guiding text for this chapter has been *Gaudium et spes*—a document that instructs the church to be sensitive to "the signs of the times." The future for the church and the world will be shaped significantly by two complementary but contending forces: globalization and localization. The former highlights increasing integration of societies and states; the latter, perhaps in response, highlights a desire for local control and recognition of distinctiveness. Although these trends are secular, they have an ecclesial counterpart to which Curran has always been sensitive: the value of a universal teaching authority and the need for pluralism and diversity in the local church.

This tension is only one characteristic of the complex theological map of Roman Catholicism, but it has two important consequences for social ethics. Ecclesially, the long-term trend of the twentieth century was the leadership of the papal office in shaping and emphasizing Catholic social teaching. Other actors, from theologians to activists, have contributed significantly to the growing role of social ministry in the church, but the universal teaching role of the papacy has been decisive. In an increasingly integrated global arena, the need for a normative vision that addresses the system (political, economic, legal) as a whole will grow in importance. Globalization has its own logic but not its own ethic; a church with a systemic perspective is an imperative. The experience of the past twenty years shows, however, that room must be made for local theologies (e.g., the theology of liberation), for the voice of local episcopal conferences, and for an intellectual balance between universal norms and a space for diversity of interpretation and application. Catholicism's global reach and multiple local churches offer a unique but demanding opportunity. As a theme, this tension—the need to address it and creative reflection across universal and local concerns—will be part of future theological work.

The ethical implications of this ecclesial theme will involve rethinking some basic concepts against the horizon of globalization. Like the fact of industrialization in the early twentieth century, globalization sets the secular context for much theological reflection in this century. At least three basic ideas from the social teaching need to be related systematically to this context: the state, the market, and the common good. The state remains the central unit of the decentralized international system, but it is challenged from above and below by integration and by the drive for ethnic, national, and economic freedom. Specifying the normative role, status, and limits of the state is one future task. The market has always challenged Catholic ethics; it now does so with new intensity and complexity, precisely because of its global scope and influence. Analytically, the market now poses the kind of question in power and influence that the state has traditionally posed for Catholic ethics. Finally, the changed status of the state and the market will require going beyond existing general statements in Catholic teaching about an international common good; future work will need to provide more substance and structure for this crucial idea. The global and the local, in their secular and ecclesial meaning, will frame much of the future in Catholic social teaching.

NOTES

1. The magisterial texts on social teaching for this chapter appear in David J. O'Brien and Thomas A. Shannon, eds., *Catholic Social Thought: The Documentary Heritage* (Maryknoll, N.Y.: Orbis Books, 1992). Hereafter, citation is by title of document, paragraph number, and page numbers from O'Brien and Shannon. Hence, *Gaudium et spes*, nos. 1–93, 166–237.
2. I have summarized some of this history in J. Bryan Hehir, "The Church in the World: Responding to the Call of the Council," *Marianist Award Lecture 1995* (Dayton, Ohio: University of Dayton Press, 1995).

3. Representative texts of this period are Henri deLubac, *Catholicism: A Study of the Corporate Destiny of Mankind* (New York: Sheed & Ward, 1958), and Yves Congar, *Lay People in the Church: A Study for the Theology of the Laity* (Westminster, Md.: Newman, 1957).
4. *Gaudium et spes,* no. 40, 189.
5. For extensive commentary on *Gaudium et spes,* see Herbert Vorgrimler, ed., *Commentary on the Documents of Vatican II,* vol. 5 (Freiburg, Germany: Herder, 1969).
6. *Justitio in mundo,* Introduction, 289.
7. *Gaudium et spes,* no. 43, 192.
8. Ibid., no. 42, 191.
9. The phrase seeks to give appropriate weight to the extensive social teaching of the pope, his own vigorous ministry of human rights, and his firm opposition to linkage between the church and political parties or any political role for priests and religious, as well as his less than active engagement with Christian democracy.
10. A sampling of essays that illustrate Curran's methodological emphasis includes *Catholic Moral Theology in Dialogue* (Notre Dame, Ind.: University of Notre Dame Press, 1976), 111–49; *Transition and Tradition in Moral Theology* (Notre Dame, Ind.: University of Notre Dame Press, 1979), 83–116; *Toward an American Catholic Moral Theology* (Notre Dame, Ind.: University of Notre Dame Press, 1987), 174–93; *Tensions in Moral Theology* (Notre Dame, Ind.: University of Notre Dame Press, 1988), 87–109, 110–18, 138–61, 162–82.
11. Charles Curran, *American Catholic Social Ethics: Twentieth Century Approaches* (Notre Dame, Ind.: University of Notre Dame Press, 1982), 284–86; *Critical Concerns in Moral Theology* (Notre Dame, Ind.: University of Notre Dame Press, 1984), 155.
12. Charles Curran, "Theological Reflections on the Social Mission of the Church," in *The Social Mission of the Church: A Theological Reflection,* ed. Edward J. Ryle (Washington, D.C.: Catholic University of America Press, 1972), 31.
13. Curran, *Critical Concerns in Moral Theology,* 156–57.
14. *Gaudium et spes,* no. 39, 189.
15. Ibid., no. 3, 177.
16. Curran, *Tensions in Moral Theology,* 87–109.
17. *Gaudium et spes,* no. 43, 193.
18. Both appear in O'Brien and Shannon, *Catholic Social Thought,* 492–71, and 572–860.
19. Curran, "Theological Reflections on the Social Mission of the Church," 40, 41, 49.

20. *Gaudium et spes,* no. 42, 191.
21. Curran, *Catholic Moral Theology in Dialogue,* 1–23.
22. Curran, "Theological Reflections on the Social Mission of the Church," 49.
23. Charles Curran, *The Church and Morality: An Ecumenical and Catholic Approach* (Minneapolis, Minn.: Fortress, 1993), 81–85.
24. Charles Curran, "The Catholic Identity of Catholic Institutions," *Theological Studies* 58 (1997): 90–108.
25. Curran, *Critical Concerns in Moral Theology,* 148–52; Curran, *Transition and Tradition in Moral Theology,* 120–22.
26. Curran, *Catholic Moral Theology in Dialogue,* 120–25.
27. Charles Curran, *Politics, Medicine and Christian Ethics: A Dialogue with Paul Ramsey* (Philadelphia: Fortress, 1973), 42–55.
28. Ibid., 49.
29. John Paul II, *The Splendor of Truth* (Boston: Pauline Books and Media, 1993), 110–16, and *The Gospel of Life* (Boston: Pauline Books and Media, 1995), 137*ff.*
30. Curran, *The Church and Morality,* 120–21.
31. J. Bryan Hehir, "Identity and Institutions" *Health Progress* (December 1995): 17–23.

PART IV

Dialogue

CHAPTER 11

Charles Curran: Ecumenical Moral Theologian Par Excellence

James M. Gustafson

For me to reread many of Charles Curran's publications over the past four decades is not only to recall but also to relive the halcyon years of ecumenism, particularly ecumenical Christian ethics and moral theology. Memories of profound intellectual and personal relationships are vivified: pedagogical ventures when Charles Curran and I shared the podium; scholarly meetings at which we read papers and responded to each other's work; one-on-one discussions in various hotels and in Caldwell Hall at the Catholic University of America; rare but significant correspondence; and other revered persons who frequently were assembled with us—Richard A. McCormick, S.J.; Bernard Häring; Paul Ramsey; and many, many others.

I believe Charles Curran and I had more agenda in common than I had with most of my Protestant colleagues and all of my Roman Catholic colleagues except Bernard Häring. Of course, Curran is far more learned than I in the Roman Catholic tradition and has published articles on many more different topics than I have. I gratefully acknowledge my indebtedness to him in *Protestant and Roman Catholic Ethics: Prospects for Rapprochement.*[1] There I note what has impressed me so strongly in preparation for this chapter—namely, the significant overlap in our theological and ethical interests. Both of us were always concerned with systematic theological issues in ethics, the use of scripture in moral theology, historical studies, theories of moral philosophy, practical moral issues, the relation of Christian particularity to universal morality, theological anthropology, and other topics. Clearly, however, the comprehensiveness of Curran's research and writing surpasses that of any of his contemporaries.

In the blush of ecumenical enthusiasm I once noted that I thought a point had been reached at which Roman Catholics and Protestants shared basic theological and ethical issues, and our work could be directed by those issues rather than historical confessional allegiances. Without defensiveness, we could look critically at materials from our own traditions, especially in light of the strengths of others. With appreciation, we could draw from each other's traditions to propose improvements in our own. Curran and I taught, as well as wrote, open to materials from both traditions as they pertained to the theological and ethical issues at hand; the evidence is in the teaching and publication of our students. Evidence for how much theological and ethical literature we used in common is replete in many paragraphs and many notes in both of our works.

Retrospectively, what I learned from him was broader and deeper than I was conscious of, and my public acknowledgment of that has been insufficient.

CRITERIA

Why have I chosen the title "Charles Curran: Ecumenical Moral Theologian Par Excellence"? Because I believe his work helped to shape, and in turn met, the important criteria for genuinely ecumenical work, and because the exemplary way in which he met these criteria continues to provide a model for able students and for what is needed now during a resurgence of particularistic traditions and polemics rather than irenics. Before I substantiate the title of this chapter I need to outline, at least, the criteria for ecumenical moral theology that I have in mind.

The first criterion is academic and intellectual mastery, to the best of one's ability, of the theological, ethical, and practical moral teachings and the religious and moral practices of one's own tradition. This mastery requires knowledge of historical developments, taking account of diversity and consensus, of change and continuity. It requires comprehensive knowledge of contemporary publications and of consensus as well as controverted issues. Such mastery is not simply amassing of information; it requires analytical skills. The ecumenical moral theologian has an agenda, a schema of critical questions to be addressed to the knowledge about the tradition and to its practices.

The second criterion is reasonably sufficient knowledge of the theological, ethical, and practical moral teachings and the religious and moral practices of another tradition *as they pertain to the issues in focus in one's own*. This requires historical knowledge of consensus and diversity, of change and continuity in the other tradition. It requires reasonably comprehensive knowledge of contemporary publications in the other tradition, of consensus and controverted issues in it. By "reasonably sufficient" and "reasonably comprehensive," I mean enough to use intelligently the same agenda, the same scheme of critical questions, that the moral theologian uses to analyze his or her own tradition.

Effectively meeting these first two criteria depends not only on intellectual and academic discipline but also on a capacity for empathy: a hermeneutic of appreciation that precedes, or functions concurrently with, a hermeneutic of suspicion. Defensiveness—a predisposition to man the barricades for one's ecclesial and theological community before one has approached another tradition—deters genuine ecumenical development. Empathy requires confidence and freedom: confidence that one's own and another tradition have justifiable reasons for their developments and thus should be taken seriously; freedom to be appreciative and critical of both without a sense of betrayal of one's own. In certain ecclesiastical circumstances, empathy has to be followed by courage—the strength and readiness to develop positions even if they run counter to current religious and ethical enthusiasms or to dissent from extrinsic ecclesiastical authority.

Subsequent criteria further develop aspects of the first two. The third criterion is the agenda, or schema, for critical analysis of one's own tradition. The author is in "dialogue" or interaction with diversity in her or his own tradition historically and concurrently, with other traditions as they pertain to critical matters, with philosophies and sciences as they pertain to fundamental and practical aspects of Christian ethics and moral theology. I itemize only major elements of the agenda.

- Is there historical diversity in the tradition, a pluralism of viewpoints? If so, which works seem to have become authoritative, and why? Which atrophied or were condemned, and why?
- What philosophical assumptions have supported traditional teaching? Can they be sustained in light of other philosophical positions—for example, "classical" or static philosophical perspectives in contrast with "historical" interpretations of reality, common good in contrast with individualistic interpretations of society, deontic or teleological ethical theories in contrast with relational ones?

- How has the historical matrix of particular teachings in fundamental or practical moral theology affected the tradition?
- What sources have been, and are, most definitive in determining what is included or excluded and what is most decisive in moral theology? How are various sources related to each other (e.g., scripture, natural reason, tradition, experience)?
- How have information and theories from various sciences been used in the development of moral theology? What is their function, or role, in formulating normative positions on particular moral questions? Do scientific evidences alter any traditional moral teachings? Do they open possibly perilous avenues of action?
- How do religious practices—the ecclesiastical functions—of a tradition affect the development of its theological and ethical teachings, and the conduct of its common life? For example, how has the sacrament of penance affected the theory and practice of moral theology?

The fourth criterion is the same or a similar agenda of analytical questions applied to another religious tradition or movement. The fifth is the use of a comparative method. The ecumenical moral theologian needs the intellectual skills of a comparativist. Comparisons can be made flatly by simply lining in parallel columns the teachings and practices of each tradition on fundamental and practical matters. "Catholics teach this about X; Protestants teach that about X." Such publications have limited value. For ecumenical moral theology, comparative work requires deeply penetrating analyses not only of what has been taught and lived but also of the reasons for similarities and differences. Materials from each tradition are evaluated in light of the theologian's own normative principles for an adequate moral theology—either those of a tradition or church or those he or she is willing to articulate and defend.

The outcomes of comparative work depend on various factors. A more irenic outcome will follow from the work of persons seeking to maximize commonality and the extent of beneficial impacts from each tradition. A more polemical outcome will follow from the work of those who are committed, often defensively, to the Truth of their own tradition or are concerned for any laxist or legalistic tendencies that appreciation of another tradition might sanction.

The sixth criterion is venturesomeness to propose a somewhat systematic, comprehensive, and defended interpretation of Christian ethics or moral theology—or at least some of its particular aspects—that attends to materials from more than one tradition. Such publication will be always identifiable as work primarily in one or another particular tradition: Roman Catholic, Eastern Orthodox, or Protestant. Its confessional, or traditional, identity is based not on extrinsic historical authority, however, but on the adequacy and persuasiveness of its arguments and their development—including any arguments for the authority of tradition. If the identity is Roman Catholic, it is because that tradition provides the most adequate basis for Christian ethics today. If the identity is Protestant or Eastern Orthodox, it is because those traditions are theologically and ethically adequate. If historically particular authorization is invoked, that authorization is defended theologically, not merely as social loyalty. It also will bear distinctive intellectual marks, however: the academic "signature" of its author. It might be driven by a dominating thesis that gives it a debatable coherence, or it might be more generously synthetic.

These criteria, obviously, have been shaped more by reflection on Curran's work and that of Lisa Sowle Cahill and other Roman Catholics, Stanley Harakas's work from the Eastern Orthodox tradition (conversant with other Christian traditions and contemporary moral philosophy while being governed by his tradition), and various Protestants' works than from an abstract disinterested theory of ecumenism. (A circularity is admitted: The criteria are inferred from materials prejudged to embody them!) They also have been shaped *against* writings from all traditions that disdain any empathetic appreciation of others and aggressively conduct implied or explicit polemics. They are not eternally definitive but are stated for their heuristic value in examining some of the work of Charles Curran.

CURRAN'S CONTRIBUTION

In Curran's publications, as in effective ecumenical ethics written by others, these criteria provide an integrated framework that penetrates his examination of the literature and his constructive proposals. Indeed, I have found no place in his work where he self-consciously articulates them in this way, nor do I find any place where he identifies himself as an ecumenical moral theologian. These criteria are not met in the serial fashion in which I have stated them. If the evidence to support the title of the chapter were organized in the foregoing sequence of criteria, not only would it be boring but, more important, it would trivialize Curran's achievements. Many passages from many of his books could be cited to support my thesis. I have not amassed bibliographical citations; I have selected a few articles and books I believe are representative: "Absolute Norms in Moral Theology" (1968),[2] *Catholic Moral Theology in Dialogue* (1972),[3] "A Methodological Overview of Fundamental Moral Theology" (1982),[4] and *The Catholic Moral Tradition Today: A Synthesis* (1999).[5]

"Absolute Norms in Moral Theology"

The material that Curran attends to in this article clearly meets my first criterion—mastery of the theologian's own tradition—and the analysis meets much of the agenda I itemize in my third criterion. The article is a critical exposition in the service of a normative evaluation of historical and contemporary Roman Catholic materials as they have been used with reference to the article's title. On the basis of historical evidences, contemporary Roman Catholic theological writings, a statement of the sources for moral theology (Bible, tradition, reason, and experience), and other materials, Curran argues that "Roman Catholic theology is not unalterably committed to a generic insistence on absolute norms in ethical conduct."[6] Indeed, he asserts with confidence that "[c]ontemporary Catholic moral theology can no longer be accused of legalism and negativism on a wide scale"[7]—thus reflecting a particular historical matrix of his own writing, as he goes on to demonstrate the importance of historical contexts for key aspects of traditional work.

The first major section of the article is an argument showing that historical diversity in the tradition militates against the claims that "natural law" is a single, unified theory that supports unqualified accounts of universal, absolute norms. Without, at this point, citing Bernard Lonergan (which he explicitly does in his conclusions) and others who distinguished the profoundly significant difference between the classical and the historical approaches to interpreting reality, Curran demonstrates from historical sources that "natural law" does not have a univocal usage in philosophical and theological aspects of the Western intellectual tradition. Aristotle did not explicitly formulate a natural law doctrine; for him fulfillment of the human *telos* of well-being depended more on externally favorable conditions than on an intrinsic tendency to perfection. Nor did the Stoics have a unified general theory of natural law; the morality espoused by particular members of that community approved of activities such as polygamy, incest, masturbation, homosexuality, and prostitution.

Curran's learning—his competent mastery of his tradition—is apparent in this brief historical account. A careful reading of Thomas Aquinas demonstrates that Aquinas's distinctions are based in part on Ulpian's tendency to identify natural law with biologically natural factors (e.g., that sexual union in humans and animals exists for procreation). Curran shows the importance of Cicero, Isidore of Seville, Gratian, and the Decretalists, as well as Aristotle for the classic locus of natural law in Catholic moral theology. Curran discusses Thomas's consideration of examples of behavior in biblical narratives that are not easily reconciled with claims for the universality and immutability of natural law and cites support for questioning traditionally nonhistorical, rationalistic interpretations of natural law from twentieth-century philosophers (e.g., John Courtney Murray and Yves Simon), as well as contemporary theologians. Historical analysis and argument lead to a sustained critique of a widely held belief that "natural law" is a sufficient moral theory from which inferences can be drawn to promulgate many of the moral rules that Catholics hold to be absolute.

The first section of Curran's article meets my first criterion (comprehensive knowledge of the theologian's own tradition), with an agenda for analysis that fits much of my third criterion (examination of historical diversity, critical examination of philosophical assumptions, and demonstration of the significance of historical contexts). It also meets an aspect of my sixth criterion by pointing to a normative position that is under development. The second section, which addresses the teaching authority of the church, meets other aspects of the third criterion.

The second and third sections change the primary focus of attention from history to intellectual and institutional processes. Curran's procedure again is critical exposition and evaluation in the service of a normative interest. From his concern for "[t]he possibility of change" he examines "the way in which the magisterium forms its moral teachings" and how "teaching authority functions."[8] His framework for analysis dominates this section in the way historical information dominates the first section: It focuses on what, in my itemization of the third criterion, I refer to as the sources of moral theology. In both sections Curran attends to another part of that criterion: which factors gain precedence and which are underutilized, and why. Vatican II and contemporary materials provide most of the information he uses. His normative position and critical judgment set the tone of this section more than in the first section.

Not surprisingly, the sources are sacred scripture, tradition, reason, and experience. (These four are inferred in comparable discussions by Protestant ethical analysts as well; they arise at least as much out of the subject matter of moral theology and Christian ethics as out of the scholar's construction.) The discussion of scripture as a source begins with a strong critical judgment: "Unfortunately, in the past Catholic moral theology has not had a scriptural basis and dimension."[9] Curran invokes Vatican

II as evidence of a shift toward the centrality of the Bible in all of Catholic theology. Interestingly, he does not cite Bernard Häring, but themes that Curran shares with his teacher are briefly listed: the covenant between God and humans, life in a community of salvation, faith as openness to the saving Word, and love of neighbor. Curran provides an outline of issues in the role of scripture in moral theology—matters that he attends to in great detail in other writings.

If scripture had been decentered in moral theology, tradition had been assumed to be more unified than historical analysis shows. "[H]istory teaches that the Church has changed traditional teaching on certain points."[10] Well-chosen examples are summarized: usury over the centuries, religious liberty, a defendant's right to silence, and contemporary controversy over the obligation of parents in a mixed marriage to raise children as Catholics. Here, with specific reference to tradition, the argument of the first section is invoked: "The fact that something was taught at an earlier time in the Church is not a guarantee that the same teaching holds true today."[11] The analysis sustains the article's main purpose: "to show that Roman Catholic moral theology is not unalterably committed to a generic insistence on absolute norms in ethical conduct."[12]

Reason, Curran agrees, is one of the means that the church must use "to apply the gospel message [not natural law] to present-day problems."[13] He quickly notes its limitations, however: Reason can lead to different conclusions about issues, and there are disagreements about the reasoning behind certain moral teachings. Reason plays an important part, "but reason alone is not an absolute and self-sufficient norm for the teaching Church" with reference to specific moral problems.[14]

The experience of Christian people, Curran argues, has played an important part in changing moral teachings; he cites usury and religious liberty as subjects on which it has made a demonstrable difference. Some moral theologians charge that recourse to experience as a basis for moral teaching undermines the authority of the church. Curran, however, suggests theological grounds for its greater importance from Vatican II: the interpretation of the church as the *whole* people of God and the indwelling of the Holy Spirit not only in the hierarchy but also in "all of the just. . . . The primary teacher in the Church is the Holy Spirit who speaks in many and diverse ways, one of which is the experience of Christian people."[15] This analysis is not license to individualism, however; Christians can be led astray by sinful egoism, prejudice, and their other limitations.

The second section of the article continues to fulfill my criteria for ecumenical moral theology: comprehensive knowledge of historical and contemporary literature and the capacity and agenda to analyze that material critically. Although Curran has stated his normative opinion only in general terms, the cumulative evidence of his analyses and arguments points to what is developed more fully in other places. He continues to provide arguments for the need to question many of the moral absolutes that the church has upheld.

The third section marshals evidences from a variety of sources to support its conclusion—namely, that there has been "an undue insistence on authority and absolute norms in the life of the Catholic."[16] Thus, the arguments are necessarily mixed: a critique of the manuals and the isolation of moral theology from spiritual theology and its consequent affinity with canon law; the church's hierarchical structure and reliance on law to gain adherence to its teachings ("Individual responsibility, creativity, and initiative are more important than mere conformity to an elaborate system of law")[17] compared to modern secular society; the embodiment in the church's structure of a pattern of medieval European society; the legalistic use of probabilism in church teaching rather than reliance on conscience ("Conscience must do for the twentieth-century Christian what probabilism did for the Catholic"[18] in earlier times); and the general aura of triumphalism that characterized pre–Vatican II Catholicism.

The critical analysis of ecclesiological and social/historical bases for emphasis on absolute norms in moral theology sustains the purpose of the article as a whole, as well as that of section three. It is governed, implicitly, by several items in my third criterion for an ecumenical moral theology. It constructs an account of Roman Catholic moral theology that is, at least, open to Protestant Christian ethics and theology and to more extensive comparisons by Catholics and Protestants.

The conclusion of the article states Curran's agenda for normative changes in the methodology of Roman Catholic moral theology, as well as the limits of his proposals. He has "not tried to prove that there are no absolute, universally valid norms of conduct in moral theology."[19] Instead, modestly, Curran has tried to prove that neither natural law nor the teaching authority of the church "*explain* the generic insistence on absolute moral norms in moral theology"[20] (emphasis added). The principal general support for this explanation, and what is left dominantly in the reader's mind, is the shift from "classical" to "historical" methodologies. Retrospectively, the reader recognizes that the article was written in a time of deep transition in the field and that Curran's aspiration that "the thrust in moral theology should be away from . . . such absolute norms"[21] has not been realized to the extent he predicted.

This is not an article in ecumenical moral theology per se. Only two footnotes cite Protestant sources, and there is no discussion of them in the text. Its limits probably were defined, at least in part, by the occasion of its publication: the widely discussed dispute at that time about whether "norms" or ""principles" on one hand and "context" or "situation" on the other should determine Christian moral judgments and conduct. Without naming this debate, Curran expounds the current transitions in Catholic moral theology. What a propaedeutic the article was and is, however, for interaction across traditions and confessions, for Curran and for sympathetic readers! My first and third criteria are well met, and indications of how Curran will meet my sixth are clear. Indeed, one could delineate in some detail Curran's normative position from what he makes explicit and from inferences.

This article contains much that Catholic and Protestant scholars need to know to isolate points of possible convergence, or at least mutual comparisons. It not only describes the moral theology of an earlier time and the moral theology developing at the time of its publication. It also analyzes and explains reasons for both, thus inviting a deeply penetrating comparative analysis. Curran as comparativist is not visible here; that aspect becomes most evident in *Politics, Medicine, and Christian Ethics: A Dialogue with Paul Ramsey* (a book I do not analyze in this chapter).[22]

Catholic Moral Theology in Dialogue

This volume is a collection of articles published in the very early 1970s. (An interesting and much more formidable task than I undertake in this chapter would be to infer a chronology of Curran's enlarging repertoire of sources from his writings.) The writings Curran uses in these essays come from a great variety of sources, including important contemporary Protestant sources. The development of each chapter is governed by a stated or implied question in Curran's agenda for an adequate and defensible moral theology. The concept of "dialogue" indicates that one of my criteria of an ecumenical moral theologian is being met—namely, the capacity for empathy. Genuine dialogue requires that a participant be able to put herself, as much as possible, into the perspective of the other to understand why the other holds the positions he does. Consistently in this book, Curran approaches information, concepts, and arguments beyond traditional limitations of moral theological writing in a nonpolemical way. A hermeneutic of appreciation precedes, or is concurrent with, a hermeneutic of suspicion; what can be learned from these materials usually is stated before they are criticized. Critical responses are based on a reasoned analysis of the writings alluded or responded to. There is no dogmatic statement—as one finds in "Koch/Preuss" and other manuals—that the errors of Protestantism, for example, will be demonstrated and refuted.

My analysis of this book, necessarily briefer than is desirable, focuses on several of the criteria for ecumenical moral theology in addition to the capacity for empathy. It takes the form of adducing evidence from key articles to sustain the claim of the title of my chapter.

I begin with Curran's knowledge of Protestant sources and how he uses them as he moves toward his own normative position. His project is not to inform readers about current Protestant theology and ethics; neither is it to demonstrate the diversity of Protestantism or the historical development of its ethics. Instead, correctly, he comes to the sources as they relate to crucial issues in Roman Catholic moral theology. His selection and analysis of them is governed by the agenda he believes to be appropriate for Roman Catholic moral theology. Within the limits of his purpose, he meets my second criterion.

In Curran's dialogue with humanism, for example, the question (which he addresses throughout his career) is whether there is a distinctively Christian ethic. Curran briefly but fairly summarizes some contemporary Protestant discussions of that question to frame and make precise his exposition and defense of his Roman Catholic position, including support for the view that ethics are universally human.[23] To highlight that the document of Vatican II on religious liberty is "a human and civil right" based on reason, he compares it with statements of the World Council of Churches that argue that it is "an implication of the Christian faith."[24] In an appreciative but critical way, Curran defends Catholic social ethics that are based on "natural law" by describing and analyzing Protestant views, such as the Lutheran theory of two realms and objections to it by other Protestants; liberal Protestantism's focus on realization of the Kingdom of God, with its "collapse" of the eschatological tension; and the effort of Karl Barth, Paul Lehmann, and others to base social ethics on a "Christological monism."[25] There is nothing unfair in Curran's exposition of these Protestant materials, brief as they are. The stage is set, so to speak, for a nuanced appreciation of the theological work of Karl Rahner—for example, that redemption encompasses the whole world—and for other ways in which Catholicism can relate the distinctively Christian dimension to universal morality, so that "[t]he denial of a distinctively Christian ethic is not as radical as it might first appear" but avoids "pseudo-problems" that some Protestant interpretations create.[26]

The issue of the relation of distinctively Christian ethics to universal morality has been addressed in different ways. One locus of discussion has been the use of scripture in moral theology. The dominant Protestant tendency, particularly in the past century, has been to ground ethics primarily in biblical theology—primarily in the New Testament. The authority of the moral teachings of the Bible varied; some Protestants, for example, defended pacifism, and others could apply love of neighbor to justify killing in war. Catholic moral theology, scholars generally believed, used biblical teachings to proof-text arguments made from "natural law." Curran notes, for example, differences in the interpretations of love between Anders Nygren's *Agape and Eros,* in which Christian and natural loves are opposed, and Catholic interpretations in which *agape* is continuous with and a perfection of natural human love.[27] He once wrote inclusively that "Catholic moral theology has not had a scriptural basis and dimension." In this book he further engages in a "dialogue" with the Bible.

Vatican II documents and other sources—from many western languages, I add with admiration—called for rethinking of the relations between scripture and moral theology, to which Curran and many others have made contributions. His dialogue with scripture also is dialogue with Protestant and Roman Catholic discussions of the subject—for example, those by Victor Paul Furnish and by Catholics Ceslaus Spicq and Rudolph Schnackenburg (which informed Protestant scholars of Catholic interpretations of traditionally Protestant "turf"). From his reading Curran lists several contributions of scripture to moral theology. Most fundamental to his systematic work, following Bernard Häring and (from Protestantism) H. Richard Niebuhr, is the "relationality-responsibility model" that decenters the traditional Catholic teleological model and the deontic model found in practical moral theology.[28] Other contributions include the call of all persons to growth toward perfection in response to God's call; the role of what Häring emphasized as conversion—the change of heart out of which action flows beyond minimalistic obedience to rules; the consequent emphasis on "interiority" in contrast to such exclusive emphasis on particular moral acts; and the importance of history in the biblical material.[29] Having shown his profound appreciation for aspects of the biblical witness, Curran reminds his readers of "dangers" in its use in moral theology: proof-texting arguments that really derive from other grounds, efforts to apply it too simply to complex moral and social issues, selectivity from the Bible in the systematization of its theology and ethics, and others.

The fifth essay in *Catholic Moral Theology in Dialogue,* "Dialogue with the Church: The Meaning of Coresponsibility," is especially significant for an examination of Curran's use of Protestant sources and for how he draws from both traditions to develop and defend a deep revision of moral theology. In this essay, the concept of responsibility becomes central—a centrality that continues through his publications in subsequent decades. Its growing importance, particularly in religious ethics, is outlined by a brief account of the notion of the "responsible society" as that concept was articulated in the first assembly of the World Council of Churches in Amsterdam in 1948, which drew heavily from British ecumenist J. H. Oldham. Clearly H. Richard Niebuhr's contrast between man-the-maker, man-the-citizen, and man-the-responder and his description of the greater adequacy of the latter over the teleological and deontic ethics of the first two types was very persuasive to Curran. Curran draws, in part, on the work of Albert R. Jonsen to make a strong case for affinity between Protestant sources—including Bonheoffer and Karl Barth, as well as Niebuhr—and contemporary Roman Catholic sources, especially Bernard Häring and Robert Johann.[30] This analysis is virtually what popular history of science calls a "paradigm shift" because theology, theoretical ethics, and practical ethics all are radically reoriented by the shift. The Catholic teleological model and the Catholic deontic model (in practical moral theology) lose their dominance; the relationality-responsibility model becomes central.

In his analysis of the foundations for the centrality of responsibility Curran notes the contributions of Barth's theology of the word of God, Emil Brunner's use of I-Thou symbolism, Joseph Sittler's plea for a more organic understanding of the God/human relationship, and especially Häring's powerful depiction of the dialogical structure of the Christian life.[31] Indeed, throughout the account of the foundations in which Curran discusses theological anthropology, eschatology, the "turn to the subject," and historical consciousness he builds his case for the model of responsibility with brief but careful use of Roman Catholic (e.g., Rahner and DeLubac) and Protestant theologians, as well as with ecclesial sources from both the World Council of Churches and Vatican II.[32] The essay concludes with Curran's interpretation of implications of the model of responsibility for personal and social ethics, as well as for ecclesiology.

Of Curran's work that I have addressed thus far, this essay meets most fully the sixth criterion for ecumenical moral theology. A constructive, or systematic, position attends empathetically but critically to another religious tradition than the author's own, and although it clearly is Roman Catholic it is very deeply informed by Protestant writings.

Curran's capacities as an ecumenical moral theologian, then, are further substantiated in the three essays I have cited from *Catholic Moral*

Theology in Dialogue. His selection from Protestant sources is apt with reference to the issues in his focus, and his reading of them in the light of his agenda is always accurate and fair. His agenda for each of the essays is clear; it provides access to analysis of perduring theological and ethical issues in both Catholicism and Protestantism. From his comparisons between the traditions he addresses very basic matters (e.g., the most adequate model for understanding morality), and he is not hesitant to amend his tradition where he finds a reasonable justification to do so. The gestures he makes toward a systematic view in all three of these essays are still palpably within the Roman Catholic tradition, but he does not defend them *because* they are traditional. In these dialogues he is nondefensively Roman Catholic because his critical exposition and evaluation of Catholic and Protestant materials provide the basis for development of a more adequate, especially comprehensive interpretation of Christian moral theology. The essay approximates my aspiration for Christian ethics and moral theology that are determined by the most adequate answers to the crucial questions, not by confessional loyalties.

"A Methodological Overview of Fundamental Moral Theology"

This article prefigures in major respects the structure and content of Curran's 1999 synthesis, *The Catholic Moral Tradition Today.* In my commentary on this article I attend to some of the specific references to Protestant literature; more speculatively, I infer ecumenically informed qualities from its general characteristics. If I am correct, Curran has not only *internalized* materials from scripture, historical and contemporary Catholicism, Protestantism, and currents of moral philosophy, he has *synthesized* them in a way that makes it difficult to name, number, and grade particular influences.

What I note in other of Curran's writings is here more fully elaborated, though in outline form. Very significant, in comparison with the moral theology of the manuals and with many of the best of Curran's contemporary colleagues—except Bernard Häring and to some extent Josef Fuchs—is the Christian theological context of the methodology he explicates. This context provides not only a background "stance" for what is more explicitly ethical; it also penetrates in sometimes overt and sometimes subtle ways the more restricted moral aspects of his work. More significantly, Curran is interested not only in theological ideas in relation to moral ideas but also in the qualities and characteristics of the Christian *life,* and the worship and devotion that shape and nourish it, in relation to the moral actions that express and are in accord with it.

"A Methodological Overview of Fundamental Moral Theology" is an overview of the *methodology* of *moral* theology, and that context determines its structure: stance, ethical model, anthropology, and decision making and norms, including conscience. By taking some liberties as an interpreter and commentator, one can read it differently—as an account of basic Christian beliefs derived from scripture and the theological tradition and of important aspects of the Christian life in the Christian church and community. In this interpretation, the moral theological structure of the article is the morphology of morality that is informed by these beliefs and motivated by faith and life in the church. The article becomes as much an essay on the Christian life in its moral expressions as it is an academic methodological overview of moral theology. This speculative analysis and interpretation gives the article a tone that is similar to much of the Protestant tradition in ethical writings: The primary focus is on the faith and life, as well as background beliefs, of the Christian community and its members, and the ethic describes the sorts of actions that do and should follow from that life.

The textual evidence for this interpretation is clear. "In my judgment the following areas must be investigated in any systematic reflection *on Christian moral life:* the perspective or stance, the ethical model; Christian anthropology; concrete Christian decision making and norms" (emphasis added).[33] The basic subject matter for systematic reflection is not theological and philosophical ideas in relation to moral ideas; it is not theological or metaphysical principles as the necessary conditions for morality; it is not biblical exegesis systematized by some theological concept (e.g., eschatology), which then orients ethics. The subject matter of the essay is not Christian moral *life,* it is *Christian* moral life.

More substantial evidence for this interpretation comes from the ordering of Curran's methodology—stance, ethical model, Christian anthropology, decision making, and norm—and from his development of each of these aspects. If one compares this essay with the textbooks from the manualist tradition, a prima facie case for my claim is palpable. The very idea of stance, not to mention making it the first aspect of a method, is not to be found in the manuals. There was a stance, of course, that can be inferred. Compared to Curran's caution that "it is impossible to say that one stance is right and another wrong,"[34] the stance of the manuals was of dogmatic certitude of the authority of the magisterium and the errors of Protestantism.

Curran's stance demonstrates the significance of "postethical" levels of moral discourse or, in other words, of background beliefs and loyalties that provide a larger framework of justification and orientation for ethics without being a sufficient condition for determining particular moral actions. Curran's own description states that a stance gives "a direction and general perspective to our understanding of some of the most basic issues in Christian ethics."[35] The issues he names are the meaning of human existence, the relation between this world and the Kingdom of God, the meaning of death for Christians, the interpretation of basic mysteries of the Christian life (e.g., sacramental and mystical aspects), and the Christian basis for universal morality (i.e., that all persons "share in the fullness of God's love").[36]

The fundamental beliefs that justify and shape the stance are aspects of *Christian theology*. They are not philosophical justifications for natural law; they are not claims for dogmatic authority by the church. Curran calls these beliefs "the fivefold Christian mysteries," which he develops and defends at greater length in other writings:

> Creation indicates the goodness of the human and human reason; . . . sin touches all reality, without . . . destroying the basic goodness of creation"; "[i]ncarnation integrates reality into the plan of God's kingdom"; [r]edemption as already present affects all reality, while resurrection destiny as future exists" both in continuity and discontinuity with the fullness of God's kingdom which will come at the end of time.[37]

In effect, these mysteries are a comprehensive systematic theology in outline; Curran the Christian theologian is prior to Curran the practical moral theologian.

Curran's own stance is developed in dialogue with strands of Protestant theology and contemporary Roman Catholic theology. His view of creation is defined in part against some radical Protestant denials of its goodness and against Catholic views that extricate natural law from the fuller theological context of the fivefold mysteries. Protestant liberalism in the extreme forms of the social gospel stressed the goodness of creation, the integrating effects of incarnation on reality, and the efficacy of redemption in the present world—all points akin to Curran's—but neglected the effects of sin and the future gift of resurrection destiny. Curran also differentiates his interpretation from aspects of Vatican II and Catholic liberation theologies.

Further commentary on "stance" is superfluous to substantiate my choice of title for this chapter. Not only is Curran's concept of stance and its content developed in sympathetic but critical interaction with Protestant sources, but the priority he gives to it resonates with the way many

Protestants have ordered Christian theological ethics—particularly writings from the decades before many Protestants focused so singularly on practical moral problems and borrowed their methodological arguments from moral philosophy. (Protestant Christian *theological* ethics has atrophied as detailed interest in many practical moral issues—for example, from medicine—occupy writers' attention, often making their publications look like pre–Vatican II moral theology.) In Curran's discussion of stance, as in the remainder of this article, is the outline of a comprehensive constructive, or systematic, position whose agenda is determined by issues any theological ethics must delineate and address in some way. Curran's response to those issues clearly is Roman Catholic, but it is informed by Protestantism in form and content. Several of my criteria for ecumenical moral theology are met.

I have attended to Curran's adoption of the ethical model, here called "relationality-responsibility,"[38] previously in this chapter, so I do not attend to its particular elaboration in this article.

As Curran develops the third aspect of his methodology, anthropology, like stance, is impregnated with Christian theological ideas and consideration of the Christian life. The section is "Christian anthropology," not philosophical or moral anthropology. The discussion, though alert to philosophical distinctions, does not consist of arguments about persons as rational agents with the capacities to deduce correct conduct from first principles or derivative axioms and to govern their conduct accordingly. Nor does it consist of arguments about human freedom in light of contemporary neurological, genetic, psychological, or social scientific evidences and explanations. Nor is it an explication of humans as sinners and distinctions between venial and mortal sins.

The section begins with a brief description, without getting into virtue theory, of how actions follow from the kind of persons we are and how the kind of persons we are, moral subjects, is constituted by our actions. What follows articulates dimensions of the *Christian* life, as gift and as task (akin, perhaps, to favored German Protestant terms: *Gabe und Aufgabe*). The task is a striving "to grow in wisdom, age, and grace before God and human beings,"[39] a call to continual conversion. Not only actions but also attitudes and dispositions that affect relationships—expressed traditionally as faith, hope, and charity—are enabled and required. There is no discussion, however, of the infusion of these theological virtues. Worship and thanksgiving ("the Christian is primarily a worshipper") acknowledge God as "the author of love, life and all good gifts."[40] God's giving and the human response mirror the basic structure of moral life. Christians are open and receptive to the world and the work of God. Note: They are not here first addressed as accountable for their obedience to moral precepts derived from natural law and church teachings. They can, and ought to, have humility of spirit; an attitude of hope; dispositions of love and justice toward their neighbors; and a sense of stewardship in using gifts, talents, selves, and resources.

Curran does not engage Protestant theological materials in his discussion of Christian anthropology. Indeed, the "tone" of this section resonates with the writings of Bernard Häring as he set Christian moral life in a deeply religious context and emphasized its positive characteristics more than living always in the consciousness of a temptation to commit a sinful act. According to my criteria, both Häring and Curran, whether consciously drawing from some Protestant traditions or retrieving neglected aspects of Catholicism are ecumenical moral theologians. Divine action and presence are prior to human response and action; God's enabling of the Christian life and its moral activities qualifies all traditional views of God primarily as lawgiver and judge who exacts retribution for human misdeeds. Moral theology, in very similar ways to some Protestant ethics, must avoid "legalism." In effect, that is the impulse of the fourth aspect of Curran's methodological overview.

Curran initially sets his deliberations about decision making in the context of contemporary writings in Protestant Christian ethics and moral philosophy. He notes and responds to two facets of Catholic moral theology that address the problems of conflicting judgments: "physicalism" as a basis for moral theology and the distinction between the objective moral order and the subjective. More adequately, however, he sets the sources of moral conflicts in fundamentally theological contexts: "eschatological tension" (the Kingdom has not come; we are still pilgrims living between the times); sin, which justifies some moral actions that would not be acceptable if there were no sin (e.g., killing in war); and finitude, a condition that sometimes makes it impossible to realize one proper value without diminishing another.

The section concludes with a discussion of conscience interpreted through Curran's relationality-responsibility model rather than through an older faculty metaphysics. "Conscience is grounded in the subject, who is called to respond to the gospel message in the midst of the multiple relationships of human existence and thereby live out the thrust for authentic self-transcendence."[41] This self-transcendence is not immune from moral error, however. Its actions are within the limitations of finitude and sin. The "church as a moral teacher... guided by the Spirit through various offices and charisms" helps to overcome these limitations.[42]

Curran does not enlist the support of Protestant theologians who sometimes have fulminated against "legalism" in Catholic moral theology and church life. He does not adduce Protestant sources that always remind Christians that they are *simil justus et peccator,* still sinners though justified. Nor does he claim that the church's moral teachings have overcome the fallibility that is an inevitable because of the finitude of any person or institution. In his conclusion about conscience he does not define his view specifically against Protestant writers (e.g., Paul Lehmann) who seem to have confidence that Christians can freely perceive in complicated circumstances what God is doing and thus what they should endorse by their actions. Perhaps it is only the imagination that leads to inferences of a wider religious and moral framework, at least congruent with some Protestant theological ethics, while also being very Roman Catholic.

No more than in Curran's other publications that I have selected does he authorize his position in this article as "ecumenical." Its authorization is not its ecumenical learning and tone, as if that would intrinsically make it more significant. My interpretation, however, emphasizes the priority of fundamental theology over practical moral theology. This analysis invites comparison and engagement between traditions on a different common ground from resolving disputes over particular moral teachings. My sixth criterion is met most impressively in this article. Curran has proposed a systematic, comprehensive interpretation of Christian ethics that attends to Protestant as well as Catholic materials, defines itself relative to Protestant and Catholic positions on crucial issues, and is Roman Catholic not because of the authority of tradition or the church. Instead, the argument to support his introduction is based on a variety of sources and grounds. It clearly bears Curran's academic "signature"; its aura is more irenic than polemic; it is an invitation to Christians from whatever tradition or church to be persuaded that a more adequate Christian moral theology is presented in the form and content of this article.

The Catholic Moral Tradition Today: A Synthesis

The Roman Catholic Church changed between 1968—the date of the first article cited in this chapter—and 1999, the publication date of Curran's most systematic and comprehensive version of his theological and ethical research and his constructive position. The title of the book itself seems to militate against my claims that he is an ecumenical moral theologian. The halcyon years of ecumenism are now only nostalgic memories entertained by aging theologians. To be sure, the Society of Christian Ethics and other academic professional associations enjoy full participation by persons from all major Christian traditions, and publications by some important scholars of a younger generation (many of them now middle aged) continue to merit the appellation I have given Curran. Highly visible and audible Protestant and Roman Catholic scholars and ecclesial officials have pulled from an irenic ecumenical center, however, to more distinctive emphases and radical claims for views that are closely bound to particular traditions.

In *The Catholic Moral Tradition Today,* the attention given to particular Protestant authors is greatly reduced relative to the 1972 and 1982 publications I have chosen as representative. Curran had not disengaged his thinking from dialogue; indeed, he continues to be appreciative and critical of Protestant writings. Like the authors of almost all current publications in Christian ethics, Curran orients part of his program with reference to the work of Stanley Hauerwas. Hauerwas's work "has many positives" from Curran's perspective: his critique of liberal individualism in favor of a more communitarian approach, as well as his emphases on virtue, character, and Christian community. Hauerwas's work is too exclusively Christian, however, and is addressed primarily to the church. It cannot provide a theological foundation for universal ethics. Its theological errors are failure to develop the doctrines of creation and incarnation that do provide Christian grounds for universal ethics—an ethics that engages and directs participation to improve social structures. It also "tends toward a triumphalist understanding of the Church" that is similar to pre–Vatican II theology by not fully facing the sinfulness and imperfection of the Christian community.[43]

The most profound impact of a Protestant thinker in this book, as in other writings on which I have commented, is fundamental to the synthesis: H. Richard Niebuhr's contribution of the relationality-responsibility model as the *root metaphor* of moral life, particularly of Christian moral life.[44] The unique morphology of Curran's moral theology, though certainly derived in part from the work of Bernard Häring and others, is attributed to a Protestant theologian. Like some others who appreciate but also criticize Niebuhr's work, Curran interprets it as being too passive; that is, it is more responsive to actions upon us than initiating action. Curran's development of the model is backed with biblical theological interpretation (e.g., of the character of sin), with implications of the doctrine of the Trinity and with interpretation of the divine-human relationship in the context of the doctrine of grace. Philosophically Curran adduces historical consciousness and the emphasis on the human subject to support it. Thus, he develops his own backing for the model in ways that relate it to his Catholic theology. It is striking how the relationality-responsibility model provides a fundamentally different cast and shape from the dominant tradition of Roman Catholic moral theology. Virtually every aspect of theoretical and practical moral theology is revalued and rearranged in comparison with the combination of teleological and deontological models that established the valuations and arrangements of the dominant tradition. Although the model is derived from a Protestant source, it is decisive in Curran's revision of the Catholic moral tradition.

The moral theological context that determines the particular emphases of Curran's synthesis is the resurgence of perspectives and authority that he thought in the 1968 article, for example, were fading away. Here Curran defines and articulates his perspective and particular moral positions against recent papal teachings, especially *Veritatis splendor,* and against the writings of Germain Grisez and John Finnis. Curran describes "proportionalism" sympathetically against critics who think it is a form of utilitarian consequentialism. Ferreting out whether ecumenical influences determine Curran's particular criticisms of Catholic documents, authors, and practices with whom he is "in dialogue" (though at this point he is less "in dialogue" and gives readers the outcome of years of dialogic research and writing) would require subtle inferences from specific critiques. Certainly on some issues (e.g., his defense of his interpretation of conscience and its proper function), Protestant sources are of no particular importance.

The synthesis meets the most relevant of my criteria for ecumenical moral theology. It demonstrates Curran's thorough knowledge of historical and especially contemporary writings from his own tradition. His analysis of critical issues is informed generally by the critical agenda I describe in the third criterion. The comparativist dimensions are located primarily within the perimeters of current controversies within the Catholic tradition, but they highlight the distinctive features of his own work. My sixth criterion, of course—movement toward synthesis—is the stated aim of this book.

The book is not ecumenical in the sense of claiming to be a systematic Christian ethics or moral theology that is authorized by drawing materials from more than one tradition into some new creative whole. Not only its title but also its content make it a definitely *Roman Catholic* moral theology. It is Roman Catholic not because tradition gives it a privileged theological authority, however; tradition is only one of its fallible sources. Nor does its Roman Catholic character rely on a polemical critique of, and response to, the historic and contemporary heresies of Protestantism. Curran acknowledges, as any Protestant also must, that his religious birthright and religious culture are inescapable and formative factors in his work. An accident of birth does not authorize his work, however; he is loyal to it out of conviction, and he revises it out of his concern for Christian moral life, personally and communally.

With all of its Roman Catholicism, this book and Curran's previous work, upon which it draws and which it synthesizes, is a book of ecumenical moral theology. It could not have been written as it is even in the first half of the twentieth century. It could not have been written as it is without decades of openness, particularly to Protestant thought and writing but also to many other sources from philosophy and relevant sciences. If a Protestant were to critique this book, she or he could not rely on some authority of a Protestant tradition or position—Lutheran, Anglican, Reformed, Barthian, Hauerwasian—to defend an analysis. The book is written so that the critic would have to engage the argument not as a Roman Catholic argument but as an argument in support of positions on the major issues that any comprehensive and systematic Christian theology and Christian ethics must address.

The book, like most of Curran's work, is addressed not primarily to other scholars, to gain attention within a narrow group of persons who write ethics for other scholars of ethics, but to the church—to Christians. Like his other work, this book is a reflection on *Christian moral life* and only about historical or contemporary arguments between scholars as they pertain to his religious moral vocation. Moral theology is an intellectually demanding practical discipline. Its efficacy is finally in Christian life and practice. Curran correctly addresses the Roman Catholic Church and its communicants. The way he addresses them, however, is not narrowly Catholic in temper, intention, or ideas.

CONCLUSION

I rest the case for my characterization of Charles Curran as an ecumenical moral theologian par excellence. He meets my criteria for that appellation as effectively as any Protestant or Roman Catholic I can name. I rest my case on the basis of the evidence of his empathetic, but critical, interpretation of Protestant writings and his absorption and revised use of them where they pertain to issues that are common to all Christian ethics. I rest my case on my interpretation of his work as appropriately informed by the Roman Catholic tradition and oriented toward the life of the Roman Catholic Church—its full membership, not only its hierarchy—but as inexplicable without his decades of ecumenical dialogue.

NOTES

1. James M. Gustafson, *Protestant and Roman Catholic Ethics: Prospects for Rapprochement* (Chicago: University of Chicago Press, 1978).
2. Charles E. Curran, "Absolute Norms in Moral Theology," in *Norm and Context in Christian Ethics,* ed. Gene H. Outka and Paul Ramsey (New York: Charles Scribner's Sons, 1968). 139–73.
3. Charles E. Curran, *Catholic Moral Theology in Dialogue* (Notre Dame, Ind.: Fides, 1972).
4. Charles E. Curran, "A Methodological Overview of Fundamental Moral Theology," in *Moral Theology: A Continuing Journey* (Notre Dame, Ind.: University of Notre Dame Press, 1982), 35–61.
5. Charles E. Curran, *The Catholic Moral Tradition Today: A Synthesis* (Washington, D.C.: Georgetown University Press, 1999).
6. Curran, "Absolute Norms,"140.
7. Ibid., 139.
8. Ibid., 152.
9. Ibid.
10. Ibid., 153.
11. Ibid., 156.
12. Ibid., 140.
13. Ibid., 156.
14. Ibid.
15. Ibid., 159.
16. Ibid., 160.
17. Ibid., 162.
18. Ibid., 163.
19. Ibid., 172.
20. Ibid.
21. Ibid., 173.
22. Charles E. Curran, *Politics, Medicine, and Christian Ethics: A Dialogue with Paul Ramsey* (Philadelphia: Fortress, 1973).
23. Curran, *Catholic Moral Theology in Dialogue,* 3–4.
24. Ibid., 7–9.
25. Ibid., 11–14.
26. Ibid., 23.
27. Ibid., 26.

28. Ibid., 28–32.
29. Ibid., 32–36.
30. Ibid., 151–56.
31. Ibid., 158–59.
32. Ibid., 157–72.
33. Curran, "Methodological Overview," 37.
34. Ibid., 38.
35. Ibid., 42.
36. Ibid., 42–43.
37. Ibid., 42.
38. Ibid., 44.
39. Ibid., 48.
40. Ibid., 49.
41. Ibid., 56.
42. Ibid., 57.
43. Curran, *Catholic Moral Tradition Today,* 47.
44. Ibid., 73–83, 118–30, 146–49, and virtually *et passim.*

CHAPTER 12

Curran's Fundamental Moral Theology in Comparison with European Catholic Approaches

Raphael Gallagher, CSSR

The manual tradition rarely used the term *fundamental moral theology*, though American moralist Thomas J. Bouquillon used it more than 100 years ago.[1] In part this nonusage is because of the inherent weakness of Bouquillon's neoscholastic methodology, but the more rounded explanation includes the fact that the manualists were more comfortable with a division of their material into what was general and what was special. General moral theology considered notions that were common to all morality, whereas special moral theology focused on precepts, practice of the virtues, sins, and commandments.

This division suited the formal objective, methodology, and sources of the manual: adequate preparation of future priests for the proper administration of the sacrament of confession in accordance with canonical prescriptions. Thus, general moral theology presented the theory of morality in its basic categories, which later would be applied in special questions.

With the collapse of the manuals—broadly coincident with the start of Charles E. Curran's teaching career—general moral theology becomes almost universally known as fundamental moral theology. The new terminology was accepted with a stunning rapidity but, in hindsight, with curious naiveté. Given the uncertainty about the meaning of moral theology from about 1965 onward, adding the adjective *fundamental* could hardly have clarified matters. There is a gap between calling something "general" and then, quite suddenly, "fundamental."

It is not surprising that the literature on fundamental moral theology in the forty-year period of the first reception of Vatican II is marked by confusion and contradiction.[2] Thus, the period of Curran's writing on the matter is part of a theological category's search for a precise meaning. In this chapter I first present some views from a European perspective, followed by Curran's own search to see if, forty years on, the matter is any clearer.

STATE OF THE QUESTION: EUROPEAN CATHOLIC APPROACHES

Some precisions are necessary. I use "European" in the narrow sense of Western Europe, with the minor exception of a Polish theologian writing in Italian. I use "Catholic" in the denominational sense of Roman Catholics of the Latin rite. "Approaches" refers to a fluid combination that covers the methodology, epistemology, and gnoseology of the material under consideration. The purpose of the research is to discover how European authors conceive moral theology and, consequent to this, what is their understanding of fundamental moral theology. I have chosen as primary sources books rather than articles from the period 1987 onward.[3] This choice facilitates a more like-to-like comparison with Curran's mature thought as it emerges.

Return of the Textbook

Pedagogically, the reappearance of textbooks is hardly a surprise after the piecemeal teaching that dominated too much in the 1970s. More surprising is the diversity offered. I judge this diversity to be linked to authors' interpretation of the 1993 encyclical *Veritatis splendor* (*VS*), a magisterial document whose publication had been heralded six years previously.[4] The interpretative weight given to *VS* after 1994 clearly divides the textbooks, and the approach toward the impending document indicates the typology of the pre-1994 books.

Ramón García de Haro is explicit.[5] The crisis of fundamental moral theology has a double causality: the casuist heritage and contemporary theological confusion. The solution must logically eradicate the causes. Moral theology is to have a precise object: the operative principles and actions that lead people to their final supernatural end, which is union with the One and Triune God through a progressive divinization in the world. With this definition, García de Haro presumes to give a foundation to the moral life, nourished by scripture and tradition. Strict adherence to the magisterium is decisive in the project of eradicating the twin causes of moral theology's troubles.[6]

Aurelio Fernandez[7] likewise sees a double root-cause for the current crisis in terms of contemporary confusion and the casuist heritage. This analysis shapes his definition of moral theology as that part of theology that studies human acts, in light of revelation, insofar as they are directed to God as our final end. Consequently, fundamental moral theology specifies the nature of the human act, its foundation, and the conditions within which it becomes moral.[8] Fernandez' textbook is explicitly written for priests, in their triple function as preachers, teachers, and confessors. Despite a formal structure that evokes aspects of Vatican II, the focus on the analysis of the act clearly is with a view to the classification of sins, given in extraordinary detail in what is symbolically the last chapter. Acknowledging that his book is necessarily provisional, Fernandez nonetheless is clear on where stability eventually is going to come from: the magisterium.[9]

Jean-Louis Bruguès's slim volume,[10] though using the terminology "general moral theology," clearly is a text on fundamentals. He too starts with a precomprehension of the crisis of morality, but in a slightly different key from García de Haro and Fernandez. Bruguès is more concerned with the effect of the cultural upheavals of 1968 and their repercussions for morality. This attitude reflects his French sensitivity. His definition of fundamental moral theology is lapidary,[11] in tone with the rest of the book. Notable, however, is his nuanced approach to the gradation of Vatican II texts—though in the final analysis he too regards *VS* as the defining text, along with the *Catechism of the Catholic Church.*[12]

José Román Flecha Andrès[13] nuances his approach by writing on fundamental moral theology, again for students, using a novel distinction. The first part treats the foundations of Christian ethics; the second expounds the basic categories that are applicable in special ethics. Perhaps this approach simply reflects a modest unease about what *fundamental* means when it is placed before moral theology. His understanding of fundamental moral theology is broader than that of García de Haro, Fernandez, and Bruguès, probably because of his more comprehensive understanding of anthropology. Nonetheless, Andrès is explicit in regarding *VS* as the defining text for the anthropological interpretation of the questions posed in his double-level analysis.[14] Also didactic in approach is the textbook of Cataldo Zuccaro,[15] though here, too, one notes a more irenic approach towards *VS*. Zuccaro considers fundamental moral theology in terms of a discourse on questions of conscience that are inherent to the journey of faith. There is a culture-conscious sensitivity in which this Italian author regards fundamental moral theology as part of the *cammino* of the faith of a pilgrim. Framing the question can be as important as shouting down the answer in such a scenario. Nonetheless, the importance of *VS* as a key dialogue partner is emphasized.[16]

The influence of *VS* is less explicit in the final two textbooks I consider, though the explanation is different for each. Helmut Weber defines moral theology as the part of theology that treats the problem of human ethics in its widest sense.[17] Weber is acutely aware of the complexity of the debates; his aim is to provide students with the minimal information necessary for a fundamental approach to moral theology. He is eager to use accessible language—not always a notable trait among German authors. His approach is decidedly theological, conscious of tradition, within an ecclesial and biblical context. He also is outside a type of German norm in his refusal to impose a strict system on the inherently complex issues of fundamental moral theology. Because of the date of publication, *VS* is integrated rather than used as a starting point. Another source confirms that Weber's likely approach to *VS* is to take it with seriousness but not as the cornerstone of a system.[18]

Giuseppe Angelini certainly is aware of *VS*, but it is not central to his textbook project.[19] His aim is to introduce first-level students to the basic concepts of fundamental moral theology, using a notably phenomenological methodology. He is less concerned with past polemics than with the new questions that are the hermeneutical key to his interpretation of scripture, tradition, and the raw material of life, so it is hardly a surprise that *VS* is not a core in the structure of his book. Angelini's concerns for the theoretical foundations of moral theology emerge from a different set of presuppositions than those in *VS*. It may be significant that Angelini has written extensively on historical aspects of moral theology.

Attempting a Global Synthesis

For another three books, though they could be used as textbooks I would identify their authors as offering their fundamental moral theology in another genre, broadly analogous to the *summa* tradition. The three are Spanish but have little else in common regarding the formal nature of moral theology or the methodology of its fundamental aspects. I speculate later on why these differences have emerged.

Enrique Colom and Angel Rodríguez Luño[20] follow an apparently Thomistic framework, but with a presupposition that radically influences the overall synthesis. The person's ultimate end is presented as sanctity according to a definite model.[21] Flowing from this view, which obviously influences the definition of moral theology, one develops a virtuous life that enables one to enter the *filii in Filio* by following the road of the imitation of Christ.[22] This is a high ideal: The moral life is quasi-subsumed into the spiritual life, using some texts of Vatican II to justify this particular interpretation of a presumed Thomistic line.

Marco Vidal's contrasting *summa* is shaped by different recomprehensions.[23] The Notification of the Congregation of the Doctrine of the Faith with respect to Vidal[24] does not refer to this work, though the date of publication of Vidal's book (October 2000) was at an advanced stage of the process of investigation. One can only presume that Vidal, while writing, was aware of the concerns being expressed in curial circles. Vidal's synthesis is "new" in that he no longer follows the negative-dialectic method of an earlier work on the topic. He opts for a synthesis that is closer to the theological circularity of *Gaudium et spes* and consciously tries to avoid problems associated with the "older" debates, such as those on the ethics of faith and the autonomy of ethics, because he now regards these issues as outdated. His *summa* revolves around an effort to ground moral theology in a solid anthropology that is rooted in an explicitly theological horizon.[25] Vidal has long been aware of this type of *lacuna* in his work (and was so reminded by Bernard Häring twenty years ago).[26] Vidal's conception of moral theology is developed within a pastoral focus, and his presentation of fundamental moral theology is intended to ground this pastorality in the manner already indicated.

The work of Eduardo López Azpitarte,[27] which was written before either of the foregoing works, could be regarded as an effort to avoid later divisions by offering a mediating position between Colom and Rodríguez Luño on one hand and Vidal on the other. Azpitarte acknowledges that we are at a time of plurality, which he judges in a positive light but that nonetheless forces the moral theologian not only to explain how one can be moral but why. The basis for proposing a moral life lived in faith is the axis on which the synthesis revolves. Notable is the effort to synthesize apparently contradictory questions, such as reason and revelation, the gnoseological and axiological qualities of morality, law and conscience, and freedom of choice and fundamental option. Though Azpitarte's *summa* is not as complete as that by Colom and Rodríguez Luño or that by Vidal, its nonpolemical tone leaves one freer to ponder the implications of questions.

One can only speculate about why these attempts at a global synthesis emerge from the Spanish world. My suggestion is that the strong sense in Spain that a "new" formulation of moral theology was needed had a widespread echo. One need not agree with the thesis of Vicente Gómez

Mier[28] of a paradigm shift provoking an epistemological revolution, first on the form and later on the content of (fundamental) moral theology. I have previously expressed reservations about the methodology of the use of a disciplinary scientific matrix and paradigm language in Gómez Mier's explanation of the changes in moral theology.[29] Yet his question arises from within a culture (here Spanish) that was more aware than others that the old manuals no longer sufficed. Although I detect a broad consensus on the need for a new synthesis within this culture, it is hardly surprising that opposite ones have been presented because the appetite for the "new" arises from different presuppositions. Where there are strong opposites, it is natural that one author or another will seek the middle ground.

Retrieval of Traditions and the Hermeneutics of Communication

Not all European moralists have taken the route of the textbook or synthesis to present their fundamental moral theology. A significant group has taken a *prise de position* as indicative of other options. Strong contrasts emerge by the nature of these options. Equity demands that an overall picture be offered that remains as close as possible to the authors' positions. Two broad categories are operative here: One group of authors is concerned with the retrieval of traditions, the other group with the hermeneutic of communication.

Servais Pinckaers[30] offers a guide of notable substance for theology students so that they can rediscover the sources that will provide a framework of basic criteria in moral judgments through a retrieval of what Pinckaers considers the original position of St. Thomas. This attitude is clear in Pinckaers's definition of Christian ethics (the term he prefers to moral theology) that he offers in contrast to other prevailing opinions.[31] The core of Pinckaers's retrieval project is the connaturality between the person and the good, as expressed in *VS* 64: He believes this connaturality became eclipsed in moral theology as a result of the malign influence of casuistry.[32] With this basic retrieval, Pinckaers proposes a recovery of St. Thomas through the sources that shaped his thought. This proposal, in turn, colors the three determining contexts for moral theology: the relationships between scripture and ethics in the first place, followed by those between Christian ethics, the life sciences, and anthropology. Pinckaers rejects even a hint of a return to casuistry, or a nonnormative epistemology akin to the sciences, or any ignoring of the importance of the natural inclinations. His project should be considered in light of a positive goal, which is that Christian ethics "... must convey a systematic overview of its field, provide basic criteria of judgment and come to terms with the entire domain of human activity."[33] St. Thomas is the core text for the retrieval; scripture, the Holy Spirit, the Gospel Law, and natural law rooted in freedom are the deeper sources to which the text will lead us.

Also broadly Thomistic in its retrieval emphasis is the work of Edward Kaczyński.[34] The inspiration is Thomistic in the sense of the rational tradition of theological reflection, though one should note the ample attention Kaczyński gives to Karol Wojtyla as professor and pope. Kaczyński's major preoccupation is to arrive at a precise meaning of what the foundation of morality means. Because of what he considers the unacceptable diversity of positions on the foundation of morality and on what precise reality is being founded, there is too much "disorder" in moral theology. For Kaczyński the foundation question is linked to two aspects: the moral order and the consideration of moral acts as good or bad. Only a retrieval of St. Thomas, in the line indicated above and in strict conformity with *VS,* is capable of restoring order to morality, in Kaczyński's view.[35]

The project of Livio Melina is a cognate one.[36] Here the central issue is presented as the truth about the good. Practical moral knowledge is the means to achieve this, but Melina insists, correctly, that this knowledge is of a particular type. The lines of Melina's retrieval lead one, again, to St. Thomas, though this time in the specific sense of the *Secunda Pars* of the *Summa Theologiae.* To be noted in the process of retrieval is the crucial role given to *VS* and to *Fides et ratio.* Other sources establish that Melina believes such an approach leads to a coherent moral theology, including its fundamental aspect.[37]

Notably different from the foregoing is the concern of a group of authors to establish a hermeneutical approach to moral theology that is capable of a communicative conversation with the world. The book edited by Bernard Hoose[38] might seem at first like part of the retrieval project, though certainly not of a Thomistic ilk. Given that the purpose of the book is to introduce students to the main issues in Christian ethics, however, it is better to interpret this work as a presentation of fundamental themes of Christian ethics that can have "credibility" and "communicability" in a pluralistic society.[39] A central element in the project of Josef Römelt certainly is the use of the hermeneutical horizon to explain how responsibility functions as the primary category of ethics in a technical democratic society (with an emphasis on Germany).[40] Responsibility is the organizing category because of the deep issues raised by theories of hermeneutics and communication.

Such issues are most obvious in the work edited by Jean-Pierre Wils and Dietmar Mieth.[41] Their concern is that the Roman Catholic moral tradition risks the marginalization of a self-imposed ghetto. As a consequence, all of the contributions to this work emphasize a dialogue with current philosophers and social scientists; ultimately, these thinkers will be decisive for the credibility and survival of Christian ethics. The actuality of a tradition is what matters, not its mere theological retrieval. This explains why many of the discourse partners in this book are nonecclesial.

CURRAN'S FUNDAMENTAL MORAL THEOLOGY

Given the time span and the number of primary sources—thirteen books between 1966 and 2000—a research method for interpreting Charles E. Curran's fundamental moral theology must be posited. I have worked with the following hypothesis: Curran has developed a theory of moral theology, with a corresponding fundamental grounding, from within the Catholic tradition, in dialogue with varying contemporary partners, and with a notable sensitivity to historical development in theology and the changed consciousness of what being human now means.

Catholic tradition—or, more accurately, traditions—shaped Curran's initial understanding of the topic.[42] It is remarkable how the material range of the topics of those traditions (human acts, moral acts, ultimate end, law, conscience, sin, and virtue) retained their fascination for Curran. Although his most recent position represents a different formal interpretation of these elements, we can understand this position only in light of the original position from which his questioning arises.

Early Indicators

By 1966 Curran was exploring the need for a reformulation of the manuals' fundamental moral theology.[43] Renewal is the key hermeneutical term. Given that Vatican II had ended only a year previously, it is not surprising that Curran proposes the broadest of scaffoldings without a notable analytic precision. Already, however, there are three elements that later emerge as decisive: the need for historical research, an emphasis on the resurrection, and a relational concept of personality. Curran sharpens the argument two years later.[44] He clearly is still working within the parameters of his formative tradition(s), as the analysis of law, act, norms, and sin suggests. Advancing his 1966 emphasis on two points—an insistence on a historically conscious methodology and greater explicitness of what relational personality means—Curran uses the idea of responsibility as the central axis. That he is concerned with the defects of the tradition(s)[45] confirms two points: He regards his project of fundamental moral theology as advancing tradition and as offering corrective categories.

The turbulence of the post-1968 years had a marked influence on Curran's next significant reflection on our topic.[46] His personal experiences[47] were forcing him to further refine some underpinning aspects of the manuals, such as the objective/subjective distinction and the explanation of natural law. Curran proposes four contexts to organize the emerging questions: the dialogue between Christian and non-Christian, changing methodology within moral theology, rethinking of theological theory, and the specifically Catholic aspect of moral theology.

We clearly are at an interim expression of Curran's thought. He expresses uncertainty about the possibility of a synthesis, yet he paradoxically expresses the hope for such a synthesis.[48] The new contexts clearly are refining his sense of tradition by defining the stance from which he views tradition. Though the word's precise meaning is unclear, the introduction of a "stance," consequent on the new contexts, marks an important point because it identifies the fivefold Christian mysteries approach (creation, incarnation, sin, redemption, and resurrection) that, from this point, becomes central to Curran's evolving fundamental moral theology.

An Emerging Formulation

We can identify a consolidation of Curran's thinking by 1977.[49] Still notable is the material similarity of topics in the general moral theology of the manuals and the use of the word "themes" in the title. Distinctive, however, is how Curran takes the traditional divisions (themes) and tries to reinterpret them by recontextualizing them. Law—whether natural, church, or positive—is accepted as a category of fundamental moral theology, but only if primacy is given respectively to the person of Christ, a People of God ecclesiology, and a rational rather than voluntarist approach to morality. Sin is given a prominent realism, but it must be interpreted through the theological category of love rather than through a neoscholastic analysis of individual acts. Conscience clearly is important, though again there is a nuance: The formative and dynamic innate role of conscience has greater weight than the *a posteriori* judgmental function.

Tentatively, Curran is moving toward a theory, though he still refuses to call his project a synthesis.[50] This emerging theory centers on the moral model within which Curran places the discourse. Curran's preferred model, relationality, is explained in terms of the two rejected models: deontology and teleology. The proposal of a "stance" in 1975 now moves a stage further in the elaboration of Curran's fundamental moral theology through the introduction of a "model" that has very specific consequences.[51]

A mature presentation of the middle phase of Curran's development can be identified in several chapters of a book published in 1982: *Moral Theology: A Continuing Journey.*[52] Stance and model are advanced with greater analytic clarity because Curran now regards the question of anthropology as entirely central. No longer simply balancing the deficiencies of the manuals, Curran is offering a more original position. This approach is obvious in his description of moral theology as a systematic discipline, within the church but with a precise service to the academic community as well. Curran, now adding the Christian anthropological dimension, has significantly sharpened his thought on our topic.[53] Two chapters of a work published in 1984 confirm this development.[54] These chapters illustrate an important trait of Curran's methodology: his willingness to dialogue with others who are working on the same questions (here, Bernard Häring, Timothy O'Connell, Daniel Maguire, Enda McDonagh, and Franz Böckle). While seeking what is good in others' views, Curran takes his distance when he is not convinced by the argument. For our purposes, what is important from these dialogues is how Curran clarifies his own position on moral theology: "Moral theology or Christian ethics is a thematic, reflexive, second-order discourse which studies the way in which the Christian life should be lived."[55]

Also notable is how the increasing emphasis on anthropology is taking on an even clearer Christian aspect.[56] The impression of a theologian reaching a surer level in his methodology is strengthened in 1986.[57] This is more than an updating of the 1977 work; the inclusion of new elements advances Curran's fundamental moral theology on two points. It is clearer how the stance works because it "serves as the first logical consideration in moral theology and is a standard or criterion"[58] Furthermore, the elements of the stance show how Curran favors an inclusive methodology; only such inclusivity is truly a criterion of substance in fundamental moral theology because stance "serves as the starting point of moral theology by forming the perspective"[59] More strikingly, this work advances Curran's anthropology by showing how the problem of the person, as subject and agent, is best solved in a Christological framework. No longer simply affirming his case, Curran cogently argues through a substantial Christological reflection that the anthropological problem is solved "in Christ." His sharp critique of those who use a Christology of the preexisting *logos* type serves as an introduction to a critique of a moral approach that is private, extrinsic, and abstract. Curran is interested in the soteriological implication of Christian morality, not its presentation in an abstractly formal system.[60] Three elements of Curran's fundamental moral theology are now in place: the fundamental stance, the operational model, and the preferred Christological anthropology.

Emergence of a Synthesis

Broadly coinciding with a new academic setting for Curran is the slow emergence of a synthesis that includes but also expands those elements. Curran repeats his mediation typology (scripture *and* tradition, faith *and* reason, nature *and* grace, etc.) that he regards as quintessentially Catholic. Never renouncing the primary ecclesial context of theology, he now begins to integrate more explicitly other contexts—such as social, ecumenical, and academic ones—with the result that an important nuance is added to the unfinished task of fundamental moral theology. If there are different contexts, it is not surprising that Curran turns his attention to two questions: the sources of morality and the different levels of morality.[61] Other contexts provoke an examination of varying sources and gradation of questions, though Curran does not renounce the primacy of the presuppositions of the Catholic context, which retains a central importance.

Consistent with an emphasis noted in his first work, Curran edges toward his synthesis through the route of historical research.[62] He is clear that the nature of the change at Vatican II is essentially *historical*, and no restorationist efforts will reverse this seismic change. History shows that there are legitimately different approaches within the manualist tradition (virtues, principles, casuistry). Not yet showing his preference, however, Curran proposes a definition that has clear consequences for our study: "Catholic moral theology involves the systematic, thematic and critical scientific reflection on the Christian moral life from the Roman Catholic perspective."[63]

If there are established different approaches, what are the consequences for fundamental moral theology? This is a major preoccupation of Curran's 1997 book, *The Origins of Moral Theology in the United States: Three Different Approaches*.[64] Curran establishes that in the United States of the nineteenth century there were three different approaches to fundamental moral theology. Aloysius Sabetti, writing a manual for seminarians as future confessors, follows the schema that Curran had rejected since 1966. Despite Curran's obvious attraction to the person of the *simpatico* Sabetti, it is hardly surprising that, again, Curran exposes the shortcomings of a legal model of morality that centers on isolated acts and is fascinated by sin. This approach is not moral theology, and it cannot yield anything about what is fundamental to such discourse.

The problem posed by the study of Thomas J. Bouquillon is different because he actually wrote on *fundamental* moral theology. Bouquillon's approach to our topic has little appeal for Curran, however, because of its ultimately legalistic framework, neoscholastic formulation, and problematic sources—especially the reliance on Francisco Suarez. Curran's clear preference is for the fundamental moral theology implied in John Hogan's writings because of Hogan's greater historical consciousness and refusal to accept an extrinsic and legal categorization of sin. Curran has found a key to retrieve a lost tradition and is now ready to express his own synthesis.[65]

At one level, this 1999 book is a reprise of the development I have noted: the primary ecclesial context; the central roles of stance and model; and the importance of person, virtues, principles, and conscience. The rejection of the manualist system that Curran tried to balance by corrective actions in 1966 is total. It is appropriate to leave the expression in Curran's own words:

> Moral theology seeks systematic and thematic understanding of the Christian moral life. . . . Moral theology (is) a second-order discourse that stands back from the lived reality. . . . This synthesis of Catholic moral tradition is analogous to fundamental moral theology. Fundamental moral theology deals with aspects of morality that are common to all instances of moral living. . . .[66]

Curran rests his case on these definitions; I find no substantial modification of them in his latest work.[67]

THE FUTURE OF FUNDAMENTAL MORAL THEOLOGY

I am aware of having taken a partial division of fundamental moral theology in Europe.[68] The choice was dictated by attempting to have a like-to-like typology between Curran and his European colleagues so that the basis for a future projection would be more homogenous. The fact that Curran pays more attention to European moral theologians than they devote to him is an important factor. Curran is too easily dismissed by many European colleagues. There are obvious ecclesiastical explanations for this rejection. More important may be an underlying factor: the difference between the Roman conception of law and the American tradition of legal pragmatism. The former is not always well understood by Curran; the latter is too easily dismissed by Europeans who fail to see in this tradition the positive characteristic of practical knowledge that underpins it.

The major strengths of Curran's position from which Europeans could learn are the soteriological Christology, the understanding of the progressive developmental nature of history, and the validity of a plurality of methods in moral theology. From some Europeans, in turn, Curran could learn to pay greater attention to hermeneutics, have a more philosophically rounded anthropology, and give more attention to the analytic aspects of questions rather than the synthetic aspects. Curran and the Europeans share a major common weakness: lack of attention to more recent studies on the interpretation of the texts of Vatican II. This problem is a matter of capital importance. Too often, European moral theologians quote *Optatam totius* 16 as a sort of mantra; others, such as Curran, refer generically to following the methodology of *Gaudium et spes*. The lack of accurate textual criticism is hindering the debate on fundamental moral theology. *Optatam totius,* for instance, was written with a view to the training of priests, whereas *Gaudium et spes* had a different finality. Such nuances should not be ignored.

Having tried to follow Curran's lifelong probings on fundamental moral theology, and having placed them in contrast with European research, the future of fundamental moral theology is not at all clear. Two crucial factors are to be noted. Curran himself acknowledges that what he has reached is *analogous* to fundamental moral theology. The dominant Europeans who show greater certitude that they know what is fundamental moral theology base their conclusions on textual readings of St. Thomas, often via *VS,* that lack an understanding of the variety and complexity of Thomistic traditions.

My conclusion, consequently, may be surprising. The term *fundamental moral theology* no longer seems correct to me. Curran strove mightily to transfer the general moral of the manuals to a fundamental moral, but even he acknowledges that his result is only an analogy. The dominant Europeans, by creating a formal system, seem to be unaware of the problem caused by the diversity of discourse in areas such as bioethics, business ethics, or social ethics. The terminology *a systematic foundation for Christian morality* may now be more accurate. Through such a discourse, the basic issues treated by Curran and the Europeans could be revisited and seen as if for the first time.

NOTES

1. Thomas J. Bouquillon, *Institutiones theologiae moralis fundamentalis* (Bruges, Belgium: Beyaert-Defoort, 1873).

2. I have chronicled part of this in Raphael Gallagher, "Fundamental Moral Theology, 1975–1979: A Bulletin-Analysis of Some Significant Writings Examined from a Methodological Stance," *Studia Moralia* 18 (1980): 147–92.
3. These clarifications are important. I make no claim to provide a thorough review of the authors considered; I hope merely to be faithful to their core insights on fundamental moral theology.
4. In the Apostolic Letter *Spiritus Domini* (1 August 1987), *AAS* 79 (1987): 1374.
5. Eugenio Cóferes Merino and Ramón García de Haro, *Teología Moral Fundamental* (Pamplona: EUNSA, 1998). I refer to the book as García de Haro's because it was edited after his death without substantially changing an earlier work on the topic.
6. Ibid., 30–34.
7. Aurelio Fernandez, *Teologia Moral: I—Moral Fundamental* (Burgos, Spain: Aldecoa, 1995).
8. Ibid., 93.
9. Writing in the prologue, he states, "Este Magistero tan solenne che reiterado constituye un buen punto de referencia para la exposición de la moral catolica."
10. Jean-Louis Bruguès, *Précis de théologie générale* (Paris: Mame, 1994).
11. "La théologie morale fondamentale s'attache à repérer les fondements de l'agir de l'homme." Ibid., 15.
12. Succinctly argued at ibid., 159–65.
13. José Román Flecha Andrés, *Teología moral fundamental* (Madrid: BAC, 1994).
14. Clearly and directly affirmed in the Presentación, ibid. xv.
15. Cataldo Zuccaro, *Morale Fondamentale* (Bologna, Italy: EDB, 1995).
16. The references to *VS* are discretely introduced into what is a reissue of the first edition of 1993.
17. Helmut Weber, *Teologia Morale Generale* (Milan, Italy: San Paolo, 1996), at 13.
18. See Helmut Weber, *Lehramt der Kirche—Fragen der Moral* (Freiburg, Germany: Johannes, 1998), for an example of the author's irenically respectful approach to the magisterium.
19. Giuseppe Angelini, *Teologia Morale Fondamentale* (Milan, Italy: Glossa, 1999).
20. Enrique Colom and Angel Rodríguez Luño, *Scelti in Cristo per essere santi: Elementi di teologia morale fondamentale* (Roma: Apollinare, 1999).
21. The writings of and studies on Blessed José María Escrivá de Balaguer are evident throughout.
22. The idea of *filii in Filio* was given its first modern development by Emile Mersch in the 1940s.

23. Marciano Vidal, *Nueva Moral Fundamental. El hogar teológico de la Ética* (Bilbao, Spain: Desclée de Brouwer, 2000).

24. The official Italian text is in *L'Osservatore Romano,* May 16, 2001, 6–7.

25. Marciano Vidal, "Por qué he escrito una 'Nueva' Moral Fundamental," *Moralia* 23 (2000): 513–26.

26. See his review of Vidal's *Moral de Actitudes, vol. I,* in *Studia Moralia* 20 (1982): 356–59.

27. Eduardo López Azpitarte, *Fundamentación de la ética cristiana* (Madrid: Paulinas, 1991).

28. Vicente Gómez Mier, *La refundación de la moral catolica—el cambio de matriz disciplinar después del Concilio Vaticano II* (Navarre, Spain: Verbo Divino, 1995).

29. See my review of Gómez Mier, *La refundación de la moral catolica,* in *Studia Moralia* 35 (1997): 521–23.

30. Servais Pinckaers, *The Sources of Christian Ethics* (Edinburgh: T & T Clark, 1995).

31. Ibid., 8.

32. I have already noted a widespread European negativity toward casuistry. Although no sane theologian would want to return to a syllogistic casuistry, it is not clear to me that a whole period of history can be so easily written off because of its "excesses" and in view of some "purer" form of moral theology for today. It is curious how little attention European moral theologians have taken of outstanding works from the United States that have helped to replace the casuist tradition in a positive context—for example, Albert R. Jonsen and Stephen Toulmin, *The Abuse of Casuistry. A History of Moral Reasoning* (Berkeley: University of California Press, 1988), and James F. Keenan and Thomas A. Shannon, eds., *The Context of Casuistry* (Washington, D.C.: Georgetown University Press, 1995).

33. Pinckaers, *Sources of Christian Ethics,* xvii.

34. Edward Kaczyński, *"Verità sul Bene" nella morale: Alcuni temi di morale fondamentale* (Rome: Millennium, 1998).

35. Ibid., 33–57.

36. From many works I would signal the recently translated Livio Melina, *Sharing in Christ's Virtues. For a renewal of Moral Theology in light of* Veritatis splendor (Washington, D.C.: Catholic University of America Press, 2001).

37. "Tesi e Questioni circa lo statuto della teologia morale fondamentale" is the report of a seminar in which Melina played a central part; see *Anthropotes* 15, no. 1 (1999): 261–74.

38. Bernard Hoose, ed., *Christian Ethics: An Introduction* (London: Cassell, 1998).

39. I have changed my judgment since my review of this work in *Studia Moralia* 38 (2000): 603–5.
40. Josef Römelt, *Vom Sinn moralisher Verantwortung. Zu den Grundlagen christlicher Ethik in komplexer Gesellschaft* (Regensburg, Germany: Pustet, 1996).
41. Jean-Pierre Wils and Dietmar Mieth, eds., *Concetti fondamentali dell'etica cristiana* (Brescia, Italy: Queriniana, 1994).
42. Curran was influenced by two main traditions. One is represented in Jozef Aertnys, Cornelius Damen, and Jan Visser, *Theologia Moralis,* 17th ed. (Turin, Italy: Marietti, 1956), the other by Marcelino Zalba, *Theologiae Moralis Compendium* (Madrid: BAC, 1958).
43. Charles E. Curran, *Christian Morality Today* (Notre Dame, Ind.: Fides, 1966).
44. Charles E. Curran, *A New Look at Christian Morality* (Notre Dame, Ind.: Fides, 1968).
45. Curran refers specifically to "the defects mentioned in the manualist concept of natural law"; ibid., 244.
46. Charles E. Curran, *Ongoing Revision: Studies in Moral Theology* (Notre Dame, Ind.: Fides, 1975).
47. Poignantly recalled in ibid., chapter 9, 260–94.
48. Compare ibid. at x and 289.
49. Charles E. Curran, *Themes in Fundamental Moral Theology* (Notre Dame, Ind.: University of Notre Dame Press, 1977).
50. "This volume does not pretend to offer a systematic treatise on fundamental moral theology." Ibid., 3.
51. This is made very clear in the exposition on conscience: ibid., 191–231.
52. Charles E. Curran, *Moral Theology: A Continuing Journey* (Notre Dame, Ind.: University of Notre Dame Press, 1982).
53. Curran notes how "in moral theology in the last few years there has been an unfortunate tendency . . . to reduce moral theology merely to the question of norms and the morality of specific actions . . . but there are other questions which are of greater or equal importance." Ibid., 37.
54. Charles E. Curran, *Critical Concerns in Moral Theology* (Notre Dame, Ind.: University of Notre Dame Press, 1984).
55. Ibid., 49.
56. Ultimately this is why Curran prefers Häring to the other authors ("his explicitly Christian approach . . ."; ibid., 68), despite criticisms Curran had entered earlier (ibid., 12–13).
57. Charles E. Curran, *Directions in Fundamental Moral Theology* (Dublin: Gill and Macmillan, 1986).

58. Ibid., 26.

59. Ibid., 28.

60. A soteriological approach bears some resemblance to the *Heilswissen* preference of Bernard Häring, in preference to *Seinswissen/Herrschaftswissen* approaches.

61. Charles E. Curran, *Towards an American Catholic Moral Theology* (Notre Dame, Ind.: University of Notre Dame Press, 1987).

62. Charles E. Curran, *History and Contemporary Issues* (New York: Continuum, 1996).

63. Ibid., 101.

64. Charles E. Curran, *The Origins of Moral Theology in the United States: Three Different Approaches* (Washington D.C.: Georgetown University Press, 1997).

65. Charles E. Curran, *The Catholic Moral Tradition Today: A Synthesis* (Washington, D.C.: Georgetown University Press, 1999).

66. Ibid., at 235–36 and xii.

67. Charles E. Curran, *Moral Theology at the End of the Century* (Marquette, Wisc.: Marquette University Press, 2000).

68. For a different approach, see James F. Keenan and Thomas F. Kopfensteiner, "Moral Theology out of Western Europe," *Theological Studies* 59 (1998): 107–35. I am aware that the methodological choices I make in this chapter exclude the possibility of analyzing other important European moral theologians in the period under review, such as Klaus Demmer, *Fundamentale Theologie des Ethischen* (Freiburg, Germany: Universitätsverlag, 1999).

CHAPTER 13

Beyond Revision: A Younger Moralist Looks at Charles E. Curran

Bryan N. Massingale

The German moral theologian Klaus Demmer, in reflecting on the cultural context of Catholic moral theology, writes:

> Moral theologians work within a long tradition, yet they also work at a specific time in that tradition. On one hand, they must keep a healthy distance from the object of their reflection so they do not force themselves on their interlocutors; on the other hand, they cannot avoid personal engagement. *Moral theology inevitably contains a biographical element that reflects the personality of theologians and their particular life story;* through this element, moral theologians convey their proximity to life. Moral theology is anything but a game of marbles played from a position of neutrality; it is a thinking exercise driven by existence itself.[1]

These remarks provide an appropriate setting for this essay, which responds to the contribution of Charles Curran—not to a particular aspect of moral theology but from a social location: specifically, from the generational perspective of a "younger" Catholic moral theologian.

This *festschrift,* in fact, serves as a generational marker. After forty years of teaching, research, publication, and recognized leadership, Curran is moving into the sunset of his career; after ten years in the profession, I have completed only the dawn of my own. How does one respond to an individual who has been a pivotal force in shaping the intellectual and ecclesial scene upon which one has entered? In light of Demmer's observations, my contribution and assessment can be best served by clarifying our respective generational and social locations through noting the "specific times" and signal events that have been formative influences on our theological careers. To this end, I first briefly describe Curran's social location and its influence on his theology, as evidenced in his published works. Then I provide an account of the signal events that I believe decisively shape the perspectives and concerns of a newer generation of moral theologians (whom I take to be those who came of age largely after Vatican II; received their graduate education during the mid- to late 1980s and early 1990s; and began their professional careers in moral theology during the 1990s). I conclude with a tentative probe concerning the agenda of Catholic moral theology that will be pursued by those who now inherit the mantle of one of its masters.

CURRAN'S SOCIAL LOCATION

Signal Events that Influenced Curran's Theology

Curran notes that during his seminary studies in Rome during the early and mid-1950s, he was trained in what he called "standard pre–Vatican II theology."[2] Elsewhere he explains what constituted the "standard" approach in moral theology: "Before Vatican II Catholic moral theology was identified with the manuals with their limited scope of determining sinfulness and degrees of sinfulness, a legal model with law as the remote and objective norm of morality, no real use of Scripture, a recognition of the role of human reason and natural law, and a predominant and growing emphasis on authoritative hierarchical teaching."[3] Curran's dissatisfaction with this system is evidenced in his enthusiastic response to the seminal ideas espoused by Bernard Häring, who put forth a moral theology that was "life-centered, biblically based, holistic, and stressed the universal call to holiness." Indeed, Curran writes that without doubt Häring "has been the greatest influence on my intellectual development."[4]

In light of this background, it comes as little surprise that the Second Vatican Council and its call for a thorough renewal of moral theology (see *Optatam totius,* 16) decisively shaped Curran's theology and career. Curran notes that Vatican II deeply affected moral theology in several areas: "focus, model, method, integration of scripture and theology, emphasis on the person, ecumenism and dialogue with the world and others."[5] A review of Curran's writings reveals that of the many sea changes that occurred in moral theology as a result of the Council—changes that made the discipline hardly recognizable from its recent past—perhaps three were most influential and significant: the shift from classical to historical consciousness; the emphasis on the human person and the attendant call to conversion and discipleship; and ecumenical openness, as evidenced in the call to dialogue with the world and all people of goodwill.[6] The essays in this volume detail how these emphases characterize Curran's approach to various issues in moral theology. For our purposes, it is important to highlight how Vatican II, with its call for a major overhaul of moral theology, almost of necessity made Curran's career that of a "bridge, a transitional figure"[7] between the demise of the moral manuals and the achievement of a new moral synthesis.

Without doubt—and by Curran's own account—the second decisive event that shaped his career and consciousness was *Humanae vitae* and its aftermath. To understand Curran rightly, it is important to realize that *Humanae vitae* is neither solely a document on a concrete moral issue nor a single event of official promulgation. *Humanae vitae* is a symbol for a continuing clash between conflicting moral approaches and divergent understandings of the church. Curran relates that the most pressing issue of the early 1960s in the Catholic world was the issue of responsible parenthood and whether married couples in pursuit of that goal could use artificial means of contraception.[8] It became apparent to Curran and his contemporaries, however, that the line of thought that led to a questioning and rejection of the official ban on artificial contraception would lead logically to a questioning of the official approach and specific conclusions on a host of other concerns in sexual and medical ethics: masturbation, homosexuality, euthanasia, and direct sterilization, among others.[9] Curran states that *Humanae vitae* brought to the fore two issues that have dominated his career, shaped his perspective, and set the agenda or focus of post–Vatican II moral theology: the existence of and grounding for absolute moral norms, and the role of the hierarchical magisterium in the moral discourse of the church—and the legitimacy of dissent from its teaching on moral matters.[10] He declares that these two issues, notwithstanding the many other concerns of postconciliar moral reflection, were "the two most prominent controversies in Catholic moral theology at the end of the twentieth century."[11]

The Second Vatican Council and the promulgation of *Humanae vitae*, then, are the decisive events that set the direction for Curran's career and influenced his approach to moral theology.

Curran's Project: Creative Fidelity to a Living Tradition

The formative influence of these events and Curran's consciousness as a "transitional figure" become evident in his description of his theological project. In what now appears to be a programmatic statement, Curran states that "moral theology is a *living tradition* based on the *creative fidelity* that should mark the pilgrim existence of the community of the disciples of Jesus."[12] Like the proverbial figure who retrieves from his storeroom things old and new (Mt. 13:52), he strives to "understand, appropriate, and live" the Catholic moral tradition in view of the demands of our own "history, culture, and time."[13] Curran further explains:

> Fidelity to the tradition does not mean merely repeating the very words of Scripture or of older church teaching. The Christian tradition is a living tradition, and fidelity involves creative fidelity which seeks to preserve in our time and place the incarnational principle. Creative fidelity is the task of the church. . . .[14]

Thus, "creative fidelity" seeks to avoid the "extremes" of what Curran calls "fundamentalism" (that is, "merely repeating the words and formulations of the past") and "modernism" (that is, an approach that would abandon or compromise core Christian realities out of the urgency of present needs).[15] Curran instead advocates an ongoing conversation between the received tradition and the "signs of the time" today, allowing each to influence, interpret, and challenge the other. He believes that this task requires knowledge of the past tradition and familiarity with the present challenges facing Christian believers and the modern world. He explains:

> A knowledge of the rich tradition of Catholic theology is important, but one must also recognize that such a tradition must be continually developed, changed, and reappropriated in the light of ongoing historical, social, and cultural changes. One must avoid both the rigidity of an inflexible traditionalism and the itch for novelty that refuses to acknowledge the importance of a tradition. The moral theologian today truly serves and conserves the tradition by recognizing it as a big tradition responding to the contemporary developments that have been momentous within both the world and the church.[16]

Because of this concern for tradition, Curran—though acknowledging that creative fidelity inevitably leads to departures from previous ethical conclusions on some issues—repeatedly emphasizes the connections or "continuities" between his approach and what has gone before. He delineates these continuities as *mediation* (the belief that the divine works through and is manifested in the human); *confidence in human reason's ability* to discover moral truth (evidenced in some understanding and use of natural law approaches); *the use of casuistry* as a method of resolving moral conflicts; and the conviction that moral theology remains *a discipline that serves both the church and individual conscience formation.* [17] Like the "bridge" he understands himself to be, Curran emphasizes the continuity of his approach with the tradition; highlights the harmony between his conclusions and the essential Christian mysteries (e.g., as evidenced in his articulated "stance");[18] and argues that his disagreements with official teachings are relatively few and involve matters that are remote from the core of the faith.[19] Hence, he contends that even his dissent is a form of "critical loyalty" and a consequence of creative fidelity to the tradition. He asserts, "The dissenter is committed to the church and is trying to bring about a change for the good of the church itself."[20]

Thus, it becomes apparent that Curran is a revisionist—not a revolutionary—with regard to the Catholic moral tradition.[21] He is a revisionist in the formal and broad meanings of the word. In a formal sense, he is a revisionist in that he aligns himself with other contemporary moralists who criticize and reject the physicalism (i.e., the identification of the moral act with its physical description) that they contend undergirds official Catholic teaching on certain issues in sexual and medical ethics.[22] He also is a revisionist in a broader sense, as defined by his colleague, Lisa Cahill:

> The revisionists mostly grew to maturity before Vatican II, and remember vividly the revitalization the council brought. These Catholics . . . *see the church as their religio-cultural home,* even as "mother" and "teacher," but they disagree that sexual and marital experience necessarily confirm all current church teaching. . . . They continue to struggle within the church to find room and a voice for *moderate reformulations of—and possibly a few exceptions to*—the Catholic view that sex belongs in indissoluble marriage and leads to parenthood.[23]

In my judgment, this excerpt is an accurate summary of Curran's social location and how it has shaped his approach to moral theology. Curran is a "churchman" in the best sense of that term: Deeply nourished by and steadfastly committed to the Catholic Church—not only to its intellectual heritage but also to the visible body of sinful, pilgrim believers that constitute it—he manifests abiding optimism in the soundness of its tradition and unwavering passion for demonstrating this tradition's enduring relevance for contemporary people of good will and moral conviction.

These qualities are most evident in Curran's comments in the aftermath of the decision to strip him of his position as a professor of Catholic moral theology:

> I have insisted that dissent on these issues is legitimate precisely because they do not involve the core or fundamental aspects of the

> Roman Catholic Christian faith. The corollary of this understanding is my continuing commitment to the Catholic Church, which remains centrally important for me in understanding and living a human, Christian existence. I am aware of the dangers of becoming disillusioned, embittered, or cynical, but I pray that in this whole process my faith will be strengthened. The Catholic faith and the Catholic Christian community are both theoretically and practically very significant for me. In making this whole occasion a teaching moment both in content and in tone, I believe that I am working in the long term for the good of the Catholic Church—my church.[24]

SOCIAL LOCATION OF THE YOUNGER MORAL THEOLOGIAN

I begin this discussion of the social location of a new generation of moral theologians and the formative events that shape us with several caveats or disclaimers. First, the events that I single out are not unique to a younger cohort. Of necessity, any living moralist is affected by and called to reflect on and out of these experiences. I believe that these events affect a younger moralist in a *distinctive* way, in that they have a formative influence on our consciousness and perspective (much the same as the way Vatican II and *Humanae vitae* affect all Catholic moralists but have had distinguishing formative effects on Curran's generation). Second, I do not claim to be a representative or typical "younger moralist." Yet although my "youthful" colleagues might cite other formative events, I believe that the following events are of such significance that they would show up in some way on many lists. Finally, because I do not believe that I am "typical," undoubtedly some personal influences color my perception and selection of the following events. Because I believe that the only way to universal insights is through particular perspectives, however, I hope that perceptions arising out of my particular situation will yield insight into analogous experiences possessed by many other younger American Catholic scholars.

What, then, are the events in church, society, and the academy that have marked my generation in distinctive and defining ways?

The Fall of the Berlin Wall and the Collapse of the Soviet Union

Today's younger generation of moralists is the first in recent times whose careers and social reflection have not been greatly affected by the realities of the Cold War. Tensions between East and West, between communism and democracy, were the driving force of U.S. foreign policy and the backdrop of much of Catholic social teaching during the latter half of the twentieth century (see *Pacem in terris, The Challenge of Peace,* and *Sollicitudo rei socialis*). With these tensions now significantly diminished, other concerns have arisen in the wake of these two seismic events; not the least of these is a resurgence of ethnic antagonisms and attempted genocides, not only in Europe but in Africa and Asia as well. The forces of "light" and "darkness" (e.g., former President Reagan's talk of the "evil empire") are in need of new ethical discernment and reflection. At the least, the question of the future course of Catholic social reflection in the post–Cold War world weighs on us in a distinctive way.

The Cloning of Dolly and the Human Genome Project

As a graduate student in the late 1980s, I led a seminar discussion on the ethics of technologically assisted means of human reproduction in a bioethics course. I remember that the professor and the class agreed that although cloning presented fascinating ethical scenarios, such discussions were of little immediate practical import because human cloning was at least thirty to forty years in the future. (I sometimes joke that Dolly made my graduate education in bioethics obsolete in less than five years!) Therein lies the point, however: We can do now what only yesterday seemed barely conceivable. What are the ethical responsibilities that fall to those who can become "the artisans of a new humanity" in ways the Second Vatican Council never imagined? If members of a previous generation had to wrestle with the reality that they were the first humans with the power to end human existence, my generation must contend with the fact that we are the first that could begin human creation literally "in our own image." This realization and the ethical questions it imposes, in my judgment, have a particular impact on the consciousness of my generation of moral theologians.

The Persian Gulf War and Globalization as the "New World Order"

Among the many ways to interpret the Persian Gulf War (e.g., as an intervention to liberate Kuwait from unjust aggression or to defend the West's access to cheap supplies of energy), I believe it serves as a symbolic marker for the triumph or dominance of what Walter Brueggemann calls an ideology of "military consumerism." Here is Brueggemann's trenchant description of this worldview:

> By "military consumerism" I refer to a construal of the world in which individual persons are reckoned as the primary units of meaning and

> reference, and individual persons, in unfettered freedom, are authorized . . . to pursue well-being, security, and happiness as they choose. This metanarrative has, as its "consumer" component, the conviction that well-being, security, and happiness are the result of getting, having, using, and consuming, activities that may be done without restraint or limit, even at the expense of others. This construal of reality has its "military" component in the conviction that having a disproportion of whatever it takes to enjoy well-being, security, and happiness is appropriate, and that the use of force, coercion, or violence, either to secure or to maintain a disproportion, is completely congruent with this notion of happiness."[25]

Brueggemann contends that this ideology of aggressive individualist consumerism has become the dominant "metanarrative" of western society; many people fear that the underside of globalization threatens to make this worldview the dominant global construal of reality as well. The dominance of individualism and the complexities of globalization not only have uniquely shaped the worldviews of a younger generation of moralists—perhaps in ways of which we are not aware—it also calls us to confront ethical challenges that our forebears did not envisage (e.g., the increasing irrelevance of the nation-state, the raw power of corporate conglomerates, and the resurgence of slavery and conscripted labor).

The AIDS Pandemic

AIDS was first identified as a disease in 1981.[26] In the twenty years since, this disease has made an indelible imprint on the consciousness of the current generation of moralists. It has affected our personal understandings of sexuality and sexual practices. Sexuality, disease, and death—and dread, fear, and anxiety—are linked for us in ways that previous generations did not experience. Many of us have friends, family members, parishioners, and colleagues who have died from AIDS or are living with HIV infection. How does one put into words the experience of mourning so many who have died so horribly and too soon? Our professional and pastoral experiences have brought us into contact with those who, in this country, were first publicly stigmatized by this disease: the gay community—a group whose members no longer can be faceless abstractions engaging in acts discussed with impersonal remove. We have had to become comfortable publicly discussing sexual practices to which the manualists made only oblique reference in Latin. In the words of an authoritative report, "AIDS changed how we think and how we love, what we teach our children and what words we say in public."[27] The experience of living in "a time of plague"[28]—of an incurable disease carried through practices by which we express our most intimate selves—without doubt is one of the defining experiences of a younger cohort of Catholic moralists.

"L'Affaire Curran"[29]

For the younger generation of moral theologians, especially those living in the United States, Curran himself and the events occasioned by Rome's judgment on his positions constitute a distinguishing formative experience. I believe that the Congregation for the Doctrine of the Faith's decision that Curran "is not suitable nor eligible to teach Catholic theology"[30] is the most significant and decisive intervention of the hierarchical magisterium in the field of moral theology since *Humanae vitae*. I argue that this verdict is far more significant than the promulgation of *Veritatis splendor* because the conclusions in that document were almost foreordained in light of previous judgments rendered on certain positions espoused by Curran. It also is far more decisive than *Veritatis splendor* because the Congregation's action was not merely a judgment on Curran's personal positions. The impact of this decision would be more limited if Curran's views were somehow idiosyncratic. As Curran often—and, in my judgment, rightly—has pointed out, however, his general approach to the discipline of moral theology and the specific conclusions he has reached on concrete moral issues are shared by the large majority of Catholic ethicists living today.[31] Thus, the judgment that Curran is not a Catholic theologian and cannot teach in the name of the church is the hierarchical magisterium's unequivocal repudiation of the major trajectory of postconciliar moral theology—that is, the moral theology in which many (if not most) of my generation was schooled.

What has been the impact of "the Curran affair" on a younger generation of Catholic moralists? Allow me to illustrate this impact in light of my own experience. I arrived in Washington to study moral theology at the Catholic University of America literally days after the Congregation's judgment was made public. Rereading Curran's account of his situation in *Faithful Dissent* brought back to mind the confusion, uncertainty, and turmoil of that period. In the immediate aftermath of the Congregation's decision, so many questions were raised: Could one complete a doctorate in moral theology at Catholic University? Should one? Would that degree be regarded as somehow tainted, in the academy or the church? How much freedom did we have in our writing and research? Could one cite or use Curran's works in our course papers? And the question raised constantly by colleagues and fellow students: Why would anyone in their right mind want to study moral theology now?

After completing my licentiate at Catholic University, I went to Rome to study for the doctorate at the Alphonsianum. In Rome, I experienced in very raw ways what I believe to be the major enduring impact of the Curran affair: the polarization and politicization of theology, especially moral theology. Here the question was not only why one would study this discipline but more often, "What kind of moral theologian are you?" In blunt terms, are you "orthodox" or a "dissenter"? For many younger moralists, the "Curran affair" was their initiation into the reality of doing moral theology in a polarized and politicized atmosphere of wariness and fear, where the decisive—and sometimes only—question was, "Do you agree or disagree with the Church's teaching on . . . ?" Of necessity, many younger moralists—"left" and "right" of "center" (for lack of better terms)—learned the art of discretion and circumspection; only in the presence of "safe" people did one risk stating a candid or unguarded opinion. I realized that one's opinions on the Curran controversy were a kind of litmus test for assessing one's "orthodoxy" and for determining things as mundane as with whom one ate and socialized and as significant as where one could teach—or whether one would be allowed to teach at all.

No single response on the Curran controversy is common to all younger moralists. It is safe to say that for most, the "Curran affair" occasioned a kind of existential crisis—a time of deep reflection on the meaning of being a moral theologian at this time in the church's life. It would be rare to find one of us who has not given a lot of thought to why he or she is doing this. Younger ethicists have varying responses to Curran and the type of moral reflection he represents, including explicit endorsement, sympathetic questioning, unmitigated rejection, and discreet circumspection. I believe that none, however, can profess that *l'affaire Curran* has had a negligible impact in his or her life.

These are the events that I believe shape the consciousness of a younger generation of moral theologians. These events are more significant because of decisive shifts now occurring in the ecclesial and academic contexts in which moral reflection takes place. I highlight two of these changed contexts in the church and the academy that are of special importance for understanding a new generation of theological ethicists.

The Ambiguity of Ecclesial Tradition and Commitment

Curran highlights the ecclesial context of Catholic moral theology. By this he intends several things, including an insistence on a pastoral orientation for moral theology and the belief that moral theology is a service to the Catholic community of believers as they constitute, along with others of good will, a community of moral discourse and conviction. Also implicit in his ecclesial context is the conviction that the Catholic moral theologian ought to be, or should strive to remain, a member of this faith community:

> I have urged progressive Roman Catholics to stay in the church and strive to change the church.... I can appreciate that some people feel they can no longer live in the church because of... issues that so personally touch them, but I have always urged people to stay and work for change within the church. The church is not a voluntary society where like-minded people gather together....[32]

At the risk of going out on a limb, I believe that many younger moralists, though agreeing with Curran, would want to add a "*but*...." Among many (I hasten to emphasize not all) younger moralists, there is a sense of unease or struggle with Catholic identity and church membership. For example, because of their race, ethnicity, gender, or sexual orientation, many experience a sense of discomfort—even estrangement—that stems from not being fully included in the life of the church. We find ourselves affected personally by what we study professionally.

Obviously this point is very sensitive and delicate, and I struggle with how best to name and articulate it. Perhaps our difference from a previous generation is that more of us are conscious of and affected by the deep ambiguity of the Catholic tradition. Because we are more aware of its deficits and *lacunae,* as well as its collusions and complicities with social evils such as racism and sexism, we find it difficult to give this tradition unqualified embrace. I must emphasize that this stance of "committed reservation" in the face of the tradition's "ideological deformations"[33] is not only intellectual but existential as well. As an African American Catholic, for example, I strongly resonate with how James Cone speaks of the hesitancy and struggle occasioned by embracing a complex and ambiguous faith heritage:

> I am still struggling with the Christian faith, arguing with its interpreters, past and present in white and black communities. That is the only way I can make it my own. As long as the Christian faith is connected with white supremacy and other horrendous evils, I must struggle with it or reject it as the work of evil white men. If I continue to embrace it, I do so with an uneasy conscience, knowing that nothing about it can be taken for granted. When I think about how many black

> people have been enslaved, segregated, and lynched by white Christians, I would have to be stone crazy to affirm that faith without rethinking its meaning. How can slaves affirm the faith of slave masters and still keep their religious sanity? This question is no less valid for black Catholics than it is . . . for oppressed people around the world.[34]

Like our elders, then, younger moralists think from within and contribute to the Catholic faith tradition. Yet the question of how to do so with integrity haunts and weighs on many of us.

Thus, for many (again, not all) Catholic moralists of a younger generation, our ecclesial commitment is undeniably real and yet paradoxical: It is a stance of commitment and reserve, of embrace and hesitancy, of membership and qualification, of belonging and exile.[35] In view of the delicacy of this point, perhaps it would be easier not to mention it at all. Yet honesty and the importance of this matter for understanding a present generation demand that it be mentioned—if only to invite others to attempt to state this issue in a better way.

Methodological and Interpretative Pluralism

By this I mean that moral theology today takes place in a new interpretative context. I hesitate to call this situation "postmodern" because this umbrella term covers a wide range of highly divergent theories.[36] What is beyond dispute, however, is that the interpretative situation today is marked by a shift from what Brueggemann calls "hegemonic interpretation" toward "a pluralistic interpretative perspective."[37] What he and others mean is this: Unlike a previous situation that assumed Christian normative truth as interpreted by white, western males was the privileged adjudicator of knowledge, that claim to normative privilege is now severely and passionately contested. Brueggemann declares, "Its unchallenged authority and credibility are over and done with."[38] The Christian tradition must now place its interpretation of reality alongside those of other religious and secular traditions. Moreover, the Christian tradition itself is the subject of various interpretations stemming from other social locations than white, male westerners.[39] Not only are there a plurality of interpretative traditions in theology, in the specific field of moral theology there are now a variety of methodological approaches (e.g., narrative and virtue ethics; deontological, teleological, and relational-responsibility models of decision making; liberation ethics, feminist analysis, and race critique). This shift in perspective and the variety of approaches now present make the achievement of ethical consensus more difficult (to say the least) and impose a demand for epistemological humility on the responsible scholar. Although all living moralists who seek to speak with credibility are affected by and must take into account this pluralistic intellectual situation, it does have a distinctive impact on a younger cohort, who have personally known and experienced little else and sometimes find it hard to appreciate their elders' apprehensions about foundationalism and nonfoundationalism.

These, then, are the protean events and contextual shifts that, in my judgment, have shaped the worldview and perspective of a younger generation of Catholic ethicists. Again, the claim is not that we are the only ones who are affected and influenced by these realities. Rather, just as Vatican II, with its promise and transitions, exercised a decisive and formative influence on Curran and his contemporaries (in ways they perhaps could only now recognize in hindsight), so these events and shifts seem to have a particular influence upon a new group of moral theologians—an influence we can be fully aware of only with the passage of time.

TOWARD A CATHOLIC ETHICS BEYOND REVISION

How, then, is the project of Curran and his generation assessed from the vantage point of this social location? In what new directions might a younger generation take Catholic moral theology? If the preceding section is somewhat venturous, this one carries even greater risk because graduate training in moral theology does not confer the gift of prognostication. Nonetheless, I believe that something, however tentative, can and must be said.

In assessing the state of moral theology in the last half of the twentieth century, Richard McCormick—a contemporary and close colleague of Curran's—notes that there seems to be a certain impasse, even "boredom," concerning the pressing questions that so engaged his generation: the preoccupation with sexual acts and their intrinsic evil, the role of hierarchical authority, and what constitutes legitimate dissent.[40] I tend to agree with this assessment, but not out of any kind of adolescent rebellion or ingratitude. It is neither appropriate nor necessary to malign the efforts of the recent past-still-present. All theological work must reflect its historical context and cultural conditioning. Moreover, the pursuits of my generation of Catholic ethicists are dependent on and indebted to the postconciliar era of study, reflection, ferment, and integrity under fire.

Yet rereading Curran's writings made me realize that I indeed have been formed by different experiences—experiences that make me acutely aware of what was not and has not yet been said. The formative experiences of a younger generation lead, then, to different questions and concerns. I summarize this agenda under two headings: a different project and a different strategy.

A Different Project: "Faithful Reconstruction"

I detail above how Curran conceives his project as one of "creative fidelity to a living tradition." Presuming the fundamental soundness of the Catholic moral tradition, Curran seeks to revise it in light of contemporary needs by pointing out the historically conditioned character of some of its concrete conclusions while emphasizing the continuity of his proposed revisions with the tradition. Where many of my generation differ is in our recognition not only of the tradition's historicity but also its deep ambiguity—and the ambiguity of postconciliar Catholic ethics as well.

To put the matter succinctly, Curran's project is "modern" and shares in the achievements and the limitations of modernity. One of the limitations of modern theological and ethical reflection is well expressed by David Tracy:

> There is an underside to all the talk about history in modern religion and theology. That underside is revealed in the *shocking silence* in most theologies of historical consciousness and historicity alike on the evil rampant in history, the sufferings of whole peoples, the destruction of nature itself. . . . [It is] a history without any sense of the radical interruptions of actual history, without a memory of historical suffering, especially the suffering caused by the pervasive systemic unconscious distortions in our history—sexism, racism, classism, anti-Semitism, homophobia, Eurocentrism.[41]

As a way of specifying this "shocking silence . . . on the suffering of whole peoples," I raise this question: Why, despite the "turn to the subject" and the embrace of historical consciousness by Curran and his contemporaries, did U.S. Catholic ethicists (on the right and the left) *not* attend to the blatant and endemic racism of American society? Why was the most pressing moral issue of the 1960s artificial contraception, rather than the Civil Rights movement or the racial violence and "white flight" of 1967 and 1968 that tore apart our nation's cities with enduring consequences today? Why this "disconnect" between professional reflection and public concern?[42] Could it be true, as I have argued elsewhere, that such a "disconnect" was possible because Catholic ethicists, being (mal)formed by the systemic distortion of American racism, did not regard

African Americans as being among the "subjects" to whom they should turn?[43]

Furthermore, because of this silence, there are not only voices that have not been heard, there also are moral questions that have not been asked by Catholic ethicists of previous generations—questions such as, "What does it mean to be a disciple of Jesus in a racist society?" "In a world in which 'black' is an illegitimate or inferior mode of being human, what are the social implications of believing that Black Americans are made in the image of God?" "How are persons of African descent to live ethically in a society that denies, questions, or attacks their humanity?" "How do we tell those whom society ignores, fears, and disdains that they are sons and daughters of God?" Not even adverting to these questions, in a society of endemic racism, makes one's ethical project inadequate and, in some quarters, even incredible.

My examples flow from my specific social location as an African-American Catholic, but they are illustrative of my main point: In view of the systemic distortions, unconscious biases, and unacknowledged collusions with human evil in the Catholic ethical tradition, it is not enough to emphasize the continuity of the tradition in the midst of change. A more thorough reconstruction is needed. Thus, I propose that the project of a younger generation of Catholic ethicists is that of *faithful reconstruction*. "Reconstruction" emphasizes the need for a more fundamental or "radical" (in the sense of *radix* or "root") rethinking and rearticulation of the demands of Christian faith than that conveyed by the term "revision." "Reconstruction," moreover, conveys the belief that there are certain aspects of the Catholic ethical tradition that, in the name of Christ, one should not hold in "fidelity" no matter how "creatively."[44]

Yet this reconstruction also aims to be "faithful" to the demands and challenges, the hope and the promise, of the "classic" events, symbols, narratives, and persons of the Christian faith—events, symbols, narratives, and persons that continually "resist definitive interpretation" and our attempts to ideologically co-opt and domesticate them.[45] The younger moralist (and all who have been influenced by the events that have distinctively formed us) is called to be faithful to "the unexpected claim to truth" that such classics—especially the classic memory of Jesus Christ—impose on reasonable and responsible minds.[46] In the stirring words of David Tracy,

> Christianity is always a memory that turns as fiercely against itself as against other pretensions to triumph. The great prophetic negations of

> all triumphalism released by the memory of Jesus of Nazareth render unreal, on inner-Christian grounds, any appeals to narrative, tradition, identity that partake of either innocence or triumph. To defend tradition is to defend that disturbing and often self-judging prophetic memory.[47]

As an example of "faithful reconstruction" I pose the following questions: What are the ethical implications of Jesus' practice of scandalously inclusive table fellowship? How does this practice challenge a community whose central act of worship is a ritual remembrance of Jesus at supper? Jesus' table fellowship, then, is an example of a "classic" that imposes an "unexpected claim to truth" that challenges the systematic distortions of the Catholic ethical tradition and provides material for its "faithful reconstruction."

Thus, "faithful reconstruction," as I understand it, is neither a simple critique nor a facile dismissal of a previous generation's efforts.[48] Instead, it is a call to create a new thing: a Catholic Christian ethics freed from the scotoma and bias of white privilege, patriarchy, and other systemic evils. The project of "faithful reconstruction" is consistent with the paradoxical nature of ecclesial commitment I detail above. It honors the unease and disquiet that many younger moral theologians feel in the face of the Catholic moral tradition. It also seeks to demonstrate to our contemporaries—many of whom are more skeptical than we (and some in fact alienated from the church)——the credibility of the Christian message in the face of the formidable challenge it receives from the metanarrative of military consumerism.

A Different Strategy: Seeking Consensus about Justice

Acute sensitivity to the evil embedded in human traditions and awareness of the untold human damage they occasion give rise to a passionate concern about justice. Indeed, a case could be made that justice is the prime virtue in a postmodern world.[49] Yet the pluralism of the contemporary world forces the question, "*Whose* justice?" In other words, in a world of competing claims and conflicting accounts of justice, how does one arrive at the consensus that is necessary for social peace, mutual coexistence, and human flourishing?

This topic obviously is broad; addressing it adequately goes beyond the purpose of this essay. I make only two points. First, although Curran does not deal extensively with this question, he is aware of it. In one place he asks, "Can one have justice in human societies if people are radically incapable of agreeing on what justice is?" [50] He posits the question to argue the need for some form of universal ethics, even with an appreciation for the particularity that marks historical consciousness. Second, attending to this issue, even if only in fragmentary ways, is an important part of the ongoing challenge to the current generation of moral theologians.[51] In view of today's intellectual and cultural pluralism, perhaps a full solution to this problem is not yet possible; perhaps providing a final resolution is not even our task. Indeed, providing a moral synthesis like Curran's recent attempt might well elude us.[52] Perhaps the task of a younger generation of Catholic ethicists is, in Brueggemann's words, to *fund:* "to provide the pieces, materials, and resources out of which a new world can be imagined. Our responsibility, then, is not a grand scheme or a coherent system, but the voicing of a lot of little pieces out of which people can put life together in fresh configurations."[53] Perhaps, then, a younger generation of Catholic moral theologians must be content to advance provisional theses and write essays containing the words *toward, beyond,* and *post.*

I have not provided a complete guide to moral theology from a "younger" perspective. That was not the purpose of this essay. I hope, however, that I have given enough of its rough contours to indicate how it is indebted to, yet departs from, the project that Curran has so intelligently and energetically advanced. I also hope that other Catholic ethicists of my generation will engage the task of articulating our social location and fill in whatever inadequacies and gaps that exist in my account. Above all, however, I hope that my generation of Catholic ethicists will pursue our project with the same pastoral sensitivity, personal courage, intellectual integrity, theological acumen, profound faith, and obvious joy with which Charles Curran has engaged his.

NOTES

1. Klaus Demmer, *Shaping the Moral Life: An Approach to Moral Theology* (Washington, D.C.: Georgetown University Press, 2000), 1–2; emphasis added.
2. Charles E. Curran, *Faithful Dissent* (Kansas City, Mo.: Sheed & Ward, 1986), 6.
3. Charles E. Curran, *Moral Theology at the End of the Century* (Milwaukee, Wisc.: Marquette University 1999), 14.
4. Curran, *Faithful Dissent,* 6.
5. Charles E. Curran, *History and Contemporary Issues: Studies in Moral Theology* (New York: Continuum, 1996), 102–03.

6. See Curran, *History and Contemporary Issues,* 102–06, and idem, *Moral Theology at End of Century,* 16–20.
7. Curran, *Faithful Dissent,* 93–94.
8. Ibid., 10.
9. Ibid., 20.
10. Curran advances this contention in several places; see *Faithful Dissent,* 13; *History and Contemporary Issues,* 107; and *Moral Theology at End of Century,* 25. For another account of the significance of *Humanae vitae* for contemporary Catholic moral theology, see John Mahoney, "The Impact of *Humanae vitae,* " in *The Making of Moral Theology: A Study of the Roman Catholic Tradition* (New York: Oxford University, 1987), 259–301.
11. Curran, *Moral Theology at End of Century,* 25.
12. Charles E. Curran, *The Living Tradition of Moral Theology* (Notre Dame, Ind.: University of Notre Dame Press, 1992), 83.
13. Ibid., ix.
14. Curran, *Faithful Dissent,* 51.
15. Charles E. Curran, *The Church and Morality: An Ecumenical and Catholic Approach* (Minneapolis: Fortress Press, 1993), 35.
16. Curran, *Living Tradition,* 93.
17. Curran, *Living Tradition,* 90–91. Elsewhere Curran writes, "Despite the significant changes and developments in recent Catholic moral theology, distinctive characteristics of the Catholic tradition continue to shape Catholic moral theology today—mediation, catholicity with a small c, opposition to individualism, and the relationship to the life of the Church" (*History and Contemporary Issues,* 101).
18. Charles E. Curran, *The Catholic Moral Tradition Today: A Synthesis* (Washington, D.C.: Georgetown University Press, 1999), 30–59.
19. Curran, *Faithful Dissent,* 60–62.
20. See Curran, *Faithful Dissent,* 163, and idem, *Tensions in Moral Theology* (Notre Dame, Ind.: University of Notre Dame Press, 1988), 64.
21. Curran expresses this matter in *Faithful Dissent,* 97–100.
22. Curran, *History and Contemporary Issues,* 44, 231–32.
23. Lisa Sowle Cahill, "Can We Get Real about Sex?" *Commonweal* 117 (14 September 1990): 498; emphases added. I regard the highlighted phrases as significant not only for understanding Curran but also for understanding the differences we will discover between him and a younger generation of moral theologians.
24. Charles E. Curran, "A Teaching Moment Continues," *America* 156 (April 25, 1987): 340.

25. Walter Brueggemann, *Theology of the Old Testament* (Minneapolis: Fortress, 1997), 718. Brueggemann also calls this consciousness "technological, military consumerism" (741).

26. For an extensive examination of the impact of two decades of living with the specter of AIDS, see Sharon Begley, "AIDS at 20: A Special Report," *Newsweek* 137 (June 11, 2001): 34–51.

27. Ibid., 36.

28. Albert Camus, *The Plague* (New York: Vintage Books, [1948], 1972), 211.

29. I borrow this title from an essay by Richard A. McCormick, first published in *America* (April 5, 1986), and reprinted in his *The Critical Calling: Reflections on Moral Dilemmas since Vatican II* (Washington, D.C.: Georgetown University Press, 1989), 111–30.

30. The complete text of this decision appears in Curran, *Faithful Dissent*, 267–70.

31. Curran, *Faithful Dissent*, 172, 176, 182–92.

32. Curran, *History and Contemporary Issues*, 259.

33. I borrow this term from my colleague, professor Shawn Copeland, in an informal conversation. See also Shawn Copeland, "Guest Editorial," *Theological Studies* 61 (December 2000): 605.

34. James Cone, "Black Liberation Theology and Black Catholics: A Critical Conversation," *Theological Studies* 61 (December 2000): 735.

35. On "exile," see John E. Fortunato, *Embracing the Exile: Healing Journeys of Gay Christians* (New York: Seabury, 1982).

36. A point well made by Margaret Farley in her essay, "How Shall We Love in a Postmodern World?" in *The Historical Development of Fundamental Moral Theology in the United States* (Readings in Moral Theology no. 11), ed. Charles E. Curran and Richard A. McCormick (Mahwah, N.J.: Paulist, 1999), 310–12.

37. Brueggemann, *Old Testament Theology*, 710.

38. Walter Brueggemann, *Texts Under Negotiation: The Bible and Postmodern Imagination* (Minneapolis: Fortress, 1993), 11.

39. David Tracy has made this point repeatedly from within the Catholic theological tradition. For example, see *On Naming the Present: God, Hermeneutics, and Church* (Maryknoll, N.Y.: Orbis Books, 1994), 131–39, and idem, "Evil, Suffering, Hope: The Search for New Forms of Contemporary Theodicy," *CTSA Proceedings* 50 (1995): 15–36.

40. Richard A. McCormick, *Corrective Vision: Explorations in Moral Theology* (Kansas City, Mo.: Sheed & Ward, 1994), 17–18. It should be noted that Curran concurs in thinking that the controversies in the aftermath of *Humanae vitae* have narrowed the focus of postconciliar Catholic ethics; see *Faithful Dissent*, 94.

41. Tracy, "Evil, Suffering, and Hope," 29; emphasis added.

42. I derive this insight from James F. Keenan, "Moral Theology and History," *Theological Studies* 62 (March 2001): 101–02.

43. Bryan Massingale, "The African American Experience and U.S. Roman Catholic Ethics: 'Strangers and Aliens No Longer'?" in *Black and Catholic: the Challenge and Gift of Black Folk: Contributions of African American Experience and World View to Catholic Theology*, ed. Jamie T. Phelps (Milwaukee, Wisc.: Marquette University, 1997), 79–101.

44. For example, see the comments of Barbara Hilkert Andolsen on the teaching concerning the salvation of Jewish believers in her "Response to John E. Thiel," *CTSA Proceedings* 54 (1999): 19–20.

45. David Tracy, *Plurality and Ambiguity* (New York: Harper and Row), 12.

46. Ibid., 15.

47. Tracy, *On Naming the Present,* 15.

48. Indeed, Curran's recent works reveal an awareness of postmodern perspectives and the questions they raise. In light of these questions, he states that his sense of universalism in ethics has been chastened. Yet it is fair to say that the questions of postmodern consciousness are not central to his theological project. See *The Catholic Moral Tradition Today,* 18–25.

49. Brueggemann, *Old Testament Theology,* 735–42; here he cites Derrida (pioneer of postmodern reflection) as speaking about the indestructability of justice.

50. Curran, *Living Tradition,* 178.

51. For example, see the insightful and provocative essay of Jean Porter, "The Search for a Global Ethic," *Theological Studies* 62 (March 2001): 105–21. I also note with appreciation Rosemary Radford Ruether's concluding words in a book review found in the same issue: "[I]s the solution the denial of any common humanity that all humans share? Difference without commonality could easily lead to new justifications of denial of 'human rights' to women or other races on the grounds of cultural difference. We need to reconstruct the concept of 'human nature' so that it is defined in and through plurality of cultures and social locations, rather than through one hegemonic center, while keeping an affirmation of human commonality that grounds solidarity and equivalent rights" (193).

52. See the title of his most recent book: *The Catholic Moral Tradition: A Synthesis.*

53. Brueggemann, *Texts under Negotiation,* 20.

Bibliography of Charles E. Curran, 1961–2002: Forty-One Years of Catholic Moral Theology

1961

The *Prevention of Conception after Rape.* Doctoral diss., Pontifical Gregorian University, Rome (excerpt published).

Invincible Ignorance of the Natural Law According to St. Alphonsus. Doctoral diss., Academia Alfonsiana, Rome (excerpt published).

1962

Morality and the Love of God. Doctrinal Pamphlet Series. New York: Paulist Press.

1963

"Catholic Convictions on Sunday Observance," *The Layman in an Age of Christian Renewal: Proceedings of the 1963 Convention of the National Council of Catholic Men,* 112–17. Revised in *Christian Morality Today* (Notre Dame, Ind.: Fides, 1966), 107–19.

1964

"Dear Ann Landers." Essay on *Ann Landers Talks to Teenagers About Sex. Sign* 43 (March): 57–58.

Note: Most of this bibliography is taken from Thomas W. O'Brien, "Bibliography of Charles E. Curran, 1961–90: Thirty Years of Catholic Moral Theology," *Horizons* 18 (fall 1991): 263–78. The editors acknowledge with gratitude the assistance of Carolyn Conti in the final preparation of the bibliography.

"Christian Marriage and Family Planning." *Jubilee* 12 (August): 8–13. Reprinted in *College of New Rochelle Alumnae News* 42, no. 2: 12–18. Revised in *Christian Morality Today* (Notre Dame, Ind.: Fides, 1966), 47–66.

"The Renewal of Theology." *Guide* 190 (August–September): 3–7. Revised in *Christian Morality Today,* 1–12.

"The Problem of Conscience and the Twentieth Century Christian." In *Ecumenical Dialogue at Harvard: The Roman Catholic-Protestant Colloquium,* edited by Samuel H. Miller and G. Ernest Wright. Cambridge, Mass.: Harvard University Press, 262–73. Revised as "The Christian Conscience Today," in *Christian Morality Today,* 13–26; also in *Conscience: Theological and Psychological Perspectives,* edited by C. Ellis Nelson (New York: Newman, 1973), 132–42; in *Psychology and Religion: A Reader,* edited by Margaret Gorman (New York: Paulist Press, 1985), 169–80. Also appears as "Conscience," in *A Christian Understanding of the Human Person: Basic Readings,* edited by Eugene Lauer and Joel Mlocko (New York: Paulist Press, 1982), 160–67.

1965

"Personal Reflections on Birth Control." *Current* 5 (spring): 5–12. Revised in *The Catholic Case for Contraception,* edited by Daniel Callahan (New York: Macmillan, 1969), 19–29. Also in *Christian Morality Today,* 67–78.

"The Mixed Marriage Promises, Arguments for Suppressing the 'Cautiones.'" *Jurist* 25 (January): 83–91. Revised in *Christian Morality Today,* 93–106.

"Moral Maturity in Christ." *Northeastern Seminarian Study Conference Proceedings,* 15–19.

"A Catechesis of Sin." *The Basilian Teacher* 9: 461–69.

"Relevance: Contemporary Moral Concerns." In *Jesus Christ Reforms His Church, 26th North American Liturgical Week.* Washington, D.C.: Liturgical Conference, 3–14. Revised as "The Relevance of Moral Theology Today," in *Christian Morality Today,* 121–38.

"Theological Foundations for a Spiritual Formation in Freedom and Responsibility." *Proceedings of the Society of Catholic College Teachers of Sacred Doctrine* 9: 164–76. Revised as "Formation in Freedom and Responsibility," in *Christian Morality Today,* 29–45.

1966

"The New Morality." *Commonweal* 86 (February 18): 581–82.

"The Birth Control Issue." *The Lamp* 64 (March): 8*ff.*

"What is the Natural Law?" *The Lamp* 64 (September): 11*ff.*

"Masturbation and Objectively Grave Matter: An Exploratory Discussion." *Catholic Theological Society of America Proceedings* 21: 95–109. Revised in *A New Look at Christian Morality* (Notre Dame, Ind.: Fides, 1968), 201–21.

Christian Morality Today. Notre Dame, Ind.: Fides.

1967

"Interview with Fr. Curran at Catholic University." *Baltimore Catholic Review* 32, no. 6 (April 28): 1, 7. Reprinted in *Catholic Mind* 65 (June 1967): 3–5.

"Christian Morality Today." *Triumph* 2 (June): 24–25.

"Current Trends in Moral Theology." *Proceedings of the Second Annual Convention of the National Association of Catholic Chaplains* (June): 1–10.

"Dialogue with Joseph Fletcher." *Homiletic and Pastoral Review* 67 (July): 821–29. Reprinted in *The Situation Ethics Debate,* edited by Harvey Cox (Philadelphia: Westminster, 1968), 187–93. Also in *A New Look at Christian Morality* (Notre Dame, Ind.: Fides, 1968), 159–75.

"The Ethical Teaching of Jesus." *Commonweal* 87 (November 24): 248–50. Reprinted in *God, Jesus and Spirit,* edited by Daniel J. Callahan (New York: Herder and Herder, 1969), 153–71. Also in *A New Look at Christian Morality* (Notre Dame, Ind.: Fides, 1968), 1–23. Published in revised form as "The Relevancy of the Gospel Ethic," in *Themes in Fundamental Moral Theology* (Notre Dame, Ind.: University of Notre Dame Press, 1977), 5–26.

"Civil Law, Moral Obligation of," "Epikeia," and "Taxation and Moral Obligation." In *The New Catholic Encyclopedia.* New York: McGraw-Hill.

"Law and Conscience in the Christian Context." In *Law for Liberty,* edited by James E. Biechler. Baltimore: Helicon, 156–71. Reprinted as "Church Law and Conscience," in *A New Look at Christian Morality,* 125–43. Revised in *Themes in Fundamental Moral Theology,* 81–98.

Updated in *Directions in Fundamental Moral Theology* (Notre Dame, Ind.: University of Notre Dame Press, 1985), 197–214.

1968

"Conversion: Turning, Turning." *The Catechist* 11 (February): 6–9. Revised and expanded as "Conversion: The Central Moral Message of Jesus," in *A New Look at Christian Morality,* 25–71. Edited version of expansion appears in *Conversion: Perspectives on Personal and Social Transformation,* edited by Walter E. Conn (New York: Alba House, 1978), 225–45.

"The Mixed Marriage Promises." *Outlook* 3, no. 2 (spring): 76–86.

"Fulfilling Human Sexuality: Bodily Possibilities." *Commonweal* 88 (June 14): 386–87.

"Sexuality and Sin: A Current Appraisal." *Homiletic and Pastoral Review* 68 (September): 1005–14, and 69 (October): 27–34. Also in *Sex: Thoughts for Contemporary Christians,* compiled by Michael J. Taylor (Garden City, N.Y.: Doubleday, 1972), 113–32. Appears in *Contemporary Problems in Moral Theology* (Notre Dame, Ind.: Fides, 1970), 159–88. Revised in *Themes in Fundamental Moral Theology,* 165–90.

"The Morality of Human Transplants." *Sign* 47: 22–29.

Absolutes in Moral Theology? (editor). Washington, D.C.: Corpus. Spanish translation by Jose M. Ruiz, S.J.: *¿Principios Absolutos en Teologia Moral?* (Santander, Spain: Editorial "Sal Terrae," 1970).

"Absolute Norms and Medical Ethics." In *Absolutes in Moral Theology?* 108–53. Excerpted in *Contemporary Problems in Moral Theology,* 97–158. Parts of this chapter, along with "Natural Law and Contemporary Moral Theology" from *Contraception: Authority and Dissent,* 151–75, combined to form chapters in *Themes in Fundamental Moral Theology,* 27–80, and (updated) in *Directions in Fundamental Moral Theology* 119–72.

"Absolute Norms in Moral Theology." In *Norm and Context in Christian Ethics,* edited by Gene H. Outka and Paul Ramsey. New York: Scribners, 139–74. Revised in *A New Look at Christian Morality,* 73–123.

"The Moral Theology of Bernard Häring." In *The New Day: Catholic Theologians of Renewal,* edited by William Jerry Boney and Lawrence E. Molumby. Richmond, Va.: John Knox, 92–102. Revised in *A New Look at Christian Morality,* 145–57.

"The Morality of Contraception." *Albertus Magnus Alumna* 5, no. 1 (winter): 4–6, 14.

A New Look at Christian Morality. Notre Dame, Ind.: Fides.

1969

"Pastoral Insights: Moral Theology Today." *Priest* 25 (February): 106–9.

"Social Ethics and Method in Moral Theology." *Continuum* 7 (winter-spring): 50–62. Updated in *Contemporary Problems in Moral Theology,* 225–41.

"The Sacrament of Penance Today." *Worship* 43 (November-December): 510–31 and 590–619 and 44 (January 1970): 2–19. Revised in *Contemporary Problems in Moral Theology,* 1–96.

"Natural Law and Contemporary Moral Theology." In *Contraception: Authority and Dissent* (New York: Herder and Herder, 1969), 151–75. Revised in *Contemporary Problems in Moral Theology,* 97–158.

Contraception: Authority and Dissent (editor). New York: Herder and Herder.

Dissent in and for the Church, with Robert E. Hunt, John F. Hunt, and Terrence R. Connelly. New York: Sheed and Ward.

The Responsibility of Dissent: The Church and Academic Freedom, with John F. Hunt, Terrence R. Connolly, Robert E. Hunt, and Robert K. Webb. New York: Sheed and Ward.

1970

"Theology and Genetics: A Multi-Faceted Dialogue." *Journal of Ecumenical Studies* 7 (winter): 61–89. Appears as "Moral Theology and Genetics," *Cross Currents* 20 (1970): 64–82. Reprinted in *Theology and the City of Man,* commemorating the sesquicentennial of St. Louis University. Spanish translation: *"Teología y Genética," Selecciones de Teología* 11 (1972): 67–80. Revised with footnotes in *Contemporary Problems in Moral Theology,* 189–224, and as "Genetics and the Human Future" in *Issues in Sexual and Medical Ethics* (Notre Dame, Ind.: University of Notre Dame, 1978), 103–36. Reprinted in *On Moral Medicine: Theological Perspectives in Medical Ethics,* edited by Stephen E. Lammers and Allen Verhey (Grand Rapids, Mich.: Eerdmans, 1987): 373–83.

"Methodological and Ecclesiological Questions in Moral Theology." *Chicago Studies* 9 (spring): 59–80. Revised in *Contemporary Problems in Moral Theology,* 242–68.

"Vyznam moralni teologie dnes." *Via: Casopis pro teologii* 3: 83–86.

"Is There a Distinctively Christian Ethic?" In *Metropolis: Christian Presence and Responsibility,* edited by Philip D. Morris. Notre Dame, Ind.: Fides, 92–120. Revised in *Catholic Moral Theology in Dialogue* (Notre Dame, Ind.: Fides, 1972), 1–23. Published in French as "Y a-t-il une éthique sociale spécifique chretienne?" *Le Supplement* 96 (February 1971): 39–58.

"Roman Catholic Theology in the United States Faces the Seventies" (presidential address). *Catholic Theological Society of America Proceedings* 25: 218–33. Revised in *Catholic Moral Theology in Dialogue,* 245–53.

"The Stance or Horizon of Moral Theology." In *The Pilgrim People: A Vision with Hope,* Proceedings of Villanova University Theology Institute, no. 4, edited by Joseph Papin. Villanova, Pa.: Villanova University Press, 85–110. Revised in *New Perspectives in Moral Theology* (Notre Dame, Ind.: Fides, 1974), 47–86.

"The Evolving Concept of Sin." *Conversations* (April): 1–3. Reprinted in *Conversations* (autumn 1973): 9–11.

Contemporary Problems in Moral Theology. Notre Dame, Ind.: Fides.

Medicine and Morals. Washington, D.C.: Corpus.

1971

"Responsibility in Moral Theology: Centrality, Foundation, and Implication for Ecclesiology." *Jurist* 31 (winter): 113–42. Also in *Who Decides For the Church?* edited by James A. Coriden (Hartford, Conn.: Canon Law Society of America, 1971), 113–42. Revised as "Dialogue with a Theology of the Church: The Meaning of Coresponsibility," in *Catholic Moral Theology in Dialogue,* 150–83.

"Homosexuality and Moral Theology: Methodological and Substantive Considerations." *Thomist* 35 (July): 447–81. Revised as "Dialogue with the Homophile Movement: The Morality of Homosexuality," in *Catholic Moral Theology in Dialogue,* 184–219. Edited version appears in *Homosexuality and Ethics,* edited by Edward Batchelor, Jr. (New York: Pilgrim, 1980), 89–95.

"La théologie morale et les sciences." *Recherches de Science Religieuse* 59 (July–September): 419–48. Published in Hungarian as "A theológiai erkölcstan es a tudomanyok," *Merleg* 9 (1973): 144–64. Published in English as "Dialogue with Science: Scientific Data, Scientific Possibilities and Moral Judgment," in *Catholic Moral Theology in Dialogue,* 65–110.

"The Role and Function of the Scriptures in Moral Theology." *Catholic Theological Society of America Proceedings* 26: 56–90. Also in *Readings in Moral Theology, No. 4: The Use of Scripture in Moral Theology,* 178–212, and *Catholic Moral Theology in Dialogue,* 24–64.

"Christian Conversion in the Writings of Bernard Lonergan." In *Foundations of Theology: Papers from the International Lonergan Congress 1970,* edited by Philip McShane. Notre Dame, Ind.: University of Notre Dame Press, 41–59. Revised in *Catholic Moral Theology in Dialogue,* 220–44.

1972

"Roman Catholic Social Ethics: Past, Present and Future." In *That They May Live: Theological Reflections on the Quality of Life,* College Theology Society Annual vol. 17, edited by George Devine. New York: Alba House, 87–121. Revised in *Catholic Moral Theology in Dialogue,* 111–49.

"Moral Theology's Crisis." *National Catholic Reporter* 8 (January 14): 9.

Crisis of Spirituality in Priestly Ministry." *American Ecclesiastical Review* 166 (February): 95–111, and 166 (March): 157–73. Revised in *The Crisis in Priestly Ministry* (Notre Dame, Ind.: Fides, 1972), 51–102.

"New Catholic Hospital Code." *Family Planning Perspectives* 4 (July): 7–8.

"Preaching the Word and Specific Moral Problems." *Jurist* 32 (summer): 355–80. Revised in *The Crisis in Priestly Ministry,* 103–46.

"Paul Hanley Furfey: Theorist of American Catholic Radicalism." *American Ecclesiastical Review* 166 (December): 651–77. Revised as "The Radical Catholic Social Ethics of Paul Hanley Furfey," in *New Perspectives in Moral Theology,* 87–121.

"The Present State of Catholic Moral Theology." In *Transcendence and Immanence: Festschrift in Honor of Joseph Papin,* vol. 1, edited by Joseph Armenti. Villanova, Pa.: Villanova University Press, 11–20. Revised in *Catholic Moral Theology in Dialogue,* 254–65.

"Theological Reflections on the Social Mission of the Church." In *The Social Mission of the Church: A Theological Reflection,* edited by Edward J. Ryle. Washington, D.C.: Catholic University of America Press, 31–54. Revised in *New Perspectives in Moral Theology,* 122–62.

The Crisis in Priestly Ministry. Notre Dame, Ind.: Fides.

Catholic Moral Theology in Dialogue. Notre Dame, Ind.: Fides. (Reprinted in 1976 by University of Notre Dame Press.)

1973

"Blueprints for Moral Living: Interview with Charles E. Curran." *U.S. Catholic* 38 (February): 6–13, and 38 (March): 28–37.

"Abortion: Law and Morality in Contemporary Catholic Theology." *Jurist* 33 (spring): 162–83. Revised in *New Perspectives in Moral Theology,* 163–93. Reprinted as "Abortion: Its Moral Aspects," in *Abortion: The Moral Issues,* edited by Edward Batchelor, Jr. (New York: Pilgrim, 1982), 115–28.

"Moral Theology: The Present State of the Discipline." *Theological Studies* 34 (September): 446–67. Revised as "Catholic Moral Theology Today," in *New Perspectives in Moral Theology,* 1–46.

"Sterilization: Roman Catholic Theory and Practice." *Linacre Quarterly* 40: 97–108. Revised in *New Perspectives in Moral Theology,* 194–211.

"Divorce: Doctrine et practique catholique aux Etats Unis." *Recherches de Science Religieuse* 61 (October–December): 575–624. Published in English as "Divorce: Catholic Theory and Practice in the United States," *American Ecclesiastical Review* 168 (January 1974): 3–34, and 168 (February 1974): 75–97. Revised in *New Perspectives in Moral Theology,* 212–76.

Politics, Medicine, and Christian Ethics: A Dialogue with Paul Ramsey. Philadelphia: Fortress.

1974

"Modern Christians Need Self-Denial." *U.S. Catholic* 39 (March): 13–14.

"Co-operation: Toward a Revision of the Concept and Its Application." *Linacre Quarterly* 41 (August): 152–67. Reprinted in *Catholic Medical Quarterly* 26, no. 5 (January 1975): 194–209. Revised as "Cooperation in a Pluralistic Society," in *Ongoing Revision in Moral Theology* (Notre Dame, Ind.: Fides/Claretian, 1975), 210–28.

"Divorce and Remarriage: Two Signs of the Times." *National Catholic Reporter* 10 (October 18): 7.

"Divorce from the Perspective of Moral Theology." *Canon Law Society of America Proceedings* 36: 1–24. Excerpts reprinted in *Origins* 4 (November 14, 1974): 329–35. Revised in *Ongoing Revision in Moral Theology,* 66–106. Published in French as "Le divorce: point de vue de la theologie morale," *Le Supplement* 113 (May 1975): 237–72.

"Human Life: The Fifth Commandment." *Chicago Studies* 13 (fall): 279–99. Reprinted in *An American Catholic Catechism* (New York: Seabury, 1975), 223–45. Revised as "The Fifth Commandment: Thou Shalt Not Kill," in *Ongoing Revision in Moral Theology,* 144–72.

"Dissent, Theology of." *New Catholic Encyclopedia* 16 (supplement 1967–74). Washington, D.C.: Publisher's Guild, 127–29.

"Is There a Catholic and/or Christian Ethic?" *Catholic Theological Society of America Proceedings* 29: 125–54. [Replies by J. Gustafson (155–60) and R. McCormick (161–64).] Revised as "Catholic Ethics, Christian Ethics and Human Ethics," in *Ongoing Revision in Moral Theology,* 1–36. Also appears in *Readings in Moral Theology, No. 2: The Distinctiveness of Christian Ethics* (New York: Paulist Press, 1980), 60–89.

"Paul Ramsey and Traditional Roman Catholic Natural Law Theory." In *Love and Society: Essays in the Ethics of Paul Ramsey,* edited by James T. Johnson and David Smith. Missoula, Mont.: Scholars Press, 47–65. Revised in *Ongoing Revision in Moral Theology,* 229–59.

Blueprints for Moral Living. Chicago: Claretian.

New Perspectives in Moral Theology. Notre Dame, Ind.: Fides.

1975

"Civil Law and Christian Morality: Abortion and the Churches." *Conversations* (spring): 1–19. Summary in *Origins* 4 (1974–75): 568–69. Revised in *Ongoing Revision in Moral Theology,* 107–43. Reprinted in *Law and Justice* 51 (Easter 1976): 45–67; in *Clergy Review* 62 (June 1977): 227–42; and in *Abortion: The Moral Issues,* edited by Edward Batchelor, Jr. (New York: Pilgrim, 1982), 143–65.

"The Lion Sleeps Tonight." *U.S. Catholic* 40 (May): 33–37.

"Commentary and Response." *Jurist* 35: 77–80.

"How My Mind Has Changed, 1960–1975." *Horizons* 2 (fall): 187–205.

"Ethical Considerations in Human Experimentation." *Duquesne Law Review* 13: 819–40. Revised in *Issues in Sexual and Medical Ethics* (Notre Dame, Ind.: University of Notre Dame Press, 1978), 71–102. Excerpt reprinted in *On Moral Education: Theological Perspectives in Medical Ethics,* edited by Stephen F. Lammers and Allen Verhey (Grand Rapids, Mich.: Eerdmans, 1987), 628–29.

"Pluralism in Catholic Moral Theology." *Chicago Studies* 14 (fall): 310–34. Revised in *Ongoing Revision in Moral Theology,* 37–65. Also in *Readings in Moral Theology No. 3: The Magisterium and Morality* (New York: Paulist Press, 1982), 364–87. Published in Italian as "II pluralismo nella teologia morale cattolica," *Rivista di Teologia Morale* 7 (1976): 311–32.

"Questions on the Quinlan Case." *National Catholic Reporter* 12 (November 21): 11.

"Growth (Hopefully) in Wisdom, Age and Grace." In *Journeys,* edited by Gregory Baum. New York: Paulist Press, 87–116. Revised as "Ongoing Revision: Personal and Theological Reflections," in *Ongoing Revision in Moral Theology,* 260–94.

Ongoing Revision in Moral Theology. Notre Dame, Ind.: Fides/Claretian.

1976

"The Gospel and Culture: Christian Marriage and Divorce Today." *Social Thought* 2 (winter): 9–28. Revised in *Issues in Sexual and Medical Ethics,* 3–29. Also in *Ministering to the Divorced Catholic,* edited by James Young (New York: Paulist Press, 1979), 15–36.

"The New Rite of Penance: Sin and Examination of Conscience." *Pastoral Life* 25, no. 4 (April): 9–15.

"Sexual Ethics: Reaction and Critique." *Linacre Quarterly* 43 (August): 147–64. Reprinted in *Catholic Mind* 75 (January 1977): 41–56. Revised as "Sexual Ethics: A Critique" in *Issues in Sexual and Medical Ethics,* 30–52. Published in French as "Ethique sexuelle: réaction et critique," *Le Supplement* 118 (September 1976): 390–411.

"There Is a Right to Die." *U.S. Catholic* 41 (September): 13–14.

"An Overview of Medical Ethics." *New Catholic World* 219 (September-October): 227–32. Revised in *Issues in Sexual and Medical Ethics,* 55–70.

"Utilitarisme et Théologie Morale Contemporaine." *Concilium* 120: 121–40 (also published in all language editions of *Concilium*). Published in English as "Utilitarianism and Contemporary Moral Theology: Situating the Debates," *Louvain Studies* 6 (1977): 239–55. Revised in *Themes in Fundamental Moral Theology,* 121–44. Updated in *Directions in Fundamental Moral Theology,* 173–96.

"Examination of Conscience." In *The Rite of Penance: Commentaries, Vol. II: Implementing the Rite,* edited by Elizabeth McMahon Jeep. Washington, D.C.: Liturgical Conference, 31–33.

1977

"The Catholic Hospital and the Ethical and Religious Directives for Catholic Health Facilities." *Linacre Quarterly* 44 (February): 18–36. Revised as "The Catholic Hospital Code, the Catholic Believer and a Pluralistic Society," in *Issues in Sexual and Medical Ethics,* 139–67.

"Disturbing Events." *National Catholic Reporter* 13 (March 4): 11.

"American and Catholic: American Catholic Social Ethics 1880–1965." *Thought* 52 (March): 50–74. Revised in *Directions in Catholic Social Ethics,* 71–104, and *Transition and Tradition in Moral Theology* (Notre Dame, Ind.: University of Notre Dame Press, 1979), 83–116.

"Theologians, Social Scientists Chart Compass Points Toward Vatican III; At the University of Notre Dame May 29–June 1, 1977." *National Catholic Reporter* 13 (June 17) 3–4.

"What Theology Isn't." *National Catholic Reporter* 13 (September 23): 11.

"Theology: Tensions." *National Catholic Reporter* 13 (September 30): 11.

"Hope for Theology." *National Catholic Reporter* 13 (October 7): 11.

"The Principle of Double Effect: Some Historical and Contemporary Observations." In *Atti del Congresso Internazionale, Vol. V: L'Agire Morale,* edited by Yves Congar et al. Naples: Edizione domenicane Italiane, 426–49. Appeared first in *Ongoing Revision in Moral Theology,* 173–209.

"Moral Theology Today: An Appraisal." In *In Libertatem Vocati Estis: Miscellanea Bernhard Häring,* edited by Henri Boelaars and R. Tremblay. Rome: Academia Alfonsiana, 171–89. Reprinted in *Studia Moralia* 15 (1977): 171–89. Revised as "An Overview and Appraisal of Contemporary Moral Theology," in *Transition and Tradition in Moral Theology,* 3–28.

"Population Control: Methods and Morality." In *Human Life,* edited by William C. Bier. New York: Fordham University Press, 53–72. Revised in *Directions in Catholic Social Ethics* (Notre Dame, Ind.: University of Notre Dame Press, 1985), 225–50, and *Issues in Sexual and Medical Ethics,* 168–97.

Themes in Fundamental Moral Theology. Notre Dame, Ind.: University of Notre Dame Press.

1978

"Ten Years Later: Reflections on the Anniversary of *Humanae Vitae.*" *Commnonweal* 105 (July 7): 425–30. Revised as second part of "Moral Theology in the Light of Reactions to *Humanae Vitae,*" in *Transition and Tradition in Moral Theology,* 29–58.

"After *Humanae Vitae:* A Decade of Lively Debate." *Hospital Progress* 59 (July): 84–89. Revised as first part of "Moral Theology in the Light of Reactions to *Humanae Vitae,*" in *Transition and Tradition in Moral Theology,* 29–58.

"Moral Theology, Psychiatry and Homosexuality." *Bulletin of the National Guild of Catholic Psychiatrists* 24: 13–34. Revised in *Transition and Tradition in Moral Theology,* 59–80.

"Abortion: Contemporary Debate in Religious and Philosophical Ethics." In *Encyclopedia of Bioethics,* vol. 1, edited by Warren T. Reich. New York: Free Press, 17–26. Revised in *Transition and Tradition in Moral Theology,* 207–27.

"Roman Catholicism." In *Encyclopedia of Bioethics,* vol. 4., edited by Warren T. Reich. New York: Free Press, 1522–34. Revised in *Transition and Tradition in Moral Theology,* 173–206.

"Social Ethics: Agenda for the Future." In *Toward Vatican III: The Work that Needs to Be Done,* edited by David Tracy. New York: Seabury, 146–62. Excerpts in *Theology Today* 35 (October 1978): 308–11. Revised in *Directions in Catholic Social Ethics,* 105–26, and *Transition and Tradition in Moral Theology,* 117–38.

Foreword. In Timothy E. O'Connell, *Principles for a Catholic Morality.* New York: Seabury, ix–xii.

Issues in Sexual and Medical Ethics. Notre Dame, Ind.: University of Notre Dame Press.

1979

"Mapping the Terrain of Ecumenical Christian Ethics." *Journal of Religion* 59 (April): 213–17.

"Aging: A Theological Perspective." *Social Thought* 5 (summer): 23–27. Revised in *Moral Theology: A Continuing Journey* (Notre Dame, Ind.: University of Notre Dame Press, 1982), 93–111.

"In Vitro Fertilization and Embryo Transfer: From a Perspective of Moral Theology." In *Appendix: HEW Support of Research Involving Human In Vitro Fertilization and Embryo Transfer,* Ethics Advisory Board, Department of Health, Education, and Welfare. Washington, D.C.: U.S. Government Printing Office. Revised in *Moral Theology: A Continuing Journey,* 112–40. Published in French as "Fécondation in vitro et transfert d'embryon du point de vue de la théologie morale," *Le Supplement* 130 (spring 1979): 307–28.

"Editorial: According to Curran, Pope in Danger of Over Centralizing." *National Catholic Reporter* 15 (September 28): 20.

"Academic Freedom: The Catholic University and Catholic Theology." *Furrow* 330 (December): 739–54. Reprinted in *Catholic Mind* 73 (February 1980): 11–26, and *Academe: Bulletin of the American Association of University Professors* 66 (April 1980): 126–35. Also appears in *Readings in Moral Theology No. 3: The Magisterium and Morality,* 388–407. Revised as "Catholic Theology and Academe," in *Moral Theology: A Continuing Journey,* 11–34

Readings in Moral Theology, No. 1: Moral Norms and Catholic Tradition (editor, with Richard A. McCormick). New York: Paulist Press.

Transition and Tradition in Moral Theology. Notre Dame, Ind.: University of Notre Dame Press.

1980

"Heresy and Error." *America* 142 (March 1): 164–66. Revised as "Theology, Hierarchical Magisterium and Church," in *Moral Theology: A Continuing Journey,* 3–10.

"Method in Moral Theology: An Overview from an American Perspective." *Studia Moralia* 18, no. 1: 107–28. Revised as "A Methodological Overview of Fundamental Moral Theology," in *Moral Theology: A Continuing Journey,* 35–62, and *Directions in Fundamental Moral Theology,* 3–28.

Readings in Moral Theology, No. 2: The Distinctiveness of Christian Ethics (editor, with Richard A. McCormick). New York: Paulist Press.

1981

"Challenge of Pluralism." Contribution to symposium, "What Is Shaping My Theology?" *Commonweal* 108 (January 30): 45–46.

"The Changing Anthropological Bases of Catholic Social Ethics." *Thomist* 45 (April): 284–318. Revised in *Directions in Catholic Social Ethics,* 5–42, and *Moral Theology: A Continuing Journey,* 173–208.

"Sinflation: Even the Moral Theologians Can Barely Keep Up: The Editors Interview Father Charles Curran." *U.S. Catholic* 46 (July): 22–26.

"Faith and Reason: John R. Cavanagh as Bridge Builder." *Linacre Quarterly* 48 (August): 215–37. Reprinted in *Bulletin of the National Guild of Catholic Psychiatrists* 27 (1981): 11–39. Revised as "Theory and Practice, Faith and Reason: A Case Study of John R. Cavanagh," in *Critical Concerns in Moral Theology* (Notre Dame, Ind.: University of Notre Dame Press, 1984), 203–32.

1982

"The Contraceptive Revolution and the Human Condition." *American Journal of Theology and Philosophy* 3, no. 2 (May): 42–59. Revised in *Moral Theology: A Continuing Journey,* 141–72. Reprinted in *On Moral Medicine: Theological Perspectives in Medical Ethics,* edited by Stephen E. Lammers and Allen Verhey (Grand Rapids, Mich.: Eerdmans, 1987), 313–23.

"A Complex Document for a Big Church." *Commonweal* 109 (August 13): 438–40.

"Charles E. Curran's *American Catholic Social Ethics:* Author's Response." *Horizons* 9: 341–47.

"*Free and Faithful in Christ:* A Critical Evaluation," *Studia Moralia* 20, no. 1: 145–75. Revised in *Critical Concerns in Moral Theology,* 3–41.

"Religion, Law and Public Policy in America." *Jurist* 42, no. 1: 14–28. Revised in *Directions in Catholic Social Ethics,* 127–46, and *Moral Theology: A Continuing Journey,* 209–26.

"Science, Morality and the Human Future." In *Science and Morality: New Directions in Bioethics,* edited by Doris Teichler-Zallen and Colleen D. Clements. Lexington, Mass.: D. C. Heath, 1–16. Revised as "Biomedical Science, Morality and the Human Future," in *Critical Concerns in Moral Theology,* 99–122.

Readings in Moral Theology, No. 3: The Magisterium and Morality (editor, with Richard A. McCormick. New York: Paulist Press.

American Catholic Social Ethics. Notre Dame, Ind.: University of Notre Dame Press.

Moral Theology: A Continuing Journey. Notre Dame, Ind.: University of Notre Dame Press.

1983

"The Relationship of Moral Theology to Other Theological Disciplines." *New Catholic World* 226 (January–February): 8–10.

"Horizons on Fundamental Moral Theology." *Horizons* 10 (spring): 86–110. Revised as "An Evaluation of Recent Works in Fundamental Moral Theology," in *Critical Concerns in Moral Theology,* 42–72.

"Discipleship: The Pastoral Minister and the Conscience of the Individual." *Clergy Review* 68 (August): 271–81. Revised in *Critical Concerns in Moral Theology,* 233–56, and *Directions in Fundamental Moral Theology,* 257–80.

"Analyse Américaine de la lettre pastorale sur la guerre et la paix; un cas d'espece catholique." *Le Supplement* 147 (December): 569–92. Published in English as "An Analysis of the American Bishops' Pastoral on Peace and War," in *Directions in Catholic Social Ethics,* 177–97, and in *Critical Concerns in Moral Theology,* 123–43.

"Moral Theology and Homosexuality." In *Homosexuality and the Catholic Church,* edited by Jeannine Gramick. Chicago: Thomas More, 138–68. Revised in *Critical Concerns in Moral Theology,* 73–98.

"The Moral Theology of the Bishops' Pastoral." In *Catholics and Nuclear War,* edited by Philip J. Murion. New York: Crossroad, 45–56. Published in Italian as "Metodologia morale della lettera pastorale dei vescovi americani su guerre e pace," *Revista di Theologia Morale* 15: 487–98.

1984

"What Does Sin Mean Today?" *New Catholic World* 227 (January/February): 22–24.

"Roman Catholic Teaching on Peace and War Within a Broader Theological Context." *Journal of Religious Ethics* 12 (spring): 61–81. Revised in *Directions in Catholic Social Ethics,* 198–224, and in *Critical Concerns in Moral Theology,* 144–70.

"The Uses and Limitations of Philosophical Ethics in Doing Theological Ethics." In *The Annual of the Society of Christian Ethics,* edited by Larry L. Rasmussen. Dallas: Society of Christian Ethics, 123–36. Revised as "What is Distinctive and Unique about Christian Ethics and Christian Morality," in *Toward an American Catholic Moral Theology* (Notre Dame, Ind.: University of Notre Dame Press, 1987), 52–64.

Readings in Moral Theology, No. 4: The Use of Scripture in Moral Theology (editor, with Richard A. McCormick). New York: Paulist Press.

Critical Concerns in Moral Theology. Notre Dame, Ind.: University of Notre Dame Press.

"The Distinction between the Moral and the Juridical Order." *Law and Justice* 82–83: 91–99.

1985

"Just Taxation in the Roman Catholic Tradition." *Journal of Religious Ethics* 13 (spring): 113–33. Revised in *Toward an American Catholic Moral Theology,* 93–118.

"The Extraordinary Synod: VII." *America* 153 (September 28): 164–67.

"Théologie morale aux États-Unis: Une analyse des vingt dernières années." *Le Supplement* 155 (December): 95–116. Published in English as "Moral Theology in the United States: An Analysis of the Last Twenty Years," in *Toward an American Catholic Moral Theology,* 20–51.

"Moral Theology in Dialogue with Biomedicine and Bioethics." *Studia Moralia* 23, no. 1: 57–79. Revised in *Toward an American Catholic Moral Theology,* 65–90.

"The Person as Moral Agent and Subject in the Light of Contemporary Christology." In *Called to Love: Towards a Contemporary Christian Ethic,* proceedings of Villanova University Theology Institute, 1985, edited by Francis A. Eigo. Villanova, Pa.: Villanova University Press, 21–46. Revised in *Directions in Fundamental Moral Theology,* 63–98.

"I vescovi USA e L'Economia: Verio il documento definitivo." *Revista di Theologia Morale* 17: 9–29.

"Anxiety in the Academy." *Tablet* 239 (November 9): 1177–78.

"Catholic Social Ethics: A New Approach." *Clergy Review* 70 (February): 41–47, and 70 (March): 83–89.

"The Tensions of the Minister as a Pilgrim in the Wounded Kingdom." In *Special Publications: National Association of Catholic Chaplains: Convention Highlights—1984* 1, no. 1 (June): 1–8.

Directions in Fundamental Moral Theology. Notre Dame, Ind.: Notre Dame University Press.

Directions in Catholic Social Ethics. Notre Dame, Ind.: University of Notre Dame Press.

1986

Correspondence between Curran and Cardinal Joseph Ratzinger and the Congregation for the Doctrine of the Faith appears in *Origins* 15, no. 41 (March 27). Curran's statements appear under the following titles: "Father Charles Curran Asked to Retract Positions"; "Some Background on Father Curran's Case"; "Curran: A Response"; "August 1984 Response by Curran to Congregation." A later part of this correspondence appears in *Origins* 15, no. 47 (May 8). Curran's statement is titled "Father Curran Refuses to Retract Views."

"Filial Responsibility for an Elderly Parent." *Social Thought* 11, no. 2: 27–39. Revised in *Toward an American Catholic Moral Theology,* 119–41.

"Counter-Reformation," "The Historical Development of Moral Theology," "Modern Roman Catholic Moral Theology," "Official Roman Catholic Social Teaching," and "Subsidiarity, Principle of." In *Westminster Dictionary of Christian Ethics,* edited by James F. Childress and John C. Macquarrie. Philadelphia: Westminster.

"The Difference between Personal Morality and Public Policy." In *Authority, Community and Conflict,* edited by Madonna Kolbenschlag. Kansas City, Mo.: Sheed and Ward. Revised in *Toward an American Catholic Moral Theology,* 194–202.

"Religious Freedom and Human Rights in the World and in the Church: A Christian Perspective." In *Religious Liberty and Human Rights in Nations and Religions,* edited by Leonard Swidler. Philadelphia: Ecumenical Press and Hippocrene Books, 142–73. Revised in *Toward an American Catholic Moral Theology,* 142–73.

"Public Dissent in the Church." *Origins* 16: 174–84. Major portions reprinted under the title "On Dissent in the Church," *Commonweal* 113 (September 12, 1986): 461–70.

Readings in Moral Theology, No. 5: Official Catholic Social Teaching (editor, with Richard A. McCormick). New York: Paulist Press.

Faithful Dissent. Kansas City, Mo.: Sheed & Ward.

1987

"A Teaching Moment Continues." *America* 156 (April 25): 336–40. Parts of this article appear in "Personal Reaction and Response," in *Tensions in Moral Theology* (Notre Dame, Ind.: University of Notre Dame Press, 1988), 50–73.

"Academic Freedom and Catholic Institutions of Higher Learning." *Journal of the American Academy of Religion* 55 (spring): 108–21. Revised in *Tensions in Moral Theology*, 32–49.

"Being Catholic and Being American." *Horizons* 14 (spring): 49–63. Revised in *Tensions in Moral Theology*, 183–202.

"Charles Curran: Why I Am Still A Roman Catholic." *National Catholic Reporter* 23 (September 4): 9–11. Parts of this article appear in revised and expanded form in "Personal Reaction and Response," in *Tensions in Moral Theology*, 50–73.

"Roman Catholic Sexual Ethics: A Dissenting View." *Christian Century* 104 (December 16): 1139–42. Revised in *Tensions in Moral Theology*, 74–86.

"Authority and Dissent in the Roman Catholic Church." In *Los Angeles Times* (October 16), 5. Revised in *Crisis* 51 (January 1987): 27–29. Expanded in *Vatican Authority and American Catholic Dissent*, edited by William W. May (New York: Crossroad, 1987), 27–34.

"Christian Ethics." In *Encyclopedia of Religion*, edited by Mircea Eliade, vol. 3. New York: Macmillan, 340–48.

"Official Catholic Social Teaching and the Common Good." In *The Common Good and U.S. Capitalism*, edited by Oliver F. Willliams and John W. Houck. Lanham, Md.: University Press of America, 111–29. Revised in *Tensions in Moral Theology*, 119–37.

"Destructive Tensions in Moral Theology." In *The Church in Anguish: Has the Vatican Betrayed Vatican II?*, edited by Hans Küng and Leonard Swidler. San Francisco: Harper & Row, 273–78.

Foreword. In James John Annarelli, *Academic Freedom and Catholic Higher Education*. New York: Greenwood, xi–xv.

Foreword. In *Theology and Authority*, edited by Richard Penaskovic. Peabody, Mass.: Hendrickson, xi–xvi.

Foreword. In Hans Küng, *Why I Am Still a Christian*. New York: Abingdon, 9–12.

"Human Dignity and the National Right to Self-Defense: American Catholic Bishops and the Nuclear Question." In *De Dignitate Hominis: Festschrift in Honor of Carlos-Josophat Pinto de Oliviera*, edited by Adrian Holdregger, Rued Imbach, and Raul Suarez de Miguel. Freiburg, Switzerland: Universitatsverlag, 567–78.

"Relating Religious-Ethical Inquiry to Economic Policy." In *The Catholic Challenge to the American Economy*, edited by Thomas M. Gannon. New York: Macmillan, 42–54. Revised as "An Analysis of the United States Bishops' Pastoral Letter on the Economy," in *Toward an American Catholic Moral Theology*, 174–93.

Toward an American Catholic Moral Theology. Notre Dame, Ind.: University of Notre Dame Press.

1988

"Catholic Social and Sexual Teaching: A Methodological Comparison." *Theology Today* 44 (January): 425–40. Revised as "Official Catholic Social and Sexual Teachings: A Methodological Comparison," in *Tensions in Moral Theology*, 87–109.

"Official Catholic Social Teaching and Conscience." In *Tensions in Moral Theology*, 162–82. Also in *History and Conscience: Studies in Honour of Father Sean O'Riordan*, edited by Raphael Gallagher and Brendan McConvrey (Dublin: Gill and Macmillan, 1989), 85–104.

"Ethical Principles of Catholic Social Teaching Behind the United States Bishops' Letter on the Economy." *Journal of Business Ethics* 7: 413–17. Revised in *Tensions in Moral Theology*, 110–18.

"Ministries for a Christian Life." In *A Catholic Bill of Rights*, edited by Leonard Swidler and Herbert O'Brien. Kansas City, Mo.: Sheed & Ward, 74–77.

"Academic Freedom in Catholic Universities." *Texas Law Review* 66, no. 7 (June): 1441–54.

"Is a Catholic College or University a Contradiction in Terms?" *National Catholic Reporter* 85 (December 23): 11.

"Authority and Structure in the Churches: Perspectives of a Catholic Theologian." In *Raising the Torch of Good News: Catholic Authority and Dialogue with the World,* edited by Bernard P. Prusak (College Theology Society Annual vol. 32 [1986]). Lanham, Md.: University Press of America, 81–104. Revised as "My Theological Dissent: The Issues," in *Tensions in Moral Theology,* 7–31.

Readings in Moral Theology, No. 6: Dissent in the Church (editor, with Richard A. McCormick). New York: Paulist Press.

Sexualität und Ethik. Frankfurt am Main, Germany: Athenäum, 1988. (German translation of selections from essays previously published in English.)

Tensions in Moral Theology. Notre Dame, Ind.: University of Notre Dame Press.

1989

"Providence and Responsibility: The Divine and Human from the Perspective of Moral Theology." *Catholic Theological Society of America Proceedings* 44: 43–64.

"Sexualethik im gegenwärtigen Katholizismus." In *Sexualität zwischen Verdrängung und Befreiung,* edited by Karl H. Auer and Anne Liese Frantsits. Vienna: Bundesverlag, 64–73.

1990

"Introduction: Why This Book?" In *Moral Theology: Challenges for the Future,* editor. New York: Paulist Press, 1–11.

"The Teaching Function of the Church in Morality." In *Moral Theology: Challenges for the Future.* New York: Paulist Press, 155–78.

"Dissent in the Church." *Los Angeles Times* (July 7), F14.

"Offentliche Discussionen." *Kirche Intern* 4, no. 11 (November): 29.

"La Morale sexuelle catholique d'hier à demain." *Lumière et la vie* 39 (Décembre): 117–31.

Catholic Higher Education, Theology, and Academic Freedom. Notre Dame, Ind.: University of Notre Dame Press.

Moral Theology: Challenges for the Future: Essays in Honor of Richard A. McCormick (editor). New York: Paulist Press.

1991

"Point of View." *Chronicle of Higher Education* (January 30), A48.

"Living Values, Changing Times, and Conscience." *New World Outlook* (May), 36–38.

"A Century of Catholic Social Teaching." *Theology Today* 48: 154–69.

"Catholic Social Teaching and Human Morality." In *One Hundred Years of Catholic Social Thought: Celebration and Challenge,* edited by John A. Coleman. Maryknoll, N.Y.: Orbis, 72–87. Revised in *The Living Tradition of Catholic Moral Theology* (Notre Dame, Ind.: University of Notre Dame Press, 1992), 160–81.

Readings in Moral Theology, No. 7: Natural Law and Theology (editor, with Richard A. McCormick). New York: Paulist Press.

1992

"The New World Order and Military Force." *New Theology Review* 5, no. 1 (February): 5–18. Revised in *The Living Tradition of Catholic Moral Theology,* 240–54.

"Moral Theology." In *A New Handbook of Christian Theology,* edited by Donald W. Musser and Joseph L. Price. Nashville, Tenn.: Abingdon, 315–18.

"Towards 2,000: Tensions, Perennial and New, Facing the Church." *American Theological Library Association Proceedings* 46: 201–95.

"Church, Academy, Law: Personal Reflections." In *Issues in Academic Freedom,* edited by George S. Worgul. Pittsburgh, Pa.: Duquesne University Press, 88–109. Revised in *The Living Tradition of Catholic Moral Theology,* 217–39.

"Sexual Ethics and the Roman Tradition." In *Religion and Sexual Health: Ethical, Theological, and Clinical Perspectives,* edited by Ronald M. Green. Dordrecht, the Netherlands: Kluwer, 17–35. Revised in *The Living Tradition of Catholic Moral Theology,* 27–57.

"What Catholic Ecclesiology Can Learn from Official Catholic Social Teaching." In *A Democratic Catholic Church: The Reconstruction of Roman Catholicism,* edited by Eugene C. Bianchi and Rosemary Radford

Ruether. New York: Crossroad, 94–112. Revised in *The Living Tradition of Catholic Moral Theology,* 134–59.

Foreword. In Robert Nugent and Jeannine Gramick, *Building Bridges: Gay and Lesbian Reality in the Catholic Church.* Mystic, Conn.: Twenty-Third Publications, v–viii.

The Living Tradition of Catholic Moral Theology. Notre Dame, Ind.: University of Notre Dame Press.

1993

"Moral Theology Since Vatican II." In *The Church in the Nineties: Its Legacy, Its Future,* edited by Pierre M. Hegy. Collegeville, Minn.: Liturgical Press, 39–41.

"Encyclical Left Church Credibility Stillborn: Documented Litmus Test for New Bishops." *National Catholic Reporter* 29, no. 34 (July 16): 14–15.

"Veritatis Splendor." Commonweal, 120, no. 18 (October 22): 14.

"A Discussion of *Ex corde ecclesiae* and Its Ordinances." *Commonweal* 120, no. 20 (November 19): 14–15.

The Church and Morality: An Ecumenical and Catholic Approach. Minneapolis: Fortress.

Readings in Moral Theology, No. 8: Dialogue about Catholic Sexual Teaching (editor, with Richard A. McCormick). New York: Paulist Press.

1994

"Anthropology." In *The New Dictionary of Catholic Social Thought,* edited by Judith A. Dwyer. Collegeville, Minn.: Liturgical Press, 44–47.

"Taxes." In *The New Dictionary of Catholic Social Thought,* edited by Judith A. Dwyer. Collegeville, Minn.: Liturgical Press, 934–36.

"Natural Law." In *The Modern Catholic Encyclopedia,* edited by Michael Glazier and Monika K. Hellwig. Collegeville, Minn.: Liturgical Press, 602–4.

"Catholic Ecclesiology Can Learn from Official Catholic Social Teaching." *AARC Light* 16, no. 6 (August): 1.

"The Elusive Idea of a Catholic University: Freedom Continues to Be the Critical Concept." *National Catholic Reporter* 30, no. 43 (October 7): 12–15. Revised in *History and Contemporary Issues: Studies in Moral Theology* (New York: Continuum, 1996), 201–15.

1995

"Roman Catholicism." In *Encyclopedia of Bioethics,* vol. 4, edited by Warren T. Reich. New York: MacMillan, 2331–37. Revised in *History and Contemporary Issues: Studies in Moral Theology,* 28–49.

"Fertility Control: Ethical Issues." In *Encyclopedia of Bioethics,* vol. 2, edited by Warren T. Reich. New York: Macmillan, 832–39. Revised in *History and Contemporary Issues: Studies in Moral Theology,* 123–39.

"*Veritatis Splendor:* A Revisionist Perspective." In *Veritatis Splendor: American Responses,* edited by Michael E. Allsopp and John J. O'Keefe. Kansas City, Mo.: Sheed & Ward, 224–43. Revised in *History and Contemporary Issues: Studies in Moral Theology,* 216–38.

"The Theory and Practice of Academic Freedom in Catholic Higher Education in the United States." *Église et théologie* 26, no. 1 (January): 79–100. A similar version appeared in *Indian Journal of American Studies* 25 (winter 1995): 23–38. Revised in *History and Contemporary Issues: Studies in Moral Theology,* 178–200.

"Is There Any Good News in the Recent Documents from the Vatican about Homosexuality?" In *Voices of Hope,* edited by Jeannine Gramick and Robert Nugent. New York: Center for Homophobia Education, 159–72.

"Thomas Joseph Bouquillon: Americanist, Neo-Scholastic, or Manualist?" *Catholic Theological Society of America Proceedings* 50: 156–73.

"The Manual and Casuistry of Aloysius Sabetti." In *The Context of Casuistry,* edited by James Keenan and Thomas Shannon. Washington, D.C.: Georgetown University Press, 188–204.

"Sozialethik, Soziallehre, 2. Nordamerika." In *Evangelisches Kirchenlexikon: Internationale Theologische Enzyklopädie,* edited by Katja Fiedler and Ekkehard Starke. Göttingen, Germany: Vandenhoeck & Ruprecht, 334–38.

"Encyclical is Positive, Problematic." *National Catholic Reporter* 31, no. 24 (April 24): 4–5.

"Academic Freedom," "Birth Control," "Häring, Bernard," "*Humanae Vitae,*" and "Moral Theology." In *Encyclopedia of Catholicism,* edited by Richard P. McBrien. San Francisco: HarperCollins, 10–12, 178–81, 603, 642, and 891–92.

"Théologie morale." In *Dictionnaire de philosophie morale,* edited by

Monique Canto-Sperber. Paris: Presses universitares de France. Revised in *History and Contemporary Issues: Studies in Moral Theology,* 13–27.

1996

"The Role of the Laity in the Thought of John Courtney Murray." In *John Courtney Murray and the Growth of Tradition,* edited by J. Leon Hooper and Todd David Whitmore. Kansas City, Mo.: Sheed & Ward, 241–61. Revised in *History and Contemporary Issues: Studies in Moral Theology,* 77–100.

"Two Traditions: Historical Consciousness Meets the Immutable." *Commonweal* 123 (October 11): 11–13. Significantly revised in *History and Contemporary Issues: Studies in Moral Theology,* 239–51.

"Natural Law." In *Dictionary of Ethics, Theology, and Society,* edited by Paul Barry Clarke and Andrew Linzey. London and New York: Routledge, 594–97.

"Häring Reflects on Ministry: A Review Essay." *National Catholic Reporter* 33, no. 3 (November 8): 21–22.

History and Contemporary Issues: Studies in Moral Theology. New York: Continuum.

Feminist Ethics and the Catholic Moral Tradition: Readings in Moral Theology No. 9 (editor, with Margaret A. Farley and Richard A. McCormick). New York: Paulist Press.

1997

"Absolute Moral Norms." In *Ethics in Crisis?* edited by John Scally. Dublin: Veritas, 25–32.

"The Catholic Identity of Catholic Institutions." *Theological Studies* 58 (March): 90–108.

"Open Letter to Tissa Balashuriya." *National Catholic Reporter* 33 (February 7): 7–10. French translation, "Postface: Tissa, bienvenue parmi les parias de la théologie," in Tissa Balashuriya, *Marie ou la libération humaine* (Villeurbanne, France: Golias, 1997), 343–49.

"Death 'as Friend'—But. . . ." *America* 176 (March 29): 12–15.

"Bioethics: An Overview." In *Essentials of Pediatric Intensive Care,* 2d ed., edited by Daniel L. Levin and Frances C. Morris. New York: Churchill Livingstone, 1063–68.

The Origins of Moral Theology in the United States: Three Different Approaches. Washington, D.C.: Georgetown University Press.

1998

"Churches and Human Rights: From Hostility/Reluctance to Acceptability." *Milltown Studies* 42: 30–58.

"Religious Freedom: Separating Church and State." In *Rome Has Spoken: A Guide to Forgotten Papal Statements and How They Have Changed through the Centuries,* edited by Maureen Fiedler and Linda Rabben. New York: Crossroad, 46–54.

"Sexual Orientation and Human Rights in American Religious Discourse: A Roman Catholic Perspective." In *Sexual Orientation and Human Rights in American Religious Discourse,* edited by Saul M. Olyan and Martha C. Nussbaum. New York: Oxford University Press, 85–100. Also appears in *Readings in Moral Theology, no. 12: The Catholic Church, Morality, and Politics* (New York: Paulist Press), 328–48.

"Roman Catholic Moral Theology." In *Introduction to Christian Theology: Contemporary North American Perspectives,* edited by Roger A. Badham. Louisville, Ky.: Westminster/John Knox, 121–36.

"A Shared Struggle: Catholic Identity." *Charities-USA* 25, no.1: 5–9.

John Paul II and Moral Theology: Readings in Moral Theology No. 10 (editor, with Richard A. McCormick). New York: Paulist Press.

1999

Foreword. In Bernard Häring, *My Hope for the Church: Critical Encouragement for the Twenty-First Century.* Liguori, Mo.: Liguori/Triumph, ix–xiv.

"Review Symposium: Author's Response." *Horizons* 26 (fall): 353–58.

"The Academic Nature of (Moral) Theology." *Horizons* 26 (fall 1999): 282–85.

The Historical Development of Fundamental Moral Theology in the United States: Readings in Moral Theology, No. 11 (editor, with Richard A. McCormick). New York: Paulist Press.

The Catholic Moral Tradition Today: A Synthesis. Washington, D.C.: Georgetown University Press.

Moral Theology at the End of the Century: The Père Marquette Lecture in Theology, 1999. Milwaukee, Wisc.: Marquette University Press.

2000

Foreword. In William H. Shannon, *Silence on Fire*. New York: Crossroad, xi–xx.

"A Marvelous Exponent of the Living Tradition." *National Catholic Reporter* (March 3): 12.

"A Spirituality Catholic and Communitarian." In *Selving: Linking Work to Spirituality*, edited by William Cleary. Milwaukee, Wisc.: Marquette University Press, 65–76.

"The Global Ethic." *The Ecumenist* 37 (spring): 6–10.

"Notes on Richard A. McCormick." *Theological Studies* 61: 533–45.

2001

"Catholic Social Teaching." *The Good Society* 10, no. 1: 1–6.

"Richard A. McCormick." In *New Catholic Encyclopedia: Jubilee Volume: The Wojtyla Years*. Detroit: Gale Group, 354–56.

"George Higgins and Catholic Social Teaching." *U.S. Catholic Historian* 19, no. 4 (fall): 59–72.

The Catholic Church, Morality, and Politics: Readings in Moral Theology No. 12 (editor, with Leslie Griffin). New York: Paulist Press.

2002

Catholic Social Teaching, 1891–Present: A Historical, Theological, and Ethical Analysis. Washington, D.C.: Georgetown University Press.

Contributors

Lisa Sowle Cahill is J. Donald Monan, S.J., Professor of Theology at Boston College. She is a past president of the Catholic Theological Society of America and the author of seven books, including *Sex, Gender and Christian Ethics* (1996) and *Family: A Christian Social Perspective* (2000).

James A. Coriden is a presbyter of the Diocese of Gary, Indiana, and professor of church law and dean emeritus at the Washington Theological Union. His recent works include *The Parish in Catholic Tradition: History, Theology and Canon Law* (1997), *Canon Law as Ministry: Freedom and Good Order for the Church* (2000), and contributions to the *New Commentary on the Code of Canon Law* (2000).

Margaret A. Farley is Gilbert L. Stark Professor of Christian Ethics at Yale University Divinity School. The author, coauthor, and coeditor of five books and multiple articles, she is a past president of the Society of Christian Ethics and the Catholic Theological Society of America.

Raphael Gallagher, a Redemptorist from Ireland, is an invited professor at the Alphonsian Academy in Rome. He is the editor of and a regular contributor to the journal of that institute, *Studia Moralia.*

James M. Gustafson was on the faculties of Yale University, the University of Chicago, and Emory University for forty-three years before he retired in 1998. He is the author of *Protestant and Roman Catholic Ethics: Prospects for Rapprochement* (1978), among other books; he was a participant in many ecumenical ventures; and he directed the dissertations of several Roman Catholic moral theologians.

J. Bryan Hehir served from 1993 to 2001 as professor of the practice in religion and society at Harvard Divinity School and the Weatherhead Center for International Affairs. In 2001 he became president of Catholic Charities USA.

Kenneth R. Himes, O.F.M., is professor of moral theology at Washington Theological Union. He is a past president of the Catholic Theological Society of America and former editor of *New Theology Review*. His most recent book is *Responses to 101 Questions on Catholic Social Teaching* (2001).

James F. Keenan, S.J., is professor of moral theology at the Weston Jesuit School of Theology. He edited *Catholic Ethicists on HIV/AIDS Prevention* (2000) and, with Joseph Kotva, Jr., *Practice What You Preach: Virtues, Ethics and Power in the Lives of Church Ministers and Their Congregations* (1999). He is working with Dan Harrington on a book titled *Jesus and Moral Theology: Building Bridges* (2002).

Kevin T. Kelly is pastor of St. Basil and All Saints, an ecumenical parish in Widnes, England, that is shared with Anglicans. As a moral theologian, he has written widely on moral and pastoral issues. His most recent books include *New Directions in Sexual Ethics: Moral Theology and the Challenge of AIDS* (1998), and *From a Parish Base: Essays in Moral and Pastoral Theology* (1999).

Daniel C. Maguire is professor of moral theology at Marquette University. He also is president of an international collegium of scholars in world religions known as the Religious Consultation on Population, Reproductive Health, and Ethics. His most recent books are *Sacred Energies: When the World's Religions Sit Down to Talk about the Future of Human Life and the Plight of this Planet* (2000) and *Sacred Choices: The Right to Contraception and Abortion in Ten World Religions* (2001).

Bryan N. Massingale is associate professor of moral theology at Saint Francis Seminary in Milwaukee, Wisconsin. He earned his doctorate from the Alphonsianum. He publishes principally in the area of social ethics and racial justice. His work has appeared in several journals and anthologies.

Timothy E. O'Connell is professor of Christian ethics at the Institute of Pastoral Studies at Loyola University Chicago. The author of eleven books, he also is a consultant to businesses and nonprofits regarding value-based conflict resolution.

Thomas A. Shannon is professor of religion and social ethics in the Department of Humanities and Arts at Worcester Polytechnic Institute. He is the author of several books and articles on bioethics and social ethics.

James J. Walter is the Austin and Ann O'Malley Professor of Bioethics and director of the bioethics institute at Loyola Marymount University. He has published several books and is a regular contributor to many theological and ethics journals in the field of bioethics.

Index